The Register of

Walter Langton

BISHOP OF COVENTRY AND LICHFIELD

1296–1321

VOLUME I

EDITED BY

J. B. HUGHES

Canterbury and York Society

The Boydell Press

2001

First published 2001

A Canterbury and York Society publication
published by The Boydell Press
an imprint of Boydell & Brewer Ltd
PO Box 9, Woodbridge, Suffolk IP12 3DF, UK
and of Boydell & Brewer Inc.
PO Box 41026, Rochester, NY 14604–4126, USA
website: http://www.boydell.co.uk

ISBN 0 907239 61 7

A catalogue record for this book is available
from the British Library

Details of previous volumes are available from Boydell & Brewer Ltd

This publication is printed on acid-free paper

Typeset by Joshua Associates Ltd, Oxford
Printed in Great Britain by
St Edmundsbury Press Ltd, Bury St Edmunds, Suffolk

The Canterbury and York Society

GENERAL EDITOR: PROFESSOR R.L. STOREY

ISSN 0262–995X

DIOCESE OF COVENTRY AND LICHFIELD

CANTERBURY AND YORK SOCIETY VOL. XCI

CONTENTS

MARITO MEO CARISSIMO

P.M.H.

ACKNOWLEDGEMENTS

The register is published by the kind permission of the Diocesan Registrar at Lichfield. I also wish to record my thanks to the staff of Lichfield Joint Record Office for their courteous assistance on my visits there. I am greatly indebted and owe special thanks to Professor Robin Storey. His enthusiasm for medieval church history inspired my own while I was an undergraduate at the University of Nottingham, and he introduced me to Latin and palaeography. Having brought Langton's register to my attention, he initially supervised my doctoral thesis on which this edition is based: it is fitting that he, as General Editor of the Society, has expertly guided the register through to publication. I also wish to thank Dr. Alison McHardy of the University of Nottingham for her guidance and support both during the completion of my doctoral thesis, and since. Thanks are due also to those who have answered queries about particular matters, especially Professor Bernard Hamilton, Professor Michael C.E. Jones, Professor David Smith, and Dr. Robert Swanson. Finally, I wish to thank my husband, Peter, for his constant support and encouragement.

BIBLIOGRAPHICAL ABBREVIATIONS

Beardwood, Records	*Records of the trial of Walter Langeton, bishop of Coventry and Lichfield, 1307–1312,* ed. A. Beardwood (Camden, 4th series, 6, 1969).
Beardwood, 'Trial'	A. Beardwood, 'The trial of Walter Langton, bishop of Lichfield, 1307–1312, *Transactions of the American Philosophical Society*, 54, part 3 (1964), 5–45.
BIHR	Borthwick Institute of Historical Research.
BRUC	A.B. Emden, *A biographical register of the university of Cambridge to A.D. 1500* (Cambridge, 1963).
BRUO	A.B. Emden, *A biographical register of the university of Oxford to A.D. 1500* (Oxford, 1957–9).
CCR	*Calendar of Close Rolls.*
CChR	*Calendar of Charter Rolls.*
CFR	*Calendar of Fine Rolls.*
Churchill, *Canterbury administration*	I.J. Churchill, *Canterbury administration: the administrative machinery of the archbishopric of Canterbury illustrated from original records* (London, 1933).
Councils and synods	*Councils and synods, with other documents relating to the English church,* ed. F.M. Powicke, C.R. Cheney (Oxford, 1964), II, i, *1205–65*; II, ii, *1265–1313.*
CPL	*Calendar of Papal Letters.*
CPR	*Calendar of Patent Rolls.*
CYS	Publications of the Canterbury and York Society.
Denton, *Winchelsey*	J.H. Denton, *Robert Winchelsey and the crown 1294–1313* (Cambridge, 1980).
DNB	*Dictionary of national biography* (1885–1901).
Fasti	J. Le Neve, *Fasti ecclesiae Anglicanae 1300–1541* (London, 1962–7).
Foss, *Judges*	E. Foss, *The judges of England* (London, 1848–64), iii.
Foulds, *Thurgarton Cartulary*	*The Thurgarton Cartulary,* ed. T. Foulds (Stamford, 1994).
HBC	*Handbook of British chronology,* 3rd edn., ed. E.B. Fryde, D.E. Greenway, S. Porter, I. Roy (Royal Historical Society, 1986).
Hughes, 'Account roll'	Jill B. Hughes, 'A 1301 sequestrator-general's account roll for the diocese of Coventry and Lichfield', *Chronology, conquest and conflict in medieval England* (Camden, 5th series, 10, 1997), 105–39.
Hughes, 'Clergy list'	Jill B. Hughes, 'A 1319 clergy list of the Tamworth and Tutbury deanery in the diocese of Coventry and Lichfield', *Staffordshire Studies*, 6 (1994), 1–25.

Hughes,   Jill B. Hughes, 'The episcopate of Walter Langton, bishop
   'Episcopate'   of Coventry and Lichfield, 1296–1321, with a calendar of
                     his register' (University of Nottingham unpublished Ph.D.
                     thesis, 3 vols., 1992).
Hughes,   Jill B. Hughes, 'Walter Langton, bishop of Coventry and
   'Family'   Lichfield, 1296–1321: his family background', *Nottingham
                     Medieval Studies*, 35 (1991), 70–6.
Hughes,   Jill B. Hughes, 'Walter Langton, bishop of Coventry and
   'Register'   Lichfield, 1296–1321, and his register', *Staffordshire Studies*,
                     9 (1997), 1–8.
JEH   *Journal of Ecclesiastical History.*
LJRO   Lichfield Joint Record Office.
Lunt, *Financial*   W.E. Lunt, *Financial relations of the papacy with England to
   relations*   1327* (Cambridge, Mass., 1939).
Matthew,   D. Matthew, *The Norman monasteries and their English
   Monasteries*   possessions* (Oxford, 1962).
MRA   *The great register of Lichfield cathedral known as Magnum
                     Registrum Album*, ed. H.E. Savage (William Salt
                     Archaeological Society, 1924).
PRO   Public Record Office.
Reg. Gandavo   *Registrum Simonis de Gandavo, diocesis Saresberiensis, A.D.
                     1297–1315*, ed. C.T. Flower, M.C.B. Dawes (CYS, 40, 41,
                     1934).
Reg. Halton   *The register of John de Halton, bishop of Carlisle A.D. 1292–
                     1324*, ed. W.N. Thompson (CYS, 12, 13, 1906–13).
Reg. Martival   *The register of Roger Martival, bishop of Salisbury, 1315–30*, i,
                     ed. K. Edwards, ii, ed. C.R. Elrington, iii, ed. S. Reynolds,
                     iv. ed. D.M. Owen (CYS, 55–9, 68, 1959–75).
Reg. Romeyn   *The register of John le Romeyn, lord archbishop of York, 1286–
                     1296*, ed. W. Brown (Surtees Society, 123, 128, 1913–17).
Reg. Sutton   *The rolls and register of Bishop Oliver Sutton, 1280–1299*, ed.
                     R.M.T. Hill (Lincoln Record Society, 39, 43, 48, 52, 60, 64,
                     69, 76, 1948–86).
Reg. Winchelsey   *Registrum Roberti Winchelsey Cantuariensis archiepiscopi*, ed.
                     R. Graham (CYS, 51, 52, 1952–6).
Robinson,   D. Robinson, *Staffordshire Record Office cumulative hand list,
   Hand list*   part 1, Lichfield Joint Record Office: diocesan, probate and church
                     commissioners' records*, 2nd edn. (Staffordshire County
                     Council, 1978).
Smith, *Guide*   David M. Smith, *Guide to Bishops' Registers of England and
                     Wales* (London, Royal Historical Society, 1981).
Storey,   R.L. Storey, *Diocesan administration in fifteenth century England*
   Diocesan   (St. Anthony's Press, York, 1959; 2nd edn. 1972).
   administration
   (1959), (1972)
TRHS   *Transactions of the Royal Historical Society.*
VCH   *Victoria County History.*

INTRODUCTION

The volume known as Walter Langton's register is deposited at Lichfield Joint Record Office, Lichfield (under reference LJRO B/A/1/1);[1] it also contains the ordination register of Langton's successor, Roger Northburgh (folios 143–216v). The register of Langton's own episcopate occupies folios 1–142; it covers the period 1297 to 1321 and it is the earliest surviving register for the medieval diocese of Coventry and Lichfield.[2] The register was re-bound and covered with oak boards edged with white pigskin in 1976, when a plan of the folios was made; this is now at the back of the volume. New end-leaves of natural grained vellum were then added. There are three paper folios measuring 21cm. by 29cm. at both the front and back of the volume.[3] Also at the front is a parchment flyleaf (folio iv) which may be contemporary with the register; on its recto is a note that the volume was inspected in the Exchequer in 1773, while on the verso is a short list of contents in a seventeenth century hand, and notes made from a roll of Bishop Meuland.[4] The register is written in a brownish ink on parchment folios of slightly irregular size, measuring approximately 21cm. by 29cm. The parchment is of medium quality and there are some natural holes (e.g. folios 4, 5, 101, 106, 107, 128, 131, 146). Some folios have tears which have been stitched (e.g. folios 96, 98, 106, 107), and some folios have ruled lines (e.g. folios 5, 5v, 8, 8v, 9, 12, 12v, 18v, 19, 21, 21v). Modern foliation in Arabic numerals has been added to the top right corner of each folio.

The condition of the register is generally good, though there is some staining and the edges of some folios are rubbed, making the writing illegible in places as Lichfield Joint Record Office does not allow the use of an ultra-violet lamp. Most of the folios have margins at both the outer and inner edges, with a wider margin being generally provided at the outer edge. An appropriate note of the

---

[1] Described in Robinson, *Hand list,* 4, and Smith, *Guide,* 53–5.

[2] Part or all of the register of Langton's predecessor, Roger Meuland or Longespée (1258–95), survived until the early seventeenth century, see R.N. Swanson, 'The rolls of Roger de Meuland, bishop of Coventry and Lichfield (1258–95)', *Journal of the Society of Archivists,* 11 (1990), 37–40.

[3] Those at the back are blank. Of those at the front, fo. i verso has a note that the register was inspected in the Exchequer in 1786; fo. ii is blank; and fo. iii has a note that the volume contains the register of Walter Langton and the register of ordinations of Roger Northburgh (1322–58).

[4] Swanson, 'Rolls of Roger de Meuland', 37, n. 2. Perhaps Meuland's register was in both roll and book format, see *Reg. Winchelsey,* i.59–60. This was the case at Lincoln, see *Reg. Sutton,* i. pp. xiii, xiv. Although rolls seem to have been used as the working record for Langton's ordination lists, the transition to book format for the definitive Lichfield registers may have been completed by Langton who had introduced similar innovations in the king's wardrobe, see *Book of prests of the king's wardrobe for 1294–5,* ed. E.B. Fryde (Oxford, 1962), p. xii; Hughes, 'Episcopate', i.1–7.

subject-matter, or of the name of the church, chapel, or vicarage for each entry is usually written in the outer margins. Notes of whether or not an incumbent had paid the half-mark fee (6s. 8d.) for the registration of his institution, or if this fee was remitted, appear periodically in the margins (e.g. **11, 16, 31, 32, 167, 317**), and occasionally more information regarding the fee is given (e.g. **43, 109, 110, 954**).[5] Numerous notes were made while an index was compiled in the seventeenth century,[6] but of chief interest amongst the contemporary marginal notes are those recording the release of Langton from prison in 1308, *registrum post egressum episcopi a carcere*, which in the calendar precede **608, 692, 820, 923, 1021**, and the hands that have been drawn pointing to entries **77*, 114, 214, 215, 354, 364*, 578, 1330**. Also worthy of note are the small faces which have been incorporated into the embellishments preceding the capital 'A' of the headings on folios 12 and 18.

The most numerous category of entries in the register are letters of institution, or of collation to those benefices in the bishop's gift, to which a memorandum of the mandate to induct is regularly appended after 1304, usually addressed to the · archdeacon or his official, or in cases of collation to prebends in Lichfield cathedral to the dean and chapter of Lichfield. From 1307 the precise date a benefice fell vacant is frequently noted, and whether the vacancy was caused by the death or resignation of the previous incumbent (e.g. **603, 608, 613, 624, 637, 642**), which may have been another innovation implemented by Langton.

The arrangement of the register

The first gathering comprising four folios was once part of a larger working register. There are 86 entries of which all the 34 institutions to benefices, a collation to a rectory, and six collations to prebends, together with two letters regarding an institution and an induction have been subsequently duplicated, but often with subtle differences:[7] the institutions, the collation to a rectory, and the two letters have been copied into the first relevant archdeaconry sections (folios 5–19v),[8] while the collations to prebends have been copied together into the short collation section (folio 21). They are listed below:

entry on folios 1–4v		*duplicated entry*
1	institution	223
3	collation to prebend	383
4	"	382
6	letter to institute	224
7	letter to induct	153

[5] Hughes, 'Account roll', 113.

[6] LJRO, *Seventeenth century index to Lichfield bishop's register B/A/1/1*, no. 71.

[7] Chiefly in the spelling of personal and placenames, but **1** has a marginal note that $\frac{1}{2}$; mark is owed [for the bishop's fee], while its copy (**223**) notes *nihil* [was paid for the fee], and **16** records the patrons as Abbot John and the convent of Dale, and its copy (**226**) the abbot and convent of Dale.

[8] See Hughes, 'Episcopate', iii.1157–8 for facsimiles of **32, 33, 34, 42, 43** and their duplicated entries **97, 98, 99, 230, 231**.

One licence for study has been entered twice, first as part of the recipient's institution (**37**) and as a licence only (**79**); the record of the institution, including the licence to study, is then duplicated (**228**). Another entry (**41**) has been cancelled by the scribe *quia alibi*; this letter is a cancelled copy of **30** which is subsequently duplicated (**282**). The institutions recorded on the first four folios have abbreviated forms of the archdeaconry names to which they pertain written in the margins (*Cestr'* for Chester, *Cov'* for Coventry, *Derb'* for Derby, *Staff'* for Stafford and *Salop'* for Shrewsbury), in addition to the usual marginal notes. Those for **1** and **11**, however, have been added by a later hand, as has the erroneous archdeaconry note for **4**, which is a collation to a prebend. Another collation to a prebend (**31**) was given a contemporary archdeaconry note in error, which has been deleted. Nevertheless, the archdeaconry notes were obviously made by the registry clerks to facilitate the copying process.

Most of the entries are in chronological order suggesting that copies of these letters were recorded at their time of issue; the exceptions may have been registered from other drafts or brief notes.[9] The last entry (**86**) has been added later and is an undated summary of the sequestrator-general's account. Three other entries too are undated (**75, 77*, 85**). Two of these, and three others, also were added at the foot of folios (**27, 61, 67, 77*, 85**), and when so recording **67** the scribe cut in two **66**. These entries and the additions made to others (**11, 24, 37, 44, 45, 53, 67, 80, 82, 84**), the shorter of which are either interlined or marginated, while the longer are squashed into the available spaces, give these folios the appearance of a working record.

Of the 41 entries that were not duplicated in the 'definitive' register, nineteen are of a routine nature, being grants of custodies, licences and letters dimissory (**2, 5, 9, 13, 15, 36, 40, 48–50, 52, 53, 55, 58, 59, 66, 74, 83, 84**),[10] but the rest are diverse in subject-matter and some are evidently important (**8, 27, 39, 61, 62, 63*, 64, 65, 67, 68*, 69*, 70–72, 73*, 75, 76, 77*, 80, 81, 85, 86**). Though part of the 'definitive' register is lost,[11] the re-copying process may not have been completed. The fact that the first four folios contain the only written record of the 41 unduplicated entries suggests they were deliberately retained from a working register: the grants of custodies and licences recorded here pre-date those in the subsequent custody section.[12] This theory is supported by the structure of the register of William Wickwane of York (1279–85), and those of Simon of Ghent (1297–1315) and Roger Martival (1315–30) of Salisbury.[13]

The headings on folios 1 and 5 of the register suggest that Langton's 'definitive' register began on folio 5. Though worn and stained, the heading on folio 1 is in normal handwriting occupying one line and may have been

---

[9] Smith, *Guide*, p. xi; C.R. Cheney, *English bishops' chanceries* (Manchester, 1950), 103.

[10] **79** too is a licence for study but it has been discounted here as this licence was incorporated into **37** which was subsequently duplicated in **228**.

[11] The earliest entry, a collation, is dated 3 Feb. 1297 (**375**), and an institution is dated simply 1297 (**151**), while the first precisely dated institution is 24 Sept. 1297 (**233**); the first ordination list is for June 1300 (**1285**), there are no ordination lists for 1313, and those for March 1314 (**1310**) and April 1321 (**1329**) are incomplete.

[12] Three entries in this section also have contemporary archdeaconry notations in the margin (**403, 405, 407**).

[13] Smith, *Guide*, p. xi, 234–5; BIHR, Reg. 3; *Reg. Gandavo*, i, p. lv; *Reg. Martival*, iv, pp. xxiii–iv.

added later, whereas that on folio 5 is in a large, elaborate script with many embellishments. The date of the second heading (2 February 1297) pre-dates by one day the earliest entry in the register (**375**).

Other evidence in the 'definitive' register confirms that working records were used in Langton's episcopal chancery. Folio 65A records the working copies of Langton's injunctions given to Haughmond Abbey, having many erasures and alterations (**949, 950**). It was not customary to preserve such injunctions if these were issued during the actual visitation of a house. It is thus probable that a fair copy was not made on this occasion and these working records became incorporated into the register: fair copies were made of the bishop's injunctions given in letter form to other religious houses (**809*–812**).

Elsewhere, groups of letters were obviously copied from a working record at periodic intervals; for example, **415–440**, which date from 17 December 1300 to 22 April 1301, seem to have been written by one clerk and at one time. Nevertheless, the 'definitive' register was sometimes used as a working record: **364*** and **365** were added at the foot of folio 20 and cut in two **363**; on folio 44 **720** similarly cuts in two **719***; and **1014** was added later at the foot of folio 69; while additional information was added to other entries at a later date (e.g. **109, 175, 457, 657, 669, 706, 716**). Entry **1167** commences as a grant *in commendam* dated 10 March 1319 to which another hand has added that the same clerk was instituted rector on 17 May 1319. This addition was written by the hand which copied the next entry (**1168**) dated 11 June 1319, indicating that the addition to **1167** was not made until that date at least. A similar example occurs on folio 14, where all the entries again seem to have been recorded by one hand at one time. Placed at the head of this folio **261** initially recorded the grant of custody of Aston upon Trent church to John de Sandale on 3 November 1304. Though subsequent entries run in date order, when Sandale was instituted rector on 1 October 1305 this was registered in the space left at the head of the folio, before the grant of custody, instead of being recorded in date sequence with **268** and **269** which bear the same date. Sandale's institution to two other rectories (**302, 638**), of which he had been initially granted custody (**298, 634**), were recorded separately in date order.

The ordination lists are a collection of individual quires and folios which were whip-stitched together before being sewn into the volume. The ordinands' names are listed in two or three columns per folio which run from folio to folio, a layout which indicates that they were originally recorded on rolls during the ceremony itself, as the working record, and then copied onto the present folios.[14]

Langton's vicars-general used working registers. Until 1307 the definitive copies of their records were written in the relevant archdeaconry sections amongst those of the bishop himself: thereafter, apart from a short commission in 1309, separate definitive registers were compiled which were later bound into the bishop's register. Part of the working register of one vicar-general has survived in the ordination section of the register. Folio 116 records six cancelled letters (**1308**) which duplicate **588–593**. This folio bears the marginal note *Staff*': the cancelled letters are recorded on folio 32v, which is the Stafford archdeaconry section of the register of M. Ralph de Leicester, vicar-general in

---

[14] Swanson, 'Rolls of Roger de Meuland', 39; Hughes, 'Episcopate', i.46.

1312–13.[15] Examination of the register of the previous vicar-general, M. Robert de Redeswell, (489–551) shows that he too used a working record. Most of his letters are in chronological order, the exceptions being 499, 506, 541, and they appear to have been written by the same hand and at one time; there is no obvious change in ink. One letter dated 30 December 1307 (511) enjoins the recipient to be at Lichfield before Purification to receive institution, but it continues by stating that, when he failed to appear, another clerk was granted the benefice: he was instituted vicar on 1 July 1308 (531). This indicates that 511 was not written-up until after the latter date, and it is probable that Redeswell's definitive register was made only when his commission had ended on 9 November 1308.[16]

Working registers continued to be used in the Lichfield episcopal chancery during the pontificates of Langton's two successors, Roger Northburgh (1322–58) and Robert Stretton (1360–85), probably through inherited working practices,[17] while evidence from other dioceses suggests that their use was commonplace.[18] This was the case at York where there are examples from the fourteenth to the early sixteenth centuries. The York *sede vacante* register for 1315–17 survives in two versions, the initial working register and the later duplicate (this is the case also for the vacancies in 1397, 1398, 1423–6, 1464–5, 1480, 1500–1, 1507–8 and 1514, as well as William Wickwane's register and part of Thomas Rotherham's).[19] The entries in the working section of this 1315–17 vacancy register are listed chronologically, without any subject or geographical divisions, and an abbreviated marginal note has been written against each indicating which section the entry should be placed in the duplicate definitive

[15] See Hughes, 'Episcopate', iii.1159 for a facsimile of these folios.

[16] When Redeswell was vicar-general again for a short time in 1309 four letters only arose from the business transacted by him (618, 701, 702, 834) and these were copied into the relevant archdeaconry sections of the bishop's register; on this occasion he probably considered it unnecessary to record such a small amount of business separately.

[17] Northburgh's clerks may have used a day book or copied entries from previously written separate sheets, see R.A Davies, 'A calendar of the archdeaconry of Stafford section of the register of Roger Northburgh, bishop of Coventry and Lichfield, with some discussion of its contents' (Unpublished Ph.D. thesis, University of Birmingham, 1986), 8. Licences and dispensations for non-residence have been entered 'untidily' in the front of Northburgh's and Stretton's registers, on folios of a smaller size, as though they were not intended for permanent preservation, see Robinson, *Hand list*, 3; LJRO B/A/1/2 (Northburgh), fos. 4v–15v; B/A/1/5i (Stretton), fos. 3–39v (this section of Stretton's second register is now bound separately), printed in *The registers or act books of the bishops of Coventry and Lichfield. Book 5, being the second register of Bishop Robert de Stretton, A.D. 1360–1385: an abstract of the contents*, ed. R.A. Wilson (William Salt Archaeological Society, new series, 8, 1905), 6–90.

[18] *The register of William Bateman, bishop of Norwich 1344–1355*, ed. P.E. Pobst (CYS, 84, 1996), i, p. xiii.; *Reg. Gandavo*, i, p. lv; *Reg. Martival*, iv, pp. xxiii–iv; *The register of John Waltham, bishop of Salisbury 1388–1395*, ed. T.C.B. Timmins (CYS, 80, 1994), p. xx, nos. 910–969; *The register of Walter Bronescombe, bishop of Exeter 1258–1280*, ed. O.F. Robinson (CYS, 82, 1995), i, pp. xii–xiii; *The register of Thomas Langley, bishop of Durham, 1406–1437*, ed. R.L. Storey (Surtees Society, 164, 166, 169, 170, 177, 182, 1956–70), i, p. xxxviii; ii, no. 376. Thanks are due to Professor Storey for this reference.

[19] Smith, *Guide*, p. xi, 232–3, 234–5, 237, 245–6; BIHR, Reg. 5A (1315–17 vacancy), Reg. 3 (Wickwane), Reg. 23 (Rotherham).

register:[20] the similarities between this volume and the first four folios of Langton's register are striking. It thus seems that the re-copying process of folios 1–4 was not completed at Lichfield and that the registrar decided to retain them for that reason.

The rest of the register has a structured format with some distinction being made of subject matter or archdeaconries, and with separate quires being used for these sections. From folio 5 onwards institutions and other business, including grants of custodies and licences after 1307, are recorded in the relevant archdeaconry sections: Chester, Coventry, Derby, Shrewsbury and Stafford. These are arranged in three groups:

folios 5–19v:	February 1297 – April 1307
folios 34–48v, 56–77:	May 1307 – February 1321
folios 78–91v:	March 1317 – October 1321.

The other sections of the register have been bound around these: the registers of M. Robert de Redeswell and M. Ralph de Leicester, vicars-general in 1307–8 and 1312–13 respectively, are on folios 27–30r and 31–33r; miscellaneous business is recorded on two gatherings comprising folios 20–25v and 49–55v; while the ordination lists from Langton's episcopate are on folios 92–141v, followed by those of Northburgh. Four smaller pieces of parchment, folios 65A, 84, 99, and 142, have also been bound into the register. Folio 65A measures approximately 20.4cm. in width and 9.5cm. in length and is a working record of injunctions given to Haughmond Abbey (**949, 950**). Folio 84 measures approximately 20.5cm. in width and 6.5cm. in length and records two items of routine business (**1185, 1186**). Folio 99 is slightly irregular in size and measures some 20cm. in width by 16cm. in length: its recto is blank, but recorded on the verso are copies of a charter, quitclaim, and letters patent by which Langton granted land and the advowson of Adlingfleet church, in York diocese, to Selby Abbey (**1291–1293**).[21] Folio 142 measures approximately 19cm. in width by 8.5cm. in length and again its recto is blank: the verso records an extract of a letter from Boniface VIII allowing friars to be ordained by any Catholic bishop (**1330**).

Each separate section of the register has a contemporary heading; in addition, the relevant archdeaconry name has been written by a contemporary hand at the head of every folio of the first archdeaconry section (folios 5–19v). The headings *Stafford'* added to folios 22v, 23r, and 24r are erroneous as these folios record grants of custodies and licences in each of the five archdeaconries. Contemporary thumb-tabs were stitched to the fore-edges of folios 18 (Shrewsbury

---

[20] There are seven notations, five of which refer to the archdeaconries: *Eb'* York, *No'* Nottingham, *Ry'* Richmond, *Est'* the East Riding, and *Cly'* Cleveland; while *Ca'* marks those entries for the section relating to the chapter of York, and *Suff'* those pertaining to the suffragan see of Durham which was vacant in 1316–17. Every entry in the working York vacancy register has been given one of these marginal notes to facilitate the copying process: BIHR, Reg. 5A (fos. 192–220 working register, fos. 119–41 and 175–86 definitive register). See Hughes, 'Episcopate', iii.1160 for facsimiles of entries on fo. 193 and their duplicate copies on fo. 137v.

[21] Hughes, 'Family', 70–1.

archdeaconry), 34 (Coventry archdeaconry), 41 (Stafford archdeaconry), 56 (Chester archdeaconry), and 92 (the ordination section); these are now grouped together at the back of the register. All are well-worn and were cut from used parchment as there are scraps of writing on the back as well as the heading on the front. There may have been thumb-tabs for other sections of the register which have not survived, but it has been impossible to determine stitch-holes on other relevant folios.

The ordination lists

Ordination lists do not survive for the whole of Langton's episcopate; the first is dated 4 June 1300 (**1285**) and the last, dated 18 April 1321 (**1329**), is incomplete. There are one or two lists for most of the intervening years, the exceptions being 1310 and 1320 (four each) and 1316, 1317, and 1319 (three each). No lists survive for 1313.[22] There are no obvious signs of incompleteness except perhaps in the recording of regular clergy between 1307 and 1314 and in the absence of lists of deacons and priests, and perhaps some subdeacons, ordained in March 1314 (**1310**).[23] However, an entry in Oliver Sutton's Lincoln register records that ordinations were celebrated on 21 December 1297 in St. Chad's church, Shrewsbury, by the bishop of St. Asaph 'acting by the authority and on behalf of the bishop of Lichfield and Coventry'.[24]

The ordinands' names are arranged in either two or three columns in the lists. Those of acolytes do occur (**1286, 1290, 1302, 1309**), but in the main it was customary to record only the names of those ordained subdeacon, deacon, and priest. In some later lists these categories are further subdivided to distinguish the religious from the secular clergy (**1320, 1323–1326**), and on one occasion an additional category of beneficed clerks, both secular and religious, occurs (**1320**).

Occasional notes against some ordinands' names suggest that either letters of holy orders or letters testimonial were issued by Langton's chancellor: *habet litteram,* or simply *habet,* has been written alongside the names of some priests (e.g. **1285**), while elsewhere *sit littera* occurs (e.g. **1303**). Sometimes more information is given, suggesting that letters were issued to the ordinands' patrons: William de Elmedon, priest, *habet litteram et cancellarius illam dedit nuncio prioris Coventr'*; William de Lillington, priest, *cancellarius dedit suppriori de Stone*; whereas the chancellor gave letters from two bundles to John de Scutard and William de Claverlee, priests (**1285**). Letters elsewhere in the register illustrate how necessary it was for a clerk to retain such a record of his ordination. When William de Nostrefeld was presented to Colton church the inquiry maintained it had no knowledge of William's orders, but he proved he had been ordained priest by his letters testimonial; he was then admitted to the benefice (**686, 687**). Ralph de Longedon had his letters of holy orders examined by suitable witnesses on 7 June 1312 (**588**); he had been ordained priest on 22 September 1302 (**1288**).

[22] See Appendix B in Volume II.
[23] For a detailed discussion of the ordination lists see D. Robinson, 'Ordinations of secular clergy in the diocese of Coventry and Lichfield, 1322–1358', *Archives*, 17, 73 (April, 1985), 3–21.
[24] *Reg. Sutton*, vii.111.

Five ordination lists record copies of a monition which would have been read out to the ordinands at the start of each service (**1313, 1320, 1321, 1323, 1324**), with eight others being briefly noted (**1315–1319, 1325, 1327, 1328**). These give the requirements of canon law for the ordination of clergy and they would have formed the basis of all pre-ordination examinations, though why they have been recorded only from 1315 is unclear.[25]

The celebrant of the first two recorded ordination services on 4 June and 17 December 1300 is not given (**1285, 1286**), but letters elsewhere in the register (**104, 331, 415–417**) show that Langton himself officiated. Although the lists do not form a complete series, Langton personally celebrated 31 of the 41 services, some of which would have lasted a very long time. These were held in a variety of churches, indicating the bishop visited the southern part of his diocese regularly.[26] In addition, Langton was granted licence to hold ordination services in the diocese of York after 29 May, 13 October, and 29 December 1298, in the church of the Friars Minor, York, on 21 February 1304, and after 24 May 1311.[27] Although no ordination lists have survived, Langton's itinerary shows him to have been in York around those dates. Acting upon the faculty of May 1311 Langton could have ordained at York on 5 June (Trinity), but a letter of that date explains that he was then unable to ordain Geoffrey de Vilers to the priesthood, as previously arranged, because of 'great personal indisposition': he was, in fact, then imprisoned at York, although he did grant a licence and institute a rector that day (**633*, 861, 951**).[28] Langton was later licensed by the archbishop of Canterbury to hold an ordination service at Southwark on 20 September 1316, during the vacancy of the see of Winchester, when he ordained clergy from several dioceses, including his own.[29]

Other bishops, some acting as suffragans, were commissioned to celebrate ordinations and to perform other sacramental duties in the diocese when Langton was unable to officiate. In addition to the bishop of St. Asaph in December 1297, John Halton, bishop of Carlisle, and two suffragan bishops, Thomas de Kirkcudbright, bishop of Whithorn, and Gilbert O'Tigernaig, the Franciscan bishop of Annaghdown, were commissioned in turn. Though their commissions are not registered, the faculty to ordain is incorporated in the heading of each ordination list (**1287, 1288, 1295–1301, 1309**).[30]

---

[25] *Councils and synods*, II, i.170, 172, 173, 179, 248, 297–306, 313; Hughes, 'Clergy list', 5–6; Hughes, 'Register', 5–6.

[26] Hughes, 'Register', 3; Appendices B, C in Volume II.

[27] *Reg. Romeyn*, ii.248; *The register of Thomas Corbridge, lord archbishop of York, 1300–1304*, ed. W. Brown, A. Hamilton Thompson (Surtees Society, 138, 141, 1925–8), ii.154; *The register of William Greenfield, lord archbishop of York*, ed. W. Brown, A. Hamilton Thompson (Surtees Society, 114, 149, 151–3, 1931–40), iv, no. 2339.

[28] See below p. xxxiv; for Langton's itinerary see Appendix D in Volume II.

[29] Lambeth Palace Library MS., The register of Walter Reynolds, fos. 174v–175v (no class reference); printed in *The registers of John de Sandale and Rigaud de Asserio, bishops of Winchester (A.D. 1316–1323)*, ed. F.J. Baigent (Hampshire Record Society, 1897), 347–9.

[30] Hughes, 'Episcopate', i.56–9.

DIOCESAN ADMINISTRATION

By the time of Langton's episcopate the location of the see was firmly established at Lichfield and the prelates styled themselves bishops of Coventry and Lichfield, although contemporary documents often refer to the diocesan as bishop of Chester.[31]

The diocese of Coventry and Lichfield was the third largest in England after York and Lincoln, and it covered an area of approximately 5,260 square miles.[32] The diocese was divided into five archdeaconries: Chester, Coventry, Derby, Shrewsbury, and Stafford. Of these, Derby and Stafford corresponded approximately to the county boundaries; Chester comprised the whole of Cheshire, Lancashire as far north as the river Ribble, a few parishes in Flintshire, and a single parish in Denbighshire; Shrewsbury comprised the northern part of Shropshire; and Coventry part of Warwickshire.[33]

The archdeaconry of Chester

The archdeaconry of Chester was in the bishop's collation, though no record of such exercise of patronage is recorded in the register. M. Robert de Redeswell, D.C.L., was archdeacon when Langton was elevated to the episcopate, having been collated before May 1289,[34] and he held office until his death before 17 January 1315 (**892**). He was succeeded by M. Richard de Havering between 18 February and 18 March 1315 (**893, 895**), and he was in office until his death in 1341.[35] As the register is silent about Havering it must be assumed that he was an absentee, particularly in light of his illustrious secular career. Redeswell, however, was resident and became one of the leading administrators of the diocese, being appointed Langton's vicar-general in 1307–8 and in 1309.

Chester was the largest and principal archdeaconry of the diocese and the only one to have a prebend attached to it, that of Bolton le Moors.[36] Redeswell was also rector of Davenham (**892**), and in March 1291 he was granted papal dispensation to hold this in plurality as the archdeaconry had 'no house of residence'.[37] This dispensation was questioned by Archbishop Winchelsey in 1296 when he accused Redeswell as well as the archdeacon of Derby, and others, of pluralism.[38] After Redeswell's death M. Richard de Vernoun was instituted to Davenham (**892**), and on 17 February 1315 he was said to be keeper

---

[31] *VCH Staffordshire*, iii.7–8; A. Hamilton Thompson, 'Diocesan organization in the Middle Ages: archdeacons and rural deans', *Proceedings of the British Academy* (1943), 165.

[32] This figure refers to the year 1517, see P. Hughes, *The reformation in England* (London, 1950), i.31–2; Hughes, 'Register', 2.

[33] Robinson, *Hand list*, 1; Smith, *Guide*, 53. For the deaneries see *VCH Cheshire*, iii.10–11; *VCH Lancashire*, ii.9; *VCH Warwickshire*, ii.6, 83; *VCH Derbyshire*, ii. 40, 41; *VCH Shropshire*, ii.4; *VCH Staffordshire*, iii.92–3, 139; *Taxatio ecclesiastica Angliae et Walliae auctoritate P. Nicholai IV circa A.D. 1291* (Record Commission, 1802), 241–7.

[34] *BRUO*, iii.2209; *Fasti*, x.12.

[35] *BRUO*, iii.2181; *Fasti*, x.12.

[36] P. Heath, 'The medieval archdeaconry and Tudor bishopric of Chester', *JEH*, 20 (1969), 244; K. Edwards, *The English secular cathedrals in the Middle Ages* (Manchester, 1949), 252.

[37] *CPL*, i.529.

[38] *Reg. Winchelsey*, i.120.

of the archdeaconry (**893**). His keepership had terminated by 18 March when a mandate to induct was once again addressed to the archdeacon (**895**).

In 1315 Archdeacon Havering made an agreement with the bishop concerning the extent of his jurisdiction whereby, for their lives only, the archdeacon was to have the primary hearing of causes, the proving and accounting of wills, synodals, Peter's Pence, and the perquisites of his chapter throughout his archdeaconry, while the bishop was to receive £20 a year from the archdeacon, and retain all rights of sequestration and other matters which pertained to him by custom.[39] A sequestrator-general's account roll indicates that Redeswell too had made such an agreement with Bishop Langton and records £20 paid by him in 1301. The need for this agreement arose from the palatine status the county of Chester enjoyed, which made it difficult for the bishop to cite offenders there to the consistory court in Lichfield, or elsewhere, without royal support. To overcome this successive bishops granted the archdeacon exclusive primary jurisdiction, enabling offenders to be tried within the county.[40]

The archdeaconry of Coventry

This archdeaconry was in the bishop's collation until November 1299, but from 1302 archdeacons of Coventry were provided by the pope, as were archdeacons of Stafford: the rise in the number of papal provisions during the fourteenth century is thus reflected in the diocese.[41] There were five archdeacons of Coventry during Langton's episcopate, and each was an absentee: M. Robert de Stafford, M. Peter de Insula, Gregory Giudice de Alatri, Richard de Anibaldis, and John Gaetani de Urbe.[42]

Robert de Stafford had been collated by Bishop Meuland before 1 December 1295 when he was granted papal dispensation to hold the archdeaconry and two rectories (Tibshelf and Checkley) in plurality. In 1299 he was also prebendary of the royal free chapel of St. Michael, Penkridge.[43] Stafford is mentioned once only in the register: on 30 March 1299 Langton granted him licence to travel to the Curia for two years on his own business and on pilgrimage (**66**). He received royal protection on 26 May, but died while overseas, and on 31 October 1299 his prebend at Penkridge was granted to another.[44]

Langton collated the next archdeacon, M. Peter de Insula, D.Cn.L., on 14 November 1299 (**60, 387**); he is not mentioned again in the register. In addition he held a rectory and prebend in the diocese of York. He had vacated the archdeaconry by 10 May 1302, and was subsequently collated archdeacon of Carlisle in November 1302, which office he retained until his death before 26 November 1311.[45]

---

[39] *MRA*, no. 675; Heath, 'Medieval archdeaconry', 245.

[40] Hughes, 'Account roll', 128, and n. 50; Heath, 'Medieval archdeaconry', 249–50; *VCH Cheshire*, iii.8–9.

[41] P. Heath, *Church and Realm 1272–1461* (1988), 125–34.

[42] *Fasti*, x.14.

[43] M. William de Kilkenny occurs as archdeacon on 28 June 1293, *CPR 1292–1301*, 29; *CPL*, i.561; *CPR 1292–1301*, 450.

[44] *CPR 1292–1301*, 400, 450.

[45] *BRUO*, ii.1003; *Reg. Halton*, i.176–7, 208; ii.41; *Fasti*, vi.34, 101.

The archdeaconry was then occupied by alien papal provisors, although it was not highly remunerated: the archdeacon's portion in the deanery of Coventry was said to be £6 13s. 4d. in 1291.[46] Gregory Giudice de Alatri was apparently the next archdeacon, but the only information concerning him is notice of his death when Richard de Anibaldis was provided on 10 May 1302.[47] He remained in office until 29 August 1320 when he exchanged the archdeaconry with John Gaetani de Urbe, cardinal deacon of St. Theodore, for a canonry and prebend in Reims cathedral (**1144**). Anibaldis' bull of provision also granted him dispensation to hold four other canonries, although he was under age and not in orders; and in February 1303 and December 1310 he received indults to visit his archdeaconry by deputy for five and three years respectively.[48] Gaetani was admitted and collated by proxy. He held office until 1335 and on 1 March 1325 he too was granted an indult to visit his archdeaconry by deputy for five years.[49]

The archdeaconry of Derby

There were two archdeacons of Derby during Langton's episcopate, M. Ellis de Napton and M. Geoffrey de Blaston,[50] both of whom were resident in office and were leading administrators in the diocese.

Napton occurs as archdeacon in July 1281 and he died in office on 12 July 1311 (**635**). He had been appointed coadjutor to Bishop Meuland by Archbishop Pecham, a position he may have held until Meuland's death in December 1295.[51] In March 1302 he was appointed one of three administrators of the diocese when the pope suspended Langton from episcopal office and sequestered the see.

Napton was also rector of Warmington (**635**), and held prebends in Derby, Eccleshall,[52] and St. John's collegiate church, Chester (**866**). In 1296 Winchelsey accused him together with the archdeacon of Chester, and others, of pluralism and judgment was deferred until Langton, then bishop elect of Coventry and Lichfield, had returned from abroad.[53] The outcome of the case is not documented, but he continued to hold his benefices in plurality until his death. When Napton's Chester prebend was granted to another clerk in September 1311 it was said that he had neglected his prebendal manse there, and provision was made for repairs to be carried out (**866**).

The archdeaconry was vacant for almost five months before Geoffrey de Blaston was collated on 19 December 1311 (**1050**); he held office until his death in February 1328. Blaston had a long career in Langton's administration: he was one of the bishop's clerks by 1300, and his commissary-general by January 1305

---

[46] *VCH Staffordshire*, iii.31; *Taxatio*, 244.
[47] *CPL*, i.602.
[48] *Fasti*, i.92; *CPL*, i.602, 608; *CPL*, ii.81.
[49] *CPL*, ii.242.
[50] *Fasti*, x.16.
[51] *MRA*, no. 643; *Registrum epistolarum Fratris Johannis Peckham, archiepiscopi Cantuariensis*, ed. T. Martin (Rolls Series, 1882–5), i.205; ii.727; iii.946; *Reg. Winchelsey*, i.59.
[52] *Fasti*, x.34; Bodleian Library MS. Ashmole 794, fo. 71v.
[53] *Reg. Winchelsey*, i.120.

(**473***) at least, which office he appears to have resigned on becoming archdeacon. He was commissioned to act for the bishop *ad hoc* on several occasions (**877, 1014, 1058**).[54] Blaston too was a pluralist both before[55] and during his archidiaconate: by August 1318 he was prebendary of the royal free chapel of Wolverhampton, and he was prebendary of Tarvin in October 1319 and at his death.[56] He may have received Tarvin when he was granted a hall in Lichfield cathedral close for life on 24 August 1311 (**803***). This hall had been occupied by M. Walter de Clipston, the bishop's nephew, when prebendary of Tarvin: if this was the prebendal manse Blaston may have succeeded Clipston in the prebend by that date also.[57] The vicar at Tarvin was Nicholas de Blaston, who had been presented by Clipston in September 1308 (**547**): Nicholas was probably a kinsman of Geoffrey.

The archdeaconry of Shrewsbury

Little information survives for the archdeaconries of Shrewsbury and Stafford and their incumbents. The archdeaconry of Shrewsbury was in the bishop's collation. In January 1299 the archdeacon was 'Master C'.[58] He was succeeded by M. Philip de Cornwall, prebendary of Ryton, who was collated on 15 January 1304 (**395**). He died shortly afterwards, before 21 January (**398**). Cornwall had been clerk to Archbishop Pecham and in December 1280 he completed the archbishop's visitation of Coventry and Lichfield diocese.[59]

After Cornwall's death the sequestrator-general, John Pupard, became keeper of the archdeaconry (**339**) and he inducted the next archdeacon M. Richard de Bernard, who was collated on 24 March 1304 (**342**). Bernard seems to have been resident (**447, 473***), and he held office throughout Langton's episcopate, and probably until September 1332. Bernard was apparently rector of Newport about 1290, but for how long is unclear.[60]

The archdeaconry of Stafford

The archdeaconry of Stafford was occupied by alien papal provisors for the whole of Langton's episcopate: M. Rayner de Vichio, papal chaplain, died

[54] *MRA*, nos. 328, 329, 333, 375, 571, 574, 575, 577, 579. After Langton's death Blaston was commissioned vicar-general by Bishop Northburgh, see LJRO MS. B/A/1/2, fos. 3–4.

[55] He was instituted rector of Quainton, Lincoln diocese, on 14 Sept. 1302 at Langton's presentation, and on 28 March 1304 he was collated prebendary of Bishopshull (**478**), but resigned both on becoming archdeacon (**734**); G. Lipscomb, *The history and antiquities of the county of Buckingham*, 4 vols. (London, 1847), i.420.

[56] *Fasti*, x.59; *CCR 1318–23*, 4; *MRA*, no. 571; Bodleian Library MS. Ashmole 794, fo. 72.

[57] *Fasti*, x.20, n. 3; 59 and note; Hughes, 'Family', 73–4.

[58] *Registrum Ricardi de Swinfield, episcopi Herefordensis, A.D. MCCLXXXIII–MCCCXVII*, ed. W.W. Capes (CYS, 6, 1909), 349.

[59] *Registrum epistolarum Fratris Johannis Peckham, archiepiscopi Cantuariensis*, ed. T. Martin (Rolls Series, 1882–5), i.154, 180.

[60] *Fasti*, x.17; *BRUO*, i.178. Richard de Geidon, then rector of Newport, died on 1 Jan. 1315 (**977**).

before 6 June 1301 when John de Brunforte was provided; Brunforte resigned on 19 January 1322.[61]

Vichio was in priest's orders by 15 May 1290 when he was granted papal dispensation to retain the rectories of Hayes, in London diocese, and Herringswell, in Norwich diocese, on condition that he resigned the latter within a year. It is uncertain when Vichio became archdeacon, but it may have been before January 1295 when he was said to be prebendary of Gaia Minor. He was granted papal licence to make a will on 22 May 1301, shortly before his death.[62]

The papal bull providing Brunforte confirms he succeeded Vichio as prebendary of Gaia Minor also: he was granted dispensation to hold them as he was then about twelve years old and had received the first tonsure only, and he was instructed to receive higher orders at the proper age. Brunforte was the son of Octavian de Brunforte, a member of Boniface VIII's household. On 27 April 1309 a benefice in the diocese of Fermo was reserved for him, to be held in addition to his archdeaconry and prebend at Lichfield.[63] Edward II granted the archdeaconry to M. Robert de Patrika a month after Langton's death. Brunforte was deposed by Bishop Northburgh and he then resigned in favour of Patrika.[64]

As both Vichio and Brunforte were absentees the administration of the archdeaconry fell to their official. In July 1311 this was M. Adam de Byrom (**726***), and he probably held this office from May 1308 at least (**524, 709**).

The rural deans

Despite a papal ruling that bishop and archdeacon should jointly appoint and dismiss rural deans, local custom prevailed in England,[65] and in the archdeaconries of Coventry, Derby, Shrewsbury, and Stafford they were appointed by the bishop during pleasure, but the archdeacon of Chester made his own appointments. However, in 1325 the commissary-general was authorized to appoint and dismiss rural deans, and in 1360 the sequestrator-general was empowered to appoint rural deans and apparitors 'whose appointment belongs to the bishop', but these may have been temporary concessions.[66]

Rural deans were beneficed locally and their duties generally included the

[61] *Fasti*, x.18–19; *CPL*, i.596; *VCH Staffordshire*, iii.31.

[62] *CPL*, i.514, 561, 596.

[63] *CPL*, i.596; *CPL*, ii.76; Hughes, 'Episcopate', i.119–20.

[64] *Fasti*, x.18–19, 42, 50; *CPR 1321–4*, 41; for Patrika see *BRUO*, iii.1434–5.

[65] *Councils and synods*, II, i.553, n. 2. In the diocese of Bath and Wells in 1319 rural deans were said to be elected annually by the clergy of their deanery, and by the early fifteenth century beneficed clergy here and in the diocese of Exeter held the office in turn, see R.M. Haines, *The administration of the diocese of Worcester in the first half of the fourteenth century* (London, 1965), 66, 67, n. 1, 73, n. 10; R.W. Dunning, 'Rural deans in England in the fifteenth century', *Bulletin of the Institute of Historical Research*, 40 (1967), 209.

[66] *VCH Staffordshire*, iii.35, 36, 38–9; *VCH Lancashire*, ii.9; *VCH Cheshire*, iii.10; C.A. Haigh, 'Finance and administration in a new diocese: Chester, 1541–1641' in *Continuity and change: personnel and administration of the church of England, 1500–1642*, ed. R. O'Day and F. Heal (Leicester, 1976), 147; Storey, *Diocesan administration* (1959), 15; *The registers or act books of the bishops of Coventry and Lichfield. Book 5, being the second register of Bishop Robert de Stretton, A.D. 1360–1385: an abstract of the contents*, ed. R.A. Wilson (William Salt Archaeological Society, new series, 8, 1905), 3–4.

supervision of clergy and their churches, and the welfare and morals of all persons within their deanery, and they held chapters of clergy, probably at monthly intervals and possibly by archidiaconal authority.[67] Because their offices were so localized rural deans were key administrative agents in the diocese: they were commissioned *ad hoc* in all five archdeaconries, particularly to induct incumbents (**7, 153, 669, 671, 905, 1045, 1142, 1240, 1264**), as custodians of sequestrated property (**36, 75, 459, 668**), for which they accounted to the sequestrator-general (**86**),[68] and on one occasion in testamentary matters (**515**). Their jurisdiction in the latter was regulated in February 1311 when Langton granted that rural deans in the archdeaconries of Coventry, Derby, Shrewsbury, and Stafford might henceforth admit probate of wills under 100s. in their deaneries (**719***), which put them on an equal footing with their counterparts in the diocese of York.[69] The rural deans of Chester archdeaconry were excluded because the archdeacon had the sole right to prove wills within his archdeaconry. However, by the fifteenth century, if not before, rural deans there had acquired the right to prove wills under £40, except those of clergy and esquires.[70]

The chancellor

Langton's chancellor is named once only in the register: M. Thomas de Abberbury[71] was in this office in March 1300 when Eudes de Derb' acknowledged his obligation to pay the bishop 50 marks (£33 6s. 8d.) for the fruits of Heanor church, which he had previously been granted *in commendam* (**366, 8, 219, 237**). Abberbury is mentioned in connection with financial matters both before and after this date (**67, 364***, **368, 370**), and other entries confirm the chancellor's fiscal involvement (**46, 85, 109, 110, 170**). Notes added to some names in an ordination list suggest that the chancellor issued letters of holy orders or letters testimonial to ordinands or their patrons (**1285**), and letters of proxy were kept in his letter-chest (**504**).

Abberbury probably held the chancellorship until his death at about the beginning of May 1307 and, when so commissioned, the office of vicar-general concurrently. He was certainly acting in some administrative capacity for Langton on 30 April 1306 after his last term as vicar-general had ended, when he wrote, under his own seal, but with the bishop's knowledge, to John Pupard, the sequestrator-general (**463**): he apparently did not use the bishop's seal *ad causas*.[72]

External evidence records that M. Robert de Weston was Langton's chancellor in December 1317 when he accompanied the bishop on a visitation

---

[67] Haines, *Administration of the diocese of Worcester*, 50, 51, n. 4, 65, 73; A. Hamilton Thompson, 'Diocesan organization in the Middle Ages: archdeacons and rural deans', *Proceedings of the British Academy* (1943), 185.

[68] Hughes, 'Account roll', 113–14, 132–9.

[69] Storey, *Diocesan administration* (1959), 11.

[70] *MRA*, no. 675; *VCH Cheshire*, iii.11.

[71] *BRUO*, i.2.

[72] Storey, *Diocesan administration* (1972), 4; Haines, *Administration of the diocese of Worcester*, 124–5.

of the archdeaconry of Coventry. Weston is not mentioned in the register, but a man of the same name witnessed an agreement made by Langton in May 1317.[73]

The official

The official presided, either in person or by commissary, as the judicial deputy of the bishop in the consistory court, which at Lichfield was usually held in the cathedral, and appeals from this court went directly to the Court of the Arches.[74] The demarcation of duties of the official and commissary-general at Lichfield are, however, difficult to determine, as they often appear indistinguishable.

Two officials only are named in the register, M. Walter de Thorp, D.Cn.L., and M. Philip de Turville. Both held benefices in the diocese, and elsewhere, until their deaths in 1321 and 1337 respectively.[75] Thorp was commissioned both official and vicar-general from the beginning of Langton's episcopate, and he relinquished the latter about mid-November 1297 (**1154, 6, 224, 22, 64, 156, 69*, 233**). Thorp left Langton's service when he was appointed dean of the Arches in July 1303, and it seems that the officiality was then vacant until Turville was commissioned on 22 November 1313: there is no mention of the official in the intervening period and presumably his duties were then carried out by the commissary-general, or other officers *ad hoc*. Turville was authorized to hear all *ex officio* or instance causes pertaining to the bishop's jurisdiction, and to correct and punish offences, with coercion (**757***). He is not mentioned in the register after March 1316 (**602, 653, 657, 767, 773, 877, 880, 972**) even though he was prebendary of Curborough until his death.[76]

The commissary-general and sequestrator-general

As the fourteenth century progressed the duties of the commissary-general and sequestrator-general were often combined.[77] In the diocese of Coventry and Lichfield this may have been from 1360, but during Langton's episcopate, although each officer received similar *ad hoc* commissions (e.g. **207, 342, 395, 473*, 859, 1047, 1050**), their primary duties remained separate, with the exception of testamentary jurisdiction from 1311 (**719***).[78] No commission of a commissary-general survives for the diocese until the beginning of Northburgh's episcopate in 1322: he was then authorized to hear and conclude causes of correction and instance, to investigate and correct crimes and excesses, to issue letters dimissory, and to do all that pertained to his office. In 1325 his authority

---

[73] T. Madox, *Formulare Anglicanum* (London, 1702), 11–12; *CCR 1313–18*, 470.

[74] Storey, *Diocesan administration* (1972), 5; C. Morris, 'A consistory court in the Middle Ages', *JEH*, 14 (1963), 151–2; *VCH Staffordshire*, iii.37.

[75] For Thorp see **3, 4, 22, 39, 156, 165, 378, 382, 1237, 1269, 1274, 1279, 1280**; *BRUO*, iii.2222; for Turville see **109, 445, 618, 702, 760**; *BRUO*, iii.1918. For both see Churchill, *Canterbury administration*, i.10, 443, 562 and note; ii.239, 242.

[76] *MRA*, no. 571; *Fasti*, x.27. After Langton's death Turville was keeper of the spiritualities *sede vacante*, see LJRO MS. B/A/1/2 fos. 1–2.

[77] Storey, *Diocesan administration* (1959), 8–16; C. Morris, 'The commissary of the bishop in the diocese of Lincoln', *JEH*, 10 (1959), 55–65.

[78] Hughes, 'Account roll', 111–12.

was extended to include jurisdiction over all cases in the bishop's consistory court at Lichfield, the appointment and removal of apparitors and rural deans, the issue of citations, and power to deprive clerks of their benefices.[79] However, a memorandum in the register (**935***) confirms that he had jurisdiction in the bishop's consistory court in 1310, and evidence from 1302 reveals he could act as the bishop's judicial officer, indicating that his duties were often similar to those of the official.[80]

Langton's commissary-generals were M. Simon de Shirleye (**287, 419, 452, 460**),[81] and he was succeeded by M. Geoffrey de Blaston, possibly by January 1304 (**395, 473*, 719***). When Blaston was collated archdeacon of Derby in December 1311 he may have resigned the commissaryship: no commissary-general is named thereafter, and in May 1319 Archdeacon Blaston was said to be the bishop's 'special commissary' (**1050, 1014**).

Despite the size of the diocese, Langton employed one sequestrator-general only, and no sub-sequestrators. Again, no commission appointing this officer has been registered, but the duties which generally fell to his office have been well-described: his primary function was as a bishop's chief collector of spiritual revenues and custodian of sequestrated property, whether benefices or the goods of intestates, and he was often granted testamentary jurisdiction by his diocesan. It was not unusual, however, for other diocesan administrators, chiefly archdeacons, their officials, or the rural deans, to be appointed *ad hoc* custodians of sequestrated property in the diocese.[82] The sequestrator-general's account for the period November 1297 to November 1298 is summarized in the register (**86**), presumably from a roll, or rolls, such as that which survives for the period January to Michaelmas 1301.[83] This account roll, three fragments of two other rolls for the period April 1309 to Michaelmas 1310, and one for the years 1315 to 1317 record episcopal revenue from spiritualities in the diocese.[84]

Langton's first sequestrator-general, M. William de Swepston, held office until November 1299 at least (**81, 86**). By March 1304 he had been succeeded by M. John Pupard, who is mentioned in office for the last time in December 1307 (**342, 344, 463**).[85] M. Richard de Northampton was commissioned by April 1310, and he was active in office until June 1314 (**840*, 715, 719*, 859, 634, 1047, 955, 1050, 963, 750, 1055, 1056**): he died on 11 June 1319 (**1008**), but Richard de Dolaby was said to be sequestrator-general in December 1317, though he is not mentioned in the register.[86]

---

[79] *VCH Staffordshire*, iii.35; LJRO MS. B/A/1/3, fos. 1, 13.

[80] *Descriptive catalogue of the muniments belonging to the marquis of Anglesey*, ed. I.H. Jeayes (Staffordshire Record Society, 1937), 116, 87.

[81] See the previous footnote.

[82] Hughes, 'Account roll', 111.

[83] LJRO MS. D30 M4; Hughes, 'Account roll', 116–39.

[84] LJRO MSS. D30 M9, D30 M5, D30 M7; Hughes, 'Account roll', 110; R.N. Swanson, 'Episcopal income from spiritualities in later medieval England: the evidence for the diocese of Coventry and Lichfield', *Midland History* (1988), 13–15.

[85] Beardwood, *Records*, 22, 75, 155.

[86] T. Madox, *Formulare Anglicanum* (London, 1702), 11–12.

The administration during Langton's suspension from episcopal office

When Boniface VIII suspended Langton from administration of his diocese between 30 March 1302 and 8 June 1303, while charges of gross misconduct were investigated,[87] he appointed three diocesan administrators: M. Thomas de Abberbury, Philip de Everdon, and M. Ellis de Napton. They were commissioned to act under apostolic authority in all matters spiritual and temporal, excepting any alienation of property and, because Langton had been thus deprived of all episcopal income, they were charged to provide sufficient maintenance for their diocesan.[88] Abberbury was Langton's vicar-general when the suspension was announced and his last letter of that commission is dated 12 April 1302 (**459**), while the first letters of the papal administrators are dated 26 July 1302 (**182, 292, 337**): Abberbury thus relinquished his former commission for that of papal administrator at some indeterminate time between those two dates. The administrators continued to act at least until 16 June 1303, the date of their last letter (**186**), after which Abberbury presumably resumed his commission as vicar-general until the bishop's return to England: Langton's first letter after his suspension was revoked is dated at London on 1 September 1303 (**392**).

Abberbury was one of Langton's most trusted officers, and his two colleagues were equally well-regarded. Everdon had been cofferer of the Wardrobe during Langton's keepership,[89] was prebendary of Wellington, having been collated in February 1299 (**31, 385, 480**), and had been granted houses in Lichfield cathedral close by the bishop in May 1300 (**412**). Napton was archdeacon of Derby. From Langton's point of view their selection as papal administrators was excellent, which may not have been accidental. One might have expected the pope to instruct Archbishop Winchelsey to appoint administrators for his suffragan see of Coventry and Lichfield, but he organized these appointments through his own officers. Langton was at the papal court when his suspension was announced, having successfully negotiated Edward I's entitlement to half the proceeds of the triennial tenth imposed by papal bull in February 1301.[90] The choice of the administrators and the way they were appointed suggests that the pope was not personally hostile to Langton, and that he may have allowed him some say in who was appointed to administer his diocese.[91] Langton may have exerted influence

[87] For the reason for Langton's suspension see below p. xxxv.

[88] *CPL*, i.601, 610; *MRA*, nos. 5, 305; Lunt, *Financial relations*, 503, dates Langton's suspension from 8 March 1302; Clement V later suspended Archbishop Winchelsey from administration of the diocese and province of Canterbury from 12 Feb. 1306 to 22 Jan. 1308, see Churchill, *Canterbury administration*, 567–8; *Reg. Winchelsey*, i, pp. xvii, xxiii–xxvii; Denton, *Winchelsey*, 211–47; Smith, *Guide*, 4, n. 10.

[89] *Book of prests of the king's wardrobe for 1294–5*, ed. E.B. Fryde (Oxford, 1962), 228.

[90] Lunt, *Financial relations*, 366–9; Denton, *Winchelsey*, 201–3; Hughes, 'Episcopate', i.233–5.

[91] In contrast, during Winchelsey's suspension Clement V appointed papal agents William Testa, archdeacon of Aran and papal collector of taxes, and William Geraud de Sore to administer the spiritualities and, eventually, the temporalities of the see of Canterbury after agreement had been reached with Edward I; Geraud was later replaced by Peter Amauvin: Churchill, *Canterbury administration*, 568; *Reg. Winchelsey*, i, p. xxv; Denton, *Winchelsey*, 239–42.

over the administrators' actions, particularly with regard to those collated to the two benefices in his patronage which fell vacant (**391, 460**),[92] as his itinerary shows that he was in England at that time.[93]

By virtue of Langton's suspension the diocese of Coventry and Lichfield was theoretically vacant but, despite the crown's claim to the temporal revenues of vacant sees,[94] there is no record that the king appointed his own keeper of the temporalities, and he seems to have accepted that they should be managed by the papal administrators, perhaps because of the favourable outcome of the negotiations concerning taxation.[95]

The register offers no evidence that the papal administrators made new appointments to any of the diocesan offices; being local men, they were probably content to re-commission the existing officers to act for them, but they would have had a new seal made for their use.[96] Presumably Abberbury and Napton continued as chancellor and archdeacon respectively, delegating those duties when necessary.

Fourteen entries document the administrators' activities and these are recorded in the relevant sections of the register, between similar business carried out before and after sequestration of the see[97] (**125, 126, 127, 182, 183*, 186, 251, 252, 292, 337, 391, 460, 461**): for the ordination service celebrated at Derby on 22 September 1302 they commissioned John Halton, bishop of Carlisle (**1288**), and presumably he, or a suffragan bishop, performed other essential sacramental duties. Elsewhere it is recorded that the administrators also issued letters dimissory.[98]

The administrators could and did act independently, sometimes outside the diocese; on 26 July 1302 they instituted three rectors in two different places, Banbury in Lincoln diocese (**182, 292**), and Lichfield (**337**). It was probably Abberbury who was at Banbury that day, as he came from the area (Adderbury), and held the manor of nearby Steeple Aston, where he was on 17 December 1302 (**183***), and on 22 April 1303 he was again in the vicinity at Abingdon (**127**); while some or all of the administrators were at York in October 1302

---

[92] Richard Abel, collated to St. Chad's collegiate church, Shrewsbury, was ten years old and the son of John Abel, escheator south of Trent, and M. Simon de Shirleye, collated master of Denhall Hospital, Cheshire, was the bishop's commissary-general.

[93] See Appendix D in Volume II.

[94] M. Howell, *Regalian right in medieval England* (London, 1962), 1.

[95] When Winchelsey was suspended from office in 1306 Clement V appointed none other than Walter Langton to administer the temporalities of Canterbury, but the king was unwilling to accept this and initially committed custody of the temporalities to Humphrey de Waledon. He eventually conceded that the temporalities should be administered by the papal agents: Lunt, *Financial relations*, 369, 503–4; *CCR 1296–1302*, 603; *CFR 1272–1307*, 538, 542, 543; Denton, *Winchelsey*, 240–2.

[96] At Canterbury Testa and Geraud had a seal made with the legend, '*Sigillum administratorum spiritualium Cant' per dominum papam deputorum*': *Reg. Winchelsey*, i, p. xxv.

[97] Winchelsey's register on the other hand shows no positive evidence of his suspension, nor records the acts of the administrators; presentations made to the administrators by the prior and chapter of Christ Church, Canterbury, are recorded in the prior's register, see Churchill, *Canterbury administration*, 568–9; Smith, *Guide*, 4.

[98] *Reg. Halton*, i.186; *The register of Bishop William Ginsborough, 1303 to 1307*, ed. J.W. Willis Bund (Worcestershire Historical Society, 1907), 126.

(**251, 461**). They may not have enjoyed a wholly harmonious association, however, as Abberbury complained on one occasion that his colleagues ought to have been with him more often (**183***).

Bishop Walter Langton

The prior and convent of Coventry and the dean and chapter of Lichfield elected Walter Langton, who was then prebendary of Sandiacre and canon of Lichfield (**375**), bishop in succession to Roger Meuland, or Longespée, on 20 February 1296. The Lichfield Chronicle records that the election was amicable and peacable, but doubts have been raised whether Langton's election was as free and spontaneous as it appears.[99] It is probable that the king, wishing his treasurer to receive the ultimate reward for loyal service to the crown, exerted some influence over the choice of the two chapters. Royal assent duly followed on 25 April, and Archbishop Winchelsey added his confirmation on 11 June, releasing the see's spiritualities; when Langton swore fealty to the king five days later, the temporalities were immediately released.[100] With Langton being detained overseas on diplomatic business concerning the war with France Boniface VIII arranged for him to be ordained priest, notifying him of this on 31 October 1296.[101] He was eventually consecrated by the bishop of Albano on 23 December 1296 at Cambrai, France, while attending peace negotiations to end the war with France, even though Winchelsey was reluctant to have his suffragan bishop consecrated outside Canterbury and by any person other than himself. Langton returned to England shortly afterwards and professed his obedience early in March 1297, first in Canterbury cathedral and then at Winchelsey's manor of Teynham, before sailing overseas again on government business, where he remained for most of the year.[102] Although he had assumed personal charge of his diocesan administration from about mid-November 1297, he did not visit his diocese until his enthronement in January 1299 (**63***) because of the political situation.[103]

An undated memorandum in the register notes that 10 marks were paid to two papal nuncios for Langton's confirmation as bishop (**364***), one of many instalments of the common service tax he would have paid to the pope. The total amount Langton paid is unknown, but the sums involved were substantial,

---

[99] Lichfield cathedral MS. Magnum Registrum Album, fo. 255; BL Cotton MS. Cleopatra D. ix, fo. 74v; *recte HBC*, 253; *Fasti*, x.1; *VCH Staffordshire*, iii.14.

[100] *CPR 1292–1301*, 188 *bis*, 193; *Reg. Winchelsey*, i.111–13; Hughes, 'Episcopate', i.224–5.

[101] *Les registres de Boniface VIII*, ed. G. Digard, M. Faucon, A. Thomas, R. Fawtier, 4 vols. (Ecole Française de Rome, 1907–39), i, no. 1380. Langton had been ordained subdeacon before 5 Feb. 1292, and deacon on 12 June 1294 to a title of patrimony in the diocese of Lincoln, see *Reg. Romeyn*, i.117; *Reg. Sutton*, vii.53.

[102] G.P. Cuttino, 'Bishop Langton's mission for Edward I 1296–1297', *Studies in British History* (University of Iowa, 11, 2, 1941), 147–83; *Les registres de Boniface VIII*, i, no. 1186; *Reg. Winchelsey*, i.127–9; Denton, *Winchelsey*, 51–2; Hughes, 'Episcopate', i.225–6.

[103] See note 111 below, and Appendix D; for the general political background see M. Prestwich, *Edward I*, (London, 1988), 412–35; *Documents illustrating the crisis of 1297–98*, ed. M. Prestwich (Camden, 4th series, 24, 1980).

being set at one third of the estimated value of the payer's gross income for a single year.[104]

Langton was an ambitious king's clerk and his career reached its zenith on his elevation to the episcopate. Having been born into a minor gentry family (**1291, 1292**),[105] he joined Edward I's household and secured steady promotion, becoming keeper of the Wardrobe in 1290, a position he retained until his appointment as treasurer in 1295:[106] he was then the most important and influential government minister until the end of the reign. Langton's position changed suddenly on Edward II's accession when he suffered the first of two arrests and terms of imprisonment. The king and bishop were apparently reconciled in 1312, with Langton being re-appointed treasurer for a short time. Thereafter he held no formal government office again, though he continued to be active politically in the intervening years until his death in 1321.[107]

The monks of Coventry and canons of Lichfield had thus elected an experienced and competent administrator as their bishop, and one who was at the heart of government affairs. Langton used the expertise he had gained during his career to govern his diocese well, efficiently juxtaposing his political and episcopal duties. He employed equally capable diocesan administrators, most of whom were masters with expertise in either canon or civil law, a select few of whom feature prominently. Langton's itinerary shows that he did spend a great deal of time outside his diocese, either in connection with his political duties, his personal difficulties, or visiting his manors, but these same letters reveal that he was not a negligent prelate: he was committed to his episcopal office and diocese and he attended to diocesan business in person whenever possible.[108]

[104] W.E. Lunt, *Papal revenues in the Middle Ages*, 2 vols. (Columbia University Press, 1934), i.82–87.

[105] Hughes, 'Family', 70–6.

[106] As a favoured king's clerk Langton also accumulated ecclesiastical benefices. First, before 13 Dec. 1289, St. Michael on Wyre (Coventry and Lichfield dioc.). By 1295 he was a papal chaplain and held fifteen benefices when he was granted his fifth papal dispensation to retain for two years the rectories of Manchester (Coventry and Lichfield dioc.), Adlingfleet, Bedale and Hemingborough (York dioc.), the mastership of St. Leonard's hospital, York (which the king granted him for life on 19 May 1293), and prebends in Dublin, Chichester, Howden (York dioc.), Auckland, and Lanchester (Durham dioc.), Lichfield (prebend of Sandiacre), St. Paul's, London, Salisbury, and Wells. Omitted from this dispensation is the deanery of the royal chapel of Bridgnorth to which the king presented him on 20 Dec. 1290 and which, on 28 Nov. 1296, he granted the then bishop-elect licence to retain for five years after his consecration, together with the mastership of St. Leonard's hospital for life, if he obtained papal dispensation. Langton's annual income in 1295 from these benefices has been estimated at £1000: Beardwood, 'Trial', 8–9; *CPR 1281–92*, 410; *CPR 1292–1301*, 15, 230, 340; A. Hamilton Thompson, 'The college of St. Mary Magdalene, Bridgnorth, with some account of its deans and prebendaries', *Archaeological Journal*, 84 (1927), 67–9; Hughes, 'Episcopate', i.215–22.

[107] Hughes, 'Register', 1; T.F. Tout, *Chapters in the administrative history of mediaeval England* (Manchester, 1920–33), ii.15–18; *HBC*, 79, 104; *CPR 1292–1301*, 149; *CPR 1307–13*, 412, 413, 440, 459; *CCR 1307–13*, 395; Beardwood, 'Trial', 6, 10, 14.

[108] For example, after attending the Lincoln parliament in 1301 Langton rejoined the king at Hailes Abbey, Glos., on 23 March before moving on to Evesham and Feckenham,

Langton thus followed contemporary practice and employed deputies infrequently. He preferred to appoint commissaries *ad hoc* (e.g. **473*, 609*, 726*, 728, 877, 880, 1058**), commissioning vicars-general and suffragan bishops only for his longer absences, chiefly abroad. He assigned vicars-general for the five occasions he went overseas, and to cover two other absences, one in 1300 when, in his capacity as treasurer, he assisted with Edward I's campaign against the Scots (although he may have gone overseas then also), and again in 1307–8 when he had been imprisoned by Edward II.[109] Letters record that Langton maintained contact with his diocese and made his wishes known during these commissions (e.g. **511, 517, 531, 539, 555, 567**). When Langton was re-arrested and held at York for a period of about five months in 1311, having been indicted for homicide, he retained personal control of his diocesan administration and conducted business there in spite of the difficulties this must have presented (**631–634, 720–726*, 730, 803, 860–864, 951, 1046**).[110]

No commissions appointing vicars-general have been recorded. Thus, the following terms, which have been established from both the register and other sources, are approximate, with the exception of Redeswell's first commission which is precisely dated:

M. Walter de Thorp, D.Cn.L., 23 December 1296 to about mid-November 1297.[111] He was also the bishop's official, and one of the leading administrators of the diocese.

M. Thomas de Abberbury, 7 June to 26 September 1300 (**238, 108**); 12 November 1301 to 12 April 1302 (**249, 459**); 28 October 1305 to 31 March 1306 (**353, 208, 356**). Another prominent administrator, he was also the bishop's chancellor until his death in May 1307, and one of three papal administrators appointed when the diocese was sequestered by Boniface VIII in 1302–3.

M. Robert de Redeswell, D.C.L., archdeacon of Chester, 16 September 1307 to 9 November 1308 (heading before **489, 551**). Although Langton was arrested between 7 August 1307 when he was at Loughborough (**1020**) as he accompanied Edward I's body on its slow journey from Burgh-by-Sands to Westminster and 27 August when he was a prisoner at Wallingford Castle (**819**),[112] he retained control of his diocesan administration until he commissioned Redes-

---

Worcs. While in this area Langton instituted four clerks to benefices, granted four licences and custody of sequestered revenues (**114, 246, 288, 334, 432–6**); and see *CPR 1292–1301*, 581–2, 584, 586, 626; Appendix D. For diocesan business while Langton was at Lincoln, see Hughes, 'Register', 2.

[109] Hughes, 'Register', 2–3; Appendices B, C, and D.

[110] Hughes, 'Register', 3–4; Beardwood, 'Trial', 14, 22–4.

[111] After his consecration Langton did not return to England until about 7 Jan. 1297; he was abroad again about 4 March. He had returned to England by mid-November and had assumed charge of his administration before 21 Dec. 1297 when he commissioned the bishop of St. Asaph to celebrate ordinations at Shrewsbury, see *Reg. Sutton*, vii.111; Appendix D. Thorp was named vicar-general on 20 June 1297, a letter was sent to Langton's unnamed 'viceregent' on 15 May 1297, and he instituted a rector on 24 Sept. 1297 (**233**): *CPR 1292–1301*, 253; *CCR 1296–1302*, 113.

[112] Beardwood, 'Trial', 10–38; Beardwood, *Records, passim*.

well on 16 September. This commission lasted until Langton's release from prison on 9 November 1308 (see the notes preceding **820, 923, 1021**), during which time he ensured his wishes were implemented (**511, 517, 531, 539, 1027**).

Redeswell was commissioned for a second term, about 10 June to 4 July 1309 (**618**, note preceding **701, 702, 834**). He too was one of the leading administrators in the diocese.

M. Ralph de Leicester, D.Cn.L.,[113] 12 May 1312 to 21 July 1313 (heading before **552, 573**).

Langton was compelled to relinquish personal control of his diocese when Boniface VIII suspended him from episcopal office between March 1302 and June 1303 while charges of gross misconduct, whereby he was said to be publicly defamed in England and elsewhere, were investigated. Three papal administrators then governed the diocese.[114] John Lovetot junior had accused Langton of taking Joan de Brianzon, Lovetot's stepmother, as his mistress, of strangling his father John Lovetot senior in bed with Joan's assistance, of simony, pluralism and the sale of papal constitutions, of rendering homage to the devil, kissing the devil on the back, and of frequently talking to him.[115] The latter charges of consorting with the devil echo those brought against the Templars in 1307 and, while they seem beyond belief to modern sensibilities, Langton's contemporaries would have considered them credible and scandalous, based as they were on past myths and superstitions.[116] Langton was, nevertheless, exonerated after the inquiry had ascertained that Lovetot senior had died non-violently and of natural causes.[117] Langton retained the king's support throughout his suspension and remained at the heart of government affairs.[118]

Lovetot's motive for bringing such charges arose from his enmity for Langton; by October 1300 he was in debt to the bishop for at least £964, some of which was in the name of his stepmother, Joan. The rancour between the two men lasted until Lovetot's death in 1302 or 1303.[119] Langton had known the family for a number of years: Lovetot senior had presented Langton, then said to be his clerk, to Adlingfleet rectory in 1292; and Langton once referred to this patron as his lord and special friend.[120] When Lovetot junior inherited his father's lands he

[113] *BRUO*, ii.1141.

[114] See above pp. xxx–xxxii.

[115] ' . . . *erat in regno Angliae et alibi publice defamatus, quod diabolo homagium feceret et eum fuerat osculatus in tergo, eique locutus multotiens*', see Lichfield cathedral MS. Magnum Registrum Album, fo. 167; *Foedera, conventiones, litterae etc.*, or *Rymer's Foedera, 1066–1383*, (Record Commission, 1816–69), I, ii.956–7; CPL, i.607; *MRA*, no. 305; Beardwood, 'Trial', 7–8; Hughes, 'Register', 4. Jeffrey Denton, however, says Langton was accused of having 'intercourse with the devil', see Denton, *Winchelsey*, 53.

[116] M. Barber, *The trial of the Templars* (Cambridge, 1978), 45, 178–82.

[117] *Foedera*, I, ii.957; *MRA*, no. 305.

[118] Hughes, 'Episcopate', i.231–5.

[119] Beardwood, 'Trial', 7–8; Beardwood, *Records*, 37, 50, 207; A. Beardwood, 'Bishop Langton's use of statute merchant recognizances', *Medievalia et Humanistica*, 9 (1955), 64; Hughes, 'Episcopate', i.332–3.

[120] *Reg. Romeyn*, i.117; BL Cotton MS. Vitellius E. xvi, fo. 108; PRO, SC1/27/78; Hughes, 'Episcopate', i.329–30, 333–5.

enfeoffed a toft and 20 acres of land in Adlingfleet, together with the advowson of the church there, to Simon Peverel who in turn enfeoffed his son, Walter Langton; he then granted the same *in mortmain* to the abbot and convent of Selby in 1305 (**1291, 1292**).[121]

During the course of Langton's suspension Edward I, the queen, the dean and chapter of Lichfield, and John Dalderby, bishop of Lincoln, wrote letters of support on his behalf to the pope, and to others at the Curia. While those from the court cannot be considered wholly impartial, the dean and chapter and John Dalderby were perhaps more pragmatic, commending him as 'a God-fearing man of pure life and devoted to his ministry', and 'an orthodox man, pure in faith and honourable in life'.[122] Langton's dedication to the church, and his concern for his diocese, his clergy, and parishioners has been confirmed by the register: he did not neglect his diocesan responsibilities.[123]

A bishop was obliged to see that canon law was observed throughout his diocese and thus had to understand it himself. Although Langton had not attended university he may have been the bishop 'notable for his knowledge of letters' whom Clement V had in mind as successor to Archbishop Winchelsey.[124] Langton was concerned that correct procedures were followed, and that canon law was observed: several ordination lists record the legal requirements for ordination (**1313, 1320, 1321, 1323, 1324**), and others note that these had been read out (**1315–1319, 1325, 1327, 1328**); and, for example, when Robert de Dotton, rector of Eccleston, had been unable to be ordained priest in accordance with canon law due to illness, Langton declared that the rector had been reasonably impeded and authorized that he should be ordained priest at the next opportunity (**883***).[125]

Institutions to vicarages routinely record that the vicar had sworn the oath of continual and personal residence in accordance with the constitutions of the papal legates Otto and Ottobon, promulgated in 1237 and 1268 respectively[126] (e.g. **118, 121, 140, 197, 203, 210, 269, 351–353**). When William de Essheborn took this oath at his institution as vicar of Castleton in the Peak it was noted that the inquiry had ascertained that he had been presented lawfully and within time, and that there had been no disregard for [canon] law (**496**). Nevertheless, five vicars were granted licences to be absent: the vicar of Colwich to be in the

[121] Hughes, 'Family', 70–1; BL Cotton MS. Vitellius E. xvi, fo. 108; *CPR 1301–7*, 342.

[122] *CCR 1296–1302*, 602, 603–4; *CCR 1302–7*, 81–2; *Foedera*, I, ii.943, 956; *The liber epistolaris of Richard de Bury*, ed. N. Denholm-Young (Roxburghe Club, 1950), 43, 44, 317, 318; *MRA*, no. 646; Hughes, 'Register', 5; Beardwood, 'Trial', 8; Denton, *Winchelsey*, 53–4; Lincolnshire Archives Office, Episcopal Register II (John Dalderby, 1300–1320), fo. 31r.

[123] Bishop Langton has been criticized by historians. For example, Tout labelled him 'a neglectful and negligent prelate': Tout, *Chapters in the administrative history of mediaeval England*' (Manchester, 1920–33), ii.16, 21. This and other disparaging remarks are quoted in Hughes, 'Register', 1.

[124] J.H. Denton, 'Canterbury archiepiscopal appointments: the case of Walter Reynolds', *Journal of Medieval History*, 1 (1975), 322–4.

[125] Geoffrey de Vilers, vicar of Nuneaton, was granted similar dispensation by Langton in 1311, see **633***, and above p. xxi.

[126] *Councils and synods*, II, i.238, 249 (10), II, ii.738, 757–8 (9).

service of M. Thomas Jorz,[127] with the assurance that he would not be troubled regarding his non-residence, provided that his vicarage was not defrauded of duties and the cure of souls neglected (**711**); the vicar of Whalley to travel to the Curia on business concerning his vicarage, on condition that it too was not defrauded of duties (**861**); and although the licences allowing the vicar of Wirksworth to go to the Curia, and the vicars of South Wingfield and Blackburn to go on pilgrimage record no such provisos (**402, 1036, 827**), these vicars too would have had similar dispensation and have been required to make suitable provision for their vicarages to be served by deputies.

There are two records of proceedings against incumbents. The first against M. Jordan de Maclesfeld, rector of Mottram in Longdendale, was presumably for unlicensed absenteeism, but he resigned his benefice before sentence was pronounced (**901***). He had apparently been granted a seven year licence to study at about the time of his institution in 1300, although this is not registered, and in May 1308 he had papal dispensation to study for a further three years without proceeding to higher orders (**174** and note). M. Simon de Radeswelle, rector of West Kirby and a kinsman of the archdeacon of Chester, was more fortunate in 1317 when his explanation for his absence was accepted as just and lawful (**806***). He too had previously been granted a seven year study licence, but this was in June 1300 (**104**). Other recipients of episcopal patronage benefited from the letters Langton received from Clement V in 1306 which enabled him lawfully to grant six clerks dispensation to hold two benefices, each with cure of souls, provided they were not defrauded of duties (**788***), and four clerks to receive holy orders and a single benefice, despite being under age (**797***).

The majority of the licences for absence were for study under the terms of Boniface VIII's constitution *Cum ex eo*, indicating that Langton was aware of the advantages of having a literate and educated clergy. At least 200 such licences were issued to 137 incumbents, although some licences for unspecified absence and others for travel overseas may also have been for educational purposes. One hundred and thirty-three of the study licences were for a single year, while 33 were granted for a two year period, with four being for the full term of seven years.[128] In addition, the register records that when five under-age clerks were presented to rectories they were to be supported from the revenues of those benefices while they studied and until they were old enough to be instituted (**419, 441, 447, 456, 494**).

Langton undertook regular visitations of his diocese, some of which are documented in the register, while others were made as he travelled about on other business (e.g. **369, 602, 901***).[129] One visitation of the deanery of Tamworth and Tutbury in January 1319 is recorded on a roll from which Langton's movements over a nine day period have been established; he then travelled approximately seven miles each day, allowing sufficient time for both judicial and pastoral business. The financial rewards for a bishop undertaking

[127] *BRUO*, ii.1023.

[128] L.E. Boyle, 'The constitution "Cum ex eo" of Boniface VIII', *Medieval Studies*, 24 (1962), 263–302; Hughes, 'Register', 5. For other periods of study see the Index of Subjects.

[129] See Appendices C and D.

visitation could be substantial: a sequestrator-general's account roll for the year 1301 records sums paid by both clergy and laity at visitation, totalling £86 19s. 6d. and £36 12s. 8d., some of which were possibly correction fines, procurations, or other charges.[130]

Much of the routine work of visitation would have been carried out by the bishop's officers, perhaps his chancellor or official, enabling several benefices to be visited in a single day. The visitation roll of January 1319 shows that in addition to the rectory or religious house where Langton chose to stay overnight, between two and eight neighbouring churches and their chapels were also visited before he proceeded to his next base.[131] When Langton visited other religious houses he presumably also visited their vicarages, and the parish churches and chapels in the vicinity (**473*, 809*–812, 949, 950**).[132] One concern of his visitation of Darley Abbey in June 1316 was the resignation of the abbot, and the provision to be made for his future support, which is set out in considerable detail (**811, 815***). Similar attention had been given to the needs of the retiring abbot of Haughmond the previous year (**950**).

During his episcopate Langton personally financed prestigious building-work on Lichfield cathedral, notably the Lady Chapel, which is modelled on the Sainte-Chapelle in Paris, the two western steeples, the crossing tower and its spire; and also in the close, where he had a new episcopal palace built in the style of Caernarvon Castle.[133] During this building activity Langton made provision for a common residence for the vicars of the cathedral, who had previously lodged unsupervised outside the close, granting them in 1315 a place in the north-western corner of the close, with all the houses built thereon. This was at a time when cathedral chapters in general were concerned about the behaviour and moral welfare of their vicars, and common halls of residence were being provided.[134]

Perhaps because of his patronage of the fabric of Lichfield cathedral Langton appears to have enjoyed good relations with the dean and chapter of Lichfield, although he was unsuccessful in his attempts to visit the chapter, the common churches of the chapter, and the prebends because of the powerful position of the dean. He did, however, visit the chapter of Coventry without difficulty.[135] One set of Langton's episcopal statutes is known from a copy made in the

---

[130] Hughes, 'Clergy list', 1–4, 14–20; Hughes, 'Register', 6; Hughes, 'Account roll', 112–13, 116–26.

[131] Hughes, 'Clergy list', 14–20.

[132] For other visitations see *The cartulary of Haughmond* Abbey, ed. U. Rees (Shropshire Archaeological Society and University of Wales Press, Cardiff, 1985), no. 452; The *coucher book of Whalley Abbey*, ed. W.A. Hulton (Chetham Society, first series, 10, 1847), 307–10; *Monasticon Anglicanum*, ed. William Dugdale (London, 1817–30), iii.46.

[133] J. Maddison, 'Building at Lichfield cathedral during the episcopate of Walter Langton (1296–1321)', in *The British Archaeological Association Conference Transactions 1987: XIII medieval archaeology and architecture at Lichfield*, ed. J. Maddison (Leeds, 1993), 65, 70–2, 80; N. Tringham, 'The palace of Bishop Walter Langton in Lichfield cathedral close', in *ibid.*, 85–100; Hughes, 'Register', 7–8.

[134] LJRO MS. D30 K2; *MRA*, nos. 94, 207; *VCH Staffordshire*, iii.156; K. Edwards, *The English secular cathedrals in the Middle Ages* (Manchester, 1949), 282–3.

[135] *VCH Staffordshire*, iii.155; Edwards, *English secular cathedrals*, 133; *MRA*, nos. 466, 643, 743.

sixteenth or seventeenth century. These were promulgated on 28 May 1300 in the chapter house of Lichfield cathedral, and were evidently intended to curb the power of the dean.[136]

Langton was terminally ill when he made his last will and testament at London on 1 November 1321,[137] and he died a few days later on the 9th. His body was then brought north to Lichfield to be buried in the cathedral *in novo opere ubi ordinavi*, that is in the Lady Chapel which was still under construction. Langton bequeathed considerable gold and silver to finance its completion, but building-work came to a halt in 1322 when Edward II forced a loan of 904 marks (£602 13s. 4d.) from the dean and chapter, the entire sum that had been reserved for this, though the chapel may have been finished by 1336. The Lady Chapel, the other building-work he financed on Lichfield cathedral, and his register are Langton's lasting memorial.[138]

EDITORIAL METHOD

The calendar shows all persons and places in the manuscript. Sixteenth or seventeenth century copies of earlier Lichfield acta, which have been recorded on hitherto blank folios and half-folios, have been briefly noted in the calendar (**149, 150, 216–218, 275, 276, 320, 321**) as they will appear in a forthcoming volume of Lichfield acta to be published by the British Academy. Placenames are given in their present forms; the manuscript spellings are given in round brackets. Placenames which have not been identified are in single inverted commas. First names have been given in modern form. Surnames are as in the manuscript, except well-known, Latinized surnames which are given in their modern form, and variant spellings are shown in the index. For those records of institutions or of collations where the mandate to induct is addressed to the archdeacon or his official, this is abbreviated in the calendar as 'Ind.: archd.'. Appendix A in Volume II provides full transcripts of entries of particular interest and these are indicated in the calendar by the addition of asterisks to their serial numbers. Square brackets are used for editorial insertions. Notes are to be found at the ends of entries.

---

[136] LJRO MS. D30 XIII, fos. 5v–6, 18v–19; Hughes, 'Episcopate', i.307–9.
[137] Printed in Beardwood, 'Trial', 39–40.
[138] Fasti, x.1; Beardwood, 'Trial', 39–40; Hughes, 'Register', 7–8.

THE REGISTER OF WALTER LANGTON

[Fo. 1] REGISTRUM DOMINI WALTERI LANGTON UNACUM NOMINIBUS CLERICORUM ORDINATORUM [1] . . .[1]
[The working register, see pp. xiv–xix of the introduction.
[1-1] Abraded.]

1 Note of the institution of Robert de Mar to a moiety of Eckington (*Ekynton*) church; patron, King Edward.[1] York, 24 Sept. 1298.
[Margin] Derby.[2] He owes $\frac{1}{2}$ mark [6s. 8d.].
> [See **223**.
> [1] *CPR 1292–1301*, 145.
> [2] In a later hand.]

2 Note that the bishop has delivered custody of Thorp church to Ralph de Cressy until the next holy orders, provided that he is then ordained subdeacon and will come to receive institution. York, 1 Oct. 1298.

3 Collation to John de Drokenesford[1] of the prebend [of Darnford][2] in Lichfield church which was M. W[alter] de Thorp's.[3] York, 24 Sept. 1298.
[Margin] He owes $\frac{1}{2}$ mark.
> [See **383**.
> [1] *DNB*, vi.19–20.
> [2] See **378**; *Fasti*, x.31.
> [3] *BRUO*, iii.2222.]

4 Collation to M. W[alter] de Thorp of the prebend of Weeford (*Weford*).[1] Lead Grange (*Ledegrange*), 16 June 1298.
[Margin] Stafford.[2] He owes $\frac{1}{2}$ [mark].
> [See **382**.
> [1] *Fasti*, x.64.
> [2] 'Stafford' in a later hand.]

5 Note that the bishop has delivered custody of Eccleston (*Eccliston*) church to William de Catun until the next holy orders. York, 4 Oct. 1298.
[Margin] Nothing [for the fee].

6 Note that Alexander de Wylghton, priest, having been presented to the vicarage in Hartington (*Hertingdon*) parish church (canonically ordained) by the abbess and convent of B.V.M. without the walls of London, of the order of St. Clare,[1] has had a letter addressed to the archdeacon of Coventry and M. W[alter] de Thorp to institute him. Acomb near York (*Acum prope Ebor'*), 4 Oct. 1298.

[Margin] Derby. Nothing [for the fee] because he is poor.
[See **224**.
[1] *VCH London*, i.516.]

7 Note that John de Whalleye, priest, has had a letter addressed to the dean of Warrington (*Wermington*) and Robert, rector of Standish (*Standissh*), to induct him to the vicarage of Whalley (*Whalleye*) church; patrons, abbot and convent of Whalley. York, 4 Oct. 1298.
[Margin] Chester. He paid $\frac{1}{2}$ mark.
[See **153**.]

8 Note that Heanor (*Henore*) church has been granted *in commendam* to Eudes de Derb' for half a year. York, 15 Oct. 1298.
[Margin] The bishop has relaxed the $\frac{1}{2}$ mark.
[See **219, 237**.
A benefice could be held *in commendam* for six months only and the recipient had to be a priest under the constitution of Pope Gregory X, Council of Lyon, 1274, clause 14, see 'Sexti Decretalium', book i.6, 15, *Corpus Juris Canonici*, ed. E. Friedberg (Graz, 1955).]

9 Note that the bishop has delivered custody of the sequestration[1] on Warmingham (*Wermingham*) church to Richard de Sitouns, clerk, until the next holy orders to be celebrated before Christmas. Letters dimissory for the order of subdeacon. York, 7 Nov. 1298.
[[1] Interlined.]

10 Institution of Simon de Wykeford to the prebend of Wilnecote (*Wylmunde-cote*) in Tamworth church; patron, Sir Ralph Basset, kt. Ind.: archd. of Stafford. York, 1298.
[Margin] Stafford.
[See **278**; Hughes, 'Clergy list', 8, 16.]

11 Institution of Henry Berchelmen, subdeacon, to Barlborough (*Barleburgh*) church; patron, Sir Walter de Goushull, kt.[1] York, 21 Nov. 1298. [2]Afterwards the date of institution was changed to 19 July [1299], and he then had letters dimissory for the orders of deacon and priest.[2]
[Margin] Derby.[3] He owes the fee.
[See **225**.
[1] For the Gousel family and the biography of Walter de Goushull see Foulds, *Thurgarton Cartulary*, pp. cxxxiv, cxl–cxliii.
[2–2] Interlined later.
[3] In a later hand.]

12 Institution of Richard de Morton, chaplain, to Buildwas (*Parva Buldewas*) chapel; patrons, abbot and convent of Buildwas (*Buldewas*). York, 28 Nov. 1298.
[Margin] Shrewsbury. He has day to pay the fee at Michaelmas next.
[See **324**.]

13 Note that the bishop has delivered custody of his sequestration on Tarporley (*Torperlegh'*) church to William de Fuleburn, clerk, until the next holy orders to be celebrated before Christmas. Letters dimissory for the order of subdeacon. York, 28 Nov. 1298.
[Margin] Nothing [for the fee].

14 Institution of William de Solihull, chaplain, to the chantry of Solihull church; patron, Lady Ela de Odinsel'. York, 7 Dec. 1298.
[Margin] Coventry. He paid the fee.
   [See **94**.]

15 Note that the bishop has delivered custody of his sequestration on Clifton Campville (*Clifton Caunvill'*) church to M. Jordan de Caunvill', clerk, until the next holy orders to be celebrated before Christmas. York, 7 Dec. 1298.

16 [Fo. 1v] Institution of Br. Simon de Radeford, canon of Dale (*la Dale*), to Kirkhallam (*Kirkehalum*) vicarage; patrons, Abbot John and the convent of Dale. York, 9 Dec. 1298.
[Margin] Derby. He paid ½ mark.
   [See **226**.]

17 Institution of William de Lutton to Ormskirk (*Ormeschurch*) vicarage; patrons, prior and convent of Burscough (*Burschou*). York, 15 Dec. 1298.
[Margin] Chester. He paid ½ mark.
   [See **154**.]

18 Collation to M. Thomas de Abberbury[1] of the prebend in Lichfield church which was M. John de Monte Majori's. Ind.: dean and chapter of Lichfield. York, 17 Dec. 1298.
[Margin] The prebend of Whittington and Berkswich (*Berkeswych*).[2]
   [See **384**.
   [1] *BRUO*, i.2.
   [2] *Fasti*, x.66–7.]

19 Institution of M. Jordan de Caunvill' to Clifton Campville church; patron, Sir Geoffrey de Caunvill', kt. Sibson (*Sibesdon*), 2 Jan. 1299.
[Margin] Coventry. He paid ½ mark.
   [See **95**.
   This church was listed under Stafford archdeaconry in 1319, see Hughes, 'Clergy list', 9–10, 17.]

20 Institution of William de Fuleburn, subdeacon, to Tarporley church; patron, Sir Reginald de Grey. Letters dimissory for the orders of deacon and priest. Coventry, 5 Jan. 1299.
[Margin] Chester. He paid ½ mark.
   [See **155**.]

21 Institution of Robert de Kenilleworth, chaplain, to Ellastone (*Athelaxton'*) vicarage; patrons, prior and convent of Kenilworth (*Kenilleworth*). Coventry, 6 Jan. 1299.
[Margin] Stafford. He paid ½ mark.
   [See **279**.]

22 Collation to M. W[alter] de Thorp of Astbury church, the collation of which has devolved to the bishop by lapse of time. Ind.: archd. Coventry, 5 Jan. 1299.
[Margin] Chester.
   [See **156**.
   If a presentation was not made within six months a bishop could present to the benefice by authority of clause 8 of the Third Lateran Council, 1179, see 'Decretalium D. Gregorii Papae IX Compilatio', iii.8, 2, *Corpus Juris Canonici* (as in 8); *Councils and synods*, II, i.566.]

23 Institution of John de Morton, chaplain, to Baschurch (*Baschirche*) vicarage; patrons, abbot and convent of Shrewsbury (*Salop'*). Lichfield, 10 Jan. 1299.
[Margin] Shrewsbury. He paid ½ mark.
   [See **325**.]

24 Institution of Nicholas de Aylesbur', clerk, to Pattingham (*Patyngham*) church; patrons, prior and convent of Launde (*Landa*). Lichfield, 8 Jan. 1299. ¹Afterwards, he had letters dimissory for the order of priest, and a letter *de impedimento*. London, 23 Mar. 1299.¹
[Margin] Stafford.
   [¹⁻¹ Interlined later. It is unclear what the dispensation was for, and this note has not been included in the subsequent copy of his institution **280**.]

25 Institution of Henry de Harenhale, chaplain, to Holy Trinity vicarage, Coventry; patrons, prior and convent of Coventry. Lichfield, 8 Jan. 1299.
[Margin] Coventry . . .¹
   [See **96**.
   ¹ Abraded.]

26 Institution of Br. Godman, canon of Shelford, to Alvaston (*Aylwaston*) vicarage; patrons, prior and convent of Shelford. Lichfield, 12 Jan. 1299.
[Margin] Derby. He paid ½ mark.
   [See **227**.
   Followed by four blank lines.]

27 Note that the bishop has excused himself from a ¹con¹vocation of canons² to be held in the middle of Lent at Lichfield, and the letter was addressed to the dean of Lichfield. Acomb, 23 Feb. [1299].
   [¹⁻¹ Interlined.
   ² Interlined.]

28 [Fo. 2] Institution of Richard de Cytouns, clerk, to Warmingham (*Wermyngham*) church; patron, the king.[1] Lichfield, 8 Jan. 1299.
[Margin] Chester. He paid.
[See **157**.
[1] *CPR 1292–1301*, 358.]

29 Institution of Roger de Bowode to Wombourn (*Womburn*) vicarage; patrons, prior and convent of Dudley (*Duddeley*). Lichfield, 8 Jan. 1299.
[Margin] Stafford. He paid.
[See **281**.]

30 Institution of Roger de Gretewych to Kingswinford (*Swyneford Regis*) church; patron, Lady Agnes de Somery. York, 23 Jan. 1299.
[Margin] Stafford. He paid and R[alph] de Leyc[ester][1] received [the fee].
[See **41, 282**.
[1] *BRUO*, ii.1141.]

31 Collation to Philip de Everdon[1] of the prebend of Wellington (*Welington*)[2] which was M. Thomas de Abberbury's. York, 15 Feb. 1299.
[Margin] Stafford.[3] Nothing [for the fee].
[See **385**.
[1] Cofferer of the king's wardrobe during Langton's keepership, see *Book of prests of the king's wardrobe for 1294–5*, ed. E.B. Fryde (Oxford, 1962), 228.
[2] *Fasti*, x.65.
[3] Deleted.]

32 Institution of M. Richard de Fillingleye to Offchurch (*Offechurch*) vicarage; patrons, prior and convent of Coventry. York, 16 Feb. 1299.
[Margin] Coventry. He paid the fee.
[See **97**.]

33 Institution of John de Herle, subdeacon, to Mancetter (*Manecestr'*) church; patron, Robert de Herle. London, 21 Mar. 1299.
[Margin] Coventry. He paid.
[See **98**.]

34 Institution of M. John de Pavely to Ladbroke (*Lodbrok'*) church; patron, Sir John de Lodbrok'. London, 20 Mar. 1299.
[Margin] Coventry. He paid.
[See **99**.]

35 Institution of William le Duyn of Brickhill (*Brikhull*) to a moiety of Malpas (*Maupas*) church; patron, Sir Richard de Sutton, kt. London, 24 Mar. 1299.
[Margin] Chester. He paid.
[See **158**.]

36 To the dean of High Peak (*de Alto Pecco*). He is to deliver to Roger Wyne, dean of [St. Edith's college] Tamworth,[1] custody of Eyam (*Eyum*) church and of its rector who is suffering with severe infirmities and requires the assistance and help of another person. He is to support and care for the rector, ensuring that the church is not defrauded of duties and that the cure of souls is not neglected; informing the bishop which of these things have been done by his letters patent before Palm Sunday. Note that Roger is to pay 100s. each year to the bishop for his alms on the octave of Michaelmas during the custody. London, 24 Mar. 1299.

[¹ *VCH Staffordshire*, iii.309–15.]

37 Institution of Simon de Hegham, subdeacon, to Barton Blount (*Barton Bakepuz*) church; patron, John Bakepuz. Licence to attend the schools for three years, paying 1 mark [13s. 4d.] each year to the bishop for his alms on the Nativity of St. John the Baptist. ¹He paid for the first year.¹ London, 26 Mar. 1299.
[Margin] Derby.
   [See **79, 228**.
   ¹⁻¹ Interlined later.]

38 Note that Geoffrey de Merston, canon of Dunstable (*Dunstaple*), was admitted and instituted to the vicarage and cure of souls of Bradbourne (*Bradeburn'*) church, without any inquiry, on Sat. 28 Mar. 1299 by precept of the bishop to William de Brikehull; a letter from the bishop of Lincoln, addressed to Bishop [Langton], by which he was moved to do this, was delivered with [the precept] to the chancellor.
[Margin] Derby.
   [See **229**.]

39 Note that the bishop has granted the houses which were Ralph de Hengham's,¹ to M. W[alter] de Thorp, and he has ratified Ralph's gift and charter. 28 Mar. 1299.
   [¹ Chief Justice of Common Pleas 1273–89, 1301–9, see Foss, *Judges*, 25, 261–4; *DNB*, ix.410–11.]

40 Note that Ralph de Cressy has had letters dimissory for the order of priest. London, 23 Mar. 1299.

41 [A cancelled copy of **30** and **282**.]

42 [Fo. 2v] Institution of Richard de Hereford, subdeacon, to Pinxton (*Penkeston*) church; patron, Lady Denise le Wyne. 30 Mar. 1299.
[Margin] Derby.
   [See **230**.]

43 Institution of Thomas de Sadington, clerk, in the person of William de Sadington, his brother and proctor, to Duffield (*Duffeld*) church; patron, Roger le Brabazon,¹ proctor or deputy of Lady Blanche, widow of Edmund, earl of Lancaster, son of King Henry III. London, 18 Apr. 1299.
[Margin] Derby. The fee was relaxed at the request of Roger le Brabazon.
   [See **231**.
   ¹ Chief Justice of King's Bench 1295–1316, see Foss, *Judges*, 25, 241–2; *DNB*, ii.1045–6.]

44   Note that the bishop has delivered custody of his sequestration on Acton Burnell (*Acton Burnel*) church to William de Clyf until the next holy orders. Letters dimissory for the order of subdeacon. London, 21 Apr. 1299. [1]Note of his institution. York, 30 June [1299].[1]
[Margin] Shrewsbury.
   [[1-1] Interlined later, see **326**.]

45   Note that the bishop has delivered custody of the moiety of Eckington church which was M. Peter de Pratellis's to Theobald de Beaumont until 1 Aug. next: patron, the king.[1] Acomb, 17 May 1299. [2]Afterwards, Theobald was instituted to the moiety on the eve of Annunciation, *viz.* 24 Mar. 1300, and he had letters to attend the schools for five years[2] [3]under the terms of the statute[4] that he shall be ordained subdeacon within a year.[3]
[Margin] Letters dimissory for all holy orders which he has not received, excepting the next holy orders because he was instituted.
   [See **236**.
   [1]   *CPR 1292–1301*, 408.
   [2-2]   Interlined later.
   [3-3]   Written down the spine.
   [4]   i.e. *Cum ex eo* published by Pope Boniface VIII on 3 Mar. 1298, see L. E. Boyle, 'The constitution "Cum ex eo" of Boniface VIII', *Medieval Studies*, 24 (1962), 263–302.]

46   Institution of Ralph de Cressi to Thorp church; patron, P[hilip] de Willugby, dean of Lincoln. York, 18 May 1299.
[Margin] Derby. The fee was relaxed by precept of the bishop's chancellor.
   [See **232**.]

47   Institution of M. William de Lancastr' to Eccleston church; patrons, prior and convent of Lancaster (*Lancastr'*). York, 18 May 1299.
[Margin] Chester. He paid $\frac{1}{2}$ mark.
   [See **159**.]

48   Note of licence to William, rector of Warrington (*Werington*), to attend the schools for three years, during which time he shall not be compelled to receive further orders. York, 22 Feb. 1299.

49   Note that the bishop granted a letter concerning the new statute published[1] to Thomas de Sadyngton, subdeacon,[2] rector of Duffield (*Duffeud*), that he shall not be compelled to receive further orders as long as he attends the schools. London, 18 Apr. 1299.
   [[1]   i.e. *Cum ex eo*.
   [2]   Interlined.]

50   Note that William de Billenia, rector of Hanbury (*Hambur'*), has had a letter that he shall not be obliged to be resident for the next three years. York, 30 May 1299.

51   Note of the institution of William de Mackeworth, deacon, to the vicarage of Weaverham (*Weverham*) parish church; patrons, abbot and convent of Vale Royal (*de Valle Regali*). York, 2 June 1299.
[Margin] Chester. He paid.
    [See **160**.]

52   Note that the bishop has delivered custody of his sequestration on Brinklow (*Brinkelowe*) church to Hugh de Upwell until the next holy orders. Acomb, 28 June 1299.

53   Note of similar custody of the sequestration on Duffield church to Alexander de Kingeston. Letters dimissory for the order of subdeacon. York, 30 June 1299. [1]Afterwards, at the presentation of Blanche, queen of Navarre (*Navarr'*), countess palatine of Champagne (*Campan'*) and Brie . . .[1]
    [[1-1] Interlined later and unfinished. Instituted rector 17 Mar. 1300, having been presented by this patron, see **235**.]

54   Institution of Adam de Kelsale to Mobberley (*Madburleye*) church; patron, William de Madburleye. Acomb, 27 June 1299.
[Margin] Chester. The bishop remitted the $\frac{1}{2}$ mark.
    [See **161**.]

55   Note that the bishop has delivered custody of his sequestration on Clowne (*Clune*) church to John de Leyc[ester] called Mauclerk until the next holy orders. Letters dimissory for the order of subdeacon. York, 12 July 1299.

56   Institution of Henry de Pollesworth, priest, to the chantry of St. Clement's chapel near the entrance of Coventry cathedral; patron, prior of Coventry. York, 18 July 1299.
[Margin] Coventry. He paid the fee.
    [See **100**.]

57   Note that Hugh de Uppewelle, who has custody of the sequestration on Brinklow (*Brinkelawe*) church, having been been ordained subdeacon by the bishop of Hereford by letters dimissory,[1] was instituted to the church at Acomb on 6 Oct. 1299.
[Margin] Coventry.
    [See **101**.
    [1] No ordination records survive from the episcopate of Richard Swinfield, bishop of Hereford (1283–1317), see Smith, *Guide*, 96.]

58   Licence to William de Billenia, [1]rector of Hanbury,[1] to attend the schools for three years. London, 18 Oct. 1299.
    [[1-1] Interlined.]

59   Licence to Thomas,[1] rector of Cound (*Coned*), to be in the service of Lady Matilda Burnel, his patron, for one year. London, 18 Oct. 1299.
    [[1] De Acton Reyners, see **323**.]

60 Collation to M. Peter de Insula[1] of the archdeaconry of Coventry. Acomb, 14 Nov. 1299.
[See **387**.
[1] *BRUO*, ii.1003; *Fasti*, x.14.
Followed by four blank lines.]

61 Note that the collation to William de [Sca]la[riis] of the prebend in [St. John's collegiate] church [Chester], which was William de Wesenham's, was renewed. York, 18 May 1299.
[Entry added later at the foot of the folio and now abraded, see **379**.]

62 [Fo. 3] PENSIONES COLLATAS ADVOCATIS DE ARCUBUS L[ONDON]. Letters patent. The bishop has granted to M. William de Foderingeye,[1] clerk, advocate of [the Court of] the Arches, London, 6 marks [£4] from the bishop's chamber (*camera*) to be paid in equal parts at Purification and the Nativity of St. John the Baptist for as long as he attends to the bishop's business in the same court of Canterbury. York, 11 Nov. 1298.
Note of similar letters of the same date to M. John de Bruton[2] and M. Henry de Derb',[3] granting respective pensions of 5 marks [£3 6s. 8d.] and 40s.
[See N. Ramsay, 'Retained legal counsel, c.1275–c.1475', *TRHS*, 35 (1985), 95–112.
[1] *BRUC*, 235.
[2] Churchill, *Canterbury administration*, i.17, 46, 308; ii.244.
[3] Auditor of causes, see Churchill, *ibid.*, i.10, 569; ii.242.]

63* Letter to the archdeacon of Canterbury, or his lieutenant. The bishop has arranged to be enthroned at Coventry on Sun. 4 Jan., and at Lichfield on Sun. 11 Jan. [1299]. He asks the archdeacon to be present to perform his office which pertains to him in this regard, as is customary, requesting a reply. York, 17 Nov. 1298.

64 Resignation (by letter) of Philip de Pontesbur' of Rodington (*Rodinton*) rectory, on account of infirmity and old age. Because his seal is unknown to many people he has had the seal of the bishop's official also affixed to his letter. Rodington, 30 Sept. 1298.

65 Letters patent. The bishop is bound and obligated by this bond to pay 40 marks [£26 13s. 4d.] to R[ichard Gravesend], bishop of London,[1] for the marriage of John de Bellehous, son and heir of Sir Thomas de Bellehous, within a month of being asked at New Temple, London. Acomb near York, 23 Jan. 1299.
[Margin] It is void because the bishop has paid, and the bond has been returned and cancelled.
[1] *HBC*, 258.]

66 Letters patent to M. Robert de Stafford, archdeacon of Coventry. Being inclined to his prayers, the bishop grants him faculty to go to the Curia to expedite his business and also on pilgrimage, remaining there for two years. He may receive wholly the fruits and revenues of his archdeaconry and other benefices, [fo. 3v] provided that he appoints proctors and ministers who will be answerable to the bishop and to his official concerning jurisdiction and other matters pertaining to the bishop, and that benefices in the diocese are not defrauded of duties and the cure of souls neglected. London, 30 Mar. 1299.

67 [Fo. 3][1] Note that at Acomb on Thurs. 19 Feb. 1299 M. Thomas de Abberbury paid £6 [2]and afterwards 20s.[2] to Adam de Aillesbur' for land and a messuage sold to the bishop and his brother, R[obert Peverel],[3] which £6 Thomas received from the [bishop's] hanaper (*de feodo sigilli*) from Purification 1298 to Purification 1299, except ½ mark which M. R[alph] de Leyc[ester] received in Thomas's absence and which he still has . . .[4]

[[1] Added at the foot of fo. 3, cutting in two **66**.
[2-2] Interlined.
[3] For Robert Peverel see Hughes, 'Family', 70–3.
[4] MS. trimmed.]

68* [Fo. 3v] Letters patent of the bishop and his brother, Robert Peverel, kt. They are bound to pay Adam Baldewyne of Aylesbury £220 in current ordinary coinage, not in sterling, before Whitsun, and a robe of the livery of their squires at Christmas each year during Adam's lifetime, for a messuage he has granted them in Wirksworth, and for other lands there and elsewhere in Derbyshire, as Adam's charter made to them purports. York, 19 Feb. 1299.

69* Commission to the official. Thomas de Charnes, subdeacon, has been presented to the vacant portion of Condover church by the patrons, the abbot and convent of Shrewsbury. The bishop has learned nothing to prevent his admission except that John de Shelton has been presented by a papal provision to be executed by the bishop. The official is to ascertain the merits of the provision; if he establishes that John's opposition lacks force or truth, he is to admit and induct Thomas, saving to the bishop the later institution. York, 28 Feb. 1299. On information from R[alph] de Leyc[ester].

70 Note that John de Pavely, [1]rector of Ladbroke,[1] acknowledged before M. Thomas de Abberbury, the bishop's lieutenant in this matter, that he is bound to pay 60 marks [£40] to Sir Eustace de la Hacche, kt., for a loan, to be paid in equal parts at Michaelmas and Easter next following. He is condemned to pay the money at the said terms. Note that the money has been acknowledged in the king's court.[2] 20 Mar. 1299.

[[1-1] Interlined.
[2] This debt has not been recorded in the *Calendars of Close Rolls*, but two other debts of Eustace's were, see *CCR 1296–1302*, 377, 608.]

71 [Fo. 4] Note that on 8 Apr. 1299 at London the bishop received 7 marks [£4 13s. 4d.] by the hands of William de Eston, his clerk, from John de Gaddesdene for custody of land in Shelton (*Selton*). He had previously received 20s. for the same custody from John by the hands of the same William, without acquittance having been issued to John.

72 Note that at York on 27 May 1299 the bishop issued an acquittance to the abbot of Whalley for 100 marks [£66 13s. 4d.], in part payment of 1000 marks [£666 13s. 4d.] for which the abbot is bound to the bishop.

73* Letter to the prior of Witham of the Carthusian order, the bishop's dearest friend. James Pilat, merchant of Douai,[1] is bound to pay him a certain amount of money for wool which he has had from him, and the king is bound to the same James for a large sum of money which the bishop[2] is unable to pay for the king at the present time. The bishop asks that the abbot, in reverence to the king, and the bishop's intercession, [should release] James from making the payment due to the abbot. The bishop will make recompense for this grace at a suitable time. York, 2 July 1299.

Note of similar letters to the abbot of Cleeve, the abbot of Boxley, and the prior of Hempton for James Pilat, and to the abbot of Dunkeswell, and the abbot of Buckfast for Bernard Pilat.[3]

[1,3] Merchants and burgesses of Flanders trading in England, see *CPR 1292–1301*, 254; *CCR 1296–1302*, 23.

[2] As the king's treasurer.]

74 Note that John de Tuwe, rector of Woodchurch (*Wodechurch*), has had a licence to attend the schools for three years according to the form of the statute. York, 3 July 1299.

75 Note that the accounts and allowances have been accounted and allowed between W[alter], bishop of Coventry and Lichfield, the former rector of Manchester (*Mammecestr'*), on the one part, and William de Gringelee, rector of Marnham,[1] and the other farmers of Manchester church, on the other part. The farmers are bound to the bishop for £36 6s. $10\frac{3}{4}$d. net for the third and last year of the farm, which they should pay him at Michaelmas and on 21 Dec. Besides this, they owe the bishop $6\frac{1}{2}$ marks [£4 6s. 8d.] from William de Hunte, chaplain,[2] then farmer of the altarage of Aston chapel, unless he has had acquittance from Richard de Immere, or from the farmers, and then Richard or the farmers will be bound for the $6\frac{1}{2}$ marks. They also owe the bishop [3]50s. from Richard de Immere, and 3s. 6d. which Richard received from the farmers;[3] 6s. which the dean of Manchester received on the bishop's behalf at the time of the vacancy, saving the archdeacon's portion; and 10s. 6d. which John de Dolma, proctor of William Sygyn, now rector, received from the farmers. Also to be accounted for by the proctor, and which ought to pertain to the bishop, from the day of St. Margaret [8 or 20 July], when he was inducted to Manchester church, to the following Michaelmas are 50s. which the proctor received from [the preceding Nativity of] St. John [the Baptist], and for the tithes of mills, hay, flax, hemp, and all the smallest tithes until Michaelmas, all of which pertain to the bishop according to an agreement made between him and the present rector. It is necessary that the proctor, the dean, and William le Hunte, then chaplain of Aston, shall be called to account. n.d.

[Margin] They have fully paid £36 6s. $10\frac{3}{4}$d., $6\frac{1}{2}$ marks, 6s., 10s. 6d.

[1] Instituted 18 May 1293, see *Reg. Romeyn*, i, no. 886. Still rector in Jan. 1303, see *The register of Thomas Corbridge, lord archbishop of York, 1300–1304*, ed. W. Brown, A. Hamilton Thompson (Surtees Society, 138, 141, 1925–8), i.138.

² Interlined.
³⁻³ Interlined.
Followed by six blank lines.]

76 Grant to Richard de Wolvy, clerk, of an annual pension of 5 marks [£3 6s. 8d.] from the bishop's chamber to be paid in equal parts at Michaelmas and Annunciation until he is provided to a benefice worth 60 marks [£40] by the bishop or another person. London, 28 Oct. 1299.

77* Note of letters close to Thomas de Charneles, who acts as rector of a moiety of Condover. He should be at York on the octave of Trinity [?21 June 1299] to discuss business about himself and his position with the bishop. It should be the end of the business that provision be made to John de Shelton, to whom on the same day, there should be provided an annual pension of 40[s.] or at least 20s. to be conferred by the abbot of Shrewsbury. And that there should be provided by the abbot from that other poor church, which is now ¹ . . . to John . . . Richard de . . . by the same abbot.¹ [1299.]

[A hand drawn in the left-hand margin points to this entry. This letter presumably refers to Charneles' presentation and Shelton's provision to the same moiety of Condover, see **69***.
¹⁻¹ Abraded.]

78 [Fo. 4v] Collation to M. William called le Conestable of the prebend in St. John's collegiate church, Chester, which was John Picard's. Note that letters were delivered to J[ohn] Picard that he shall be answerable for the fee. London, 18 Oct. 1299.
[See **386**.]

79 Licence to Simon,¹ rector of Barton Blount, to attend the schools for three years. London, 26 Mar. 1299.
[¹ De Hegham, see **37, 228**.]

80 Note that on Fri. 23 Oct. 1299 Sir Richard St. Valery, kt., and Sir John de Harecurt, kt., Thomas de Abberbury, and John de Neuburg' were present with the treasurer¹ in the treasurer's garden near his vinery at his houses near Westminster. Richard St. Valery has granted and demised the manor of Hinton Waldrist (*Heemton*) in fee to the treasurer in these terms:² the treasurer will give to Richard, in advance, 1000 marks [£666 13s. 4d.] in crocard,³ or half in crocard and half in sterling, [which] John de Neuburg' will settle with Richard in good faith for the treasurer before the quindene of Martinmas, ⁴and the treasurer will give 1000 marks to Richard⁴ for the first ten years; after the first ten years, the treasurer will give Richard £200 each year for the manor. The parties agreed that a fine⁵ for the manor should be drawn up in this form in the king's court, and they confirmed the covenant by pledging faith on Sat. 24 Oct., but John de Harecurt was not present that day.

[¹ Bishop Langton.
² Richard St. Valery frequently borrowed money from Langton and made a statute merchant recognizance to him for £200 on 7 Nov. 1299. According to Beardwood the coercion Langton subsequently used on Richard, including imprisonment, was to compel him to grant him the manors of Norton St. Valery and Hinton Waldrist

(Berks.) in fee, but this letter shows that he had previously granted Hinton Waldrist
to Langton in fee, see A. Beardwood, 'Bishop Langton's use of statute merchant
recognizances', *Medievalia et Humanistica*, 9 (1955), 59–60, 63; Beardwood, 'Trial',
30, 35; Beardwood, *Records*, 262–70.
[3] Base coin.
[4–4] Marginated with a line indicating it should be placed here in the text.
[5] i.e. a final concord.]

81 Note that the bishop has written to his sequestrator, M. W[illiam] de
Swepeston, that he was unable to admit Roger de Verdun, who has been
presented to Biddulph (*Bidulf*) church by Henry de Verdun, because he is under
age. [Roger] is be supported in the schools from part of the revenues of the
church, which the bishop has commanded to be held under his sequestration,
until he ordains otherwise. 5 Nov. 1299.

82 Institution of Otto de Grandisson,[1] in the person of John Gusyn of
Grandson, his proctor, to Manchester (*Mamecestr'*) church; patron, King
E[dward].[2] York, 18 Nov. 1299. [3]On the same day he had licence to attend
the schools for two years.[4] Afterwards, on 29 Mar. 1300, he had a letter to attend
the schools for five years according to the form of the statute, and letters
dimissory for the order of subdeacon.[3]
[Margin] Chester. Nothing [for the fees].
   [See **162**.
   [1] The nephew of Sir Otto de Grandisson, see C.L. Kingsford, 'Sir Otho de Grandison
      1238?-1328', *TRHS*, 3rd. series, 3 (1909), 184–5.
   [2] *CPR 1292–1301*, 440.
   [3–3] Interlined later.
   [4] *BRUC*, 267, 676; *CPR 1292–1301*, 629; *CPL*, i.594.]

83 Licence to M. William de Lanc' to attend the schools for one year. York,
19 Nov. 1299.
[Margin] Eccleston.

84 Note that the bishop has delivered custody of his sequestration on North
Meols (*North Moeles*) church to M. Henry de Hampton until Purification next.
York, 21 Dec. 1299.
   [1]Afterwards on 1 Jan. [1300] at York[2] he had custody until the next holy
orders, and letters dimissory for the order of subdeacon; patrons, abbot and
convent of Evesham.[1]
[Margin] He owes the fee.
   [[1–1] Added later.
   [2] MS. *Ebor' eodem anno* interlined.
   Followed by three blank lines.]

85 Note that the chancellor has paid 20s. to Richard de Lympodeshei from the
bishop's hanaper by order of the bishop. n.d.
   [This and a later payment to Richard (**301**) must be connected with Langton's
attempt to acquire the manor of Souldern, Oxon., see Beardwood, 'Trial', 17–18;
Beardwood, *Records*, 276–83.
   Followed by ten blank lines.]

86   Note that M. William de Swepston was the bishop's sequestrator from 24
Nov. 1297 to 1 Nov. 1298. He received £201 2s. 10¾d. from which he paid £159
6s. 8d. to Gilbert, the bishop's receiver ¹by several acquittances¹, leaving £41 16s.
2¾d. which he has ready to pay to the receiver. William has the names of [those]
who ought to pay him £93 14s. 2½d. and other unspecific amounts (*incerta*) from
sequestrations ² . . . by the account of the [rural] deans which will be made at . . .²
Total sum £294 17s. 1¼d.

   [¹⁻¹ Interlined.
   ²⁻² Abraded.]

REGISTRUM :W[ALTERI]: COVENTREN' ET LICH' EPISCOPI A FESTO PURIFICA-
CIONIS ANNO DOMINI M°:CC^{mo}: NONAGESIMO SEXTO: ET CONSECRACIONIS EJUSDEM
EPISCOPI PRIMO [2 FEB. 1297].

[The 'definitive' register.]

ARCHIDIACONATUS COVENTR'.

87 Institution of Peter de Ilmendon to Maxstoke (*Macstok'*) church; patron,
Lady Ela de Oddingeseles. London, 27 Feb. 1298.

88 Institution of M. William de Billesleghe to the vicarage of St. Michael's
church, Coventry; patrons, prior and convent of the same. 2 Mar. 1298.

89 Institution of Gilbert de Hamelhamste, subdeacon, to Southam (*Sutham*)
church; patrons, prior and convent of Coventry. London, 5 Apr. 1298.

90 Institution of Nicholas de Bermingham, priest, to Arley church; patron,
Lady Ela de Oddingseles. St. Albans (*Sanctum Albanum*), 23 Apr. 1298.

91 Institution of William Prudd, clerk, to Marton (*Merton*) vicarage; patron,
prioress of Nuneaton (*Nuneton*). 29 Apr. 1298.

92 Institution of John de Croxton, priest, to the chantry of St. Thomas the
Martyr's chapel near the entrance of Holy Trinity church, Coventry; patrons,
prior and convent of the same. 22 May 1298.

93 Institution of Nicholas de Guldeford, clerk, to Chesterton (*Cestreton*)
church; patron, the king.[1] 16 Oct. 1298.
    [[1] *CPR 1292–1301*, 292.]

94 Institution of William de Solihull, chaplain, to the chantry of Solihull
church; patron, Lady Ela de Oddingseles. York, 7 Dec. 1298.
    [See **14**.]

95 Institution of M. Jordan de Caunvill' to Clifton Campville church; patron,
Sir Geoffrey de Caunvill', kt. Sibson (*Sibbesdon*), 2 Jan. 1299.
[Margin] Stafford.[1]
    [See **19**.
    [1] In a later hand.]

[Fo. 5v] ARCHIDIACONATUS COVENTR'.

96 Institution of Henry de Harenhale, chaplain, to the vicarage of Holy Trinity
church, Coventry; patrons, prior and convent of the same. Lichfield, 8 Jan. 1299.
    [See **25**.]

97 Institution of M. Richard de Fillangleye to Offchurch (*Offechurche*) vicarage;
patrons, prior and convent of Coventry. York, 16 Feb. 1299.
    [See **32**.]

98   Institution of John de Herle, subdeacon, to Mancetter (*Manecestre*) church; patron, Robert de Herle. London, 21 Mar. 1299.
  [See **33**.]

99   Institution of M. John de Pavely to Ladbroke church; patron, Sir John de Lodbrok', kt. London, 20 Mar. 1299.
  [See **34**.]

100   Institution of Henry de Pollesworth, priest, to the chantry of St. Clement's chapel near the entrance of Coventry cathedral; patrons, prior and convent of Coventry. York, 18 July 1299.
  [See **56**.]

101   Institution of Hugh de Uppewell, subdeacon, to Brinklow church; patron, . . .¹ Acomb, 6 Oct. 1299.
  [See **57**.
  ¹ Blank space.]

102   Institution of Nicholas de Dunneschurche, chaplain, to Leamington (*Estlemyngton*) vicarage; patrons, prior and convent of St. Oswald [Nostell]. York, 7 Jan. 1300.

ANNUS [M].CCC^us. INCIPIT.

103   Institution of Gilbert de Kynesbur', priest, to a moiety of St. Peter's church, Kingsbury (*Kynesbur'*); patrons, prioress and nuns of Holy Trinity of the wood [Markyate]. Lichfield, 30 May 1300.

104   Institution of Simon de Redeswell, subdeacon, to Whitnash (*Whytenassh*) church; patrons, prior and convent of Kenilworth (*Kenillworth*). Licence to study for seven years according to the terms of the statute. Eckington, 4 June 1300.

105   Institution by Thomas de Abberbury, vicar-general, of Alan de Pollesworth, priest, to Coleshill (*Coleshull*) vicarage; patrons, prioress and convent of Holy Trinity of the wood, Markyate. Shawbury (*Shaghebur'*), 11 July 1300.

106   Institution by Thomas, vicar-general, of Warin de Waleton, priest, to Bishops Itchington (*Ichinton Episcopi*) vicarage; patron, M. A[dam de Waleton], precentor of Lichfield.¹ Lichfield (*Lych'*), 23 July 1300.
  [¹ *Fasti*, x.7.]

[Fo. 6] COVEN'.

107   Institution by M. Thomas de Abberbury, vicar-general, of John de Berevill', priest, to Church Lawford (*Churchelalleford*) church; patron, Br. Thomas called Boyn, proctor-general in England of the abbot and convent of St. Mary, Saint-Pierre-sur-Dives (*super Divam*). Church Lawford (*Lalleford*), 11 June 1300.

108 Institution by Thomas de Abberbury, vicar-general, of Ralph de Doninton, priest, to Newnham (*Newenham*) vicarage; patrons, prior and convent of Kenilworth. Coventry, 26 Sept. 1300.

109 Institution of M. Philip de Turvill'[1] to Bedworth (*Bedeworth*) church; patron, William de Charneles, lord of the same. Coventry, 26 Sept. 1300.
[2]He has a letter dated 5 Aug. 1301[3] to remain in the schools for three years.[2]
[Margin] The chancellor has relaxed the fee.

[[1] *BRUO*, iii.1918.
[2-2] Added later.
[3] MS. *non. Augusti anno Domini .M°. CCC. primo*, but see **445** which records this licence dated *kal. Julii* (1 July 1301).]

110 Institution of Richard de Blaby, deacon, to Wolston (*Wolricheston*) vicarage; patron, Br. Thomas called Boyn, proctor of the abbot and convent of St. Mary, Saint-Pierre-sur-Dives. Letters dimissory for the order of priest. York, 14 Oct. 1300.
[Margin] The chancellor has relaxed the fee.

111 Institution of Henry de Lodbrok', priest, to Kenilworth vicarage; patrons, prior and convent of the same. York, 9 Nov. 1300.

112 Institution of Thomas le Bretoun, clerk, to Church Lawford church; patron, Br. Thomas Boyn, proctor-general in England of the abbot and convent of St. Mary, Saint-Pierre-sur-Dives. Northampton (*Norht'*), 24 Dec. 1300.

113 Institution of Thomas de Hinkelegh, acolyte, to Birmingham (*Bermingham*) church; patron, Lady Isabella, widow of Sir William de Bermingham. Reepham (*Refham*), 14 Feb. 1301.
[Birmingham church became vacant on 4 Dec. 1300. It was then placed under the bishop's sequestration and 12s. 11d. was received from it, see **466**; Hughes, 'Account roll', n. 73.]

114 Institution of William de Edrichesleye, clerk, to Grendon church; patron, Sir Ralph de Grendon. Hailes Abbey (*Hayles*), 23 Mar. 1301.
[Grendon church also had been placed under the bishop's sequestration prior to this institution and 13s. 7d. was received from it, see Hughes, 'Account roll', n. 71.
A hand drawn in the left-hand margin points to this entry.]

115 Institution of Robert de Halughton, priest, to Rugby (*Rokeby*) chapel; patron, Sir Peter de Leyc[ester]. Acomb, 2 July 1301.

116 Institution of Ingram de Yerdele, chaplain, to Birdingbury (*Burthingbur'*) church; patron, Sir John Paynel, kt. York, 31 Aug. 1301.

117 Institution by the vicar-general of Henry, son of John de Pollesworth to Polesworth vicarage; patrons, abbess and convent of Polesworth. Kenilworth, 28 Nov. 1301.

118   Institution of Richard de Bradewell, deacon, to the vicarage of Bolsover (*Bollesovere*) church,[1] with charge of personal residence,[2] which he swore; patrons, abbot and convent of Darley (*Derleye*). Acomb (*Akum*), 12 Apr. 1304.

> [1 In Derby archdeaconry.
> 2 In his constitutions in 1268 the papal legate Ottobon decreed that vicars should be resident and adequately ordained, being at least in deacons' orders and proceeding to the priesthood within a year, reiterating the earlier decrees of the papal legate Otto in 1237 and the Council of Oxford in 1222, see *Councils and synods*, II, i.112–13, cl.21; 249, cl.10; II, ii.758–9, cl.9.]

119   [Fo. 6v] Institution by the vicar-general of William, son of Gerard de Allespath to Alspath (*Allespath*) vicarage; patrons, Br. Adam, subprior, Br. Alexander, sacrist, Br. Henry de Stretton, monks of Coventry church, deputies of the prior, who is overseas, and the convent of the same. Kenilworth, 28 Nov. 1301.

120   Institution by the vicar-general of Maurice de Steberlegh' to the chapel of All Saints near Coventry cathedral; patron, prior of Coventry. Coventry, 15 Dec. 1301.

121   Institution of Ralph de Derset, priest, to the vicarage of Burton Dassett (*Magna Dersetta*) church; patrons, prior and convent of Arbury (*Horbur'*)[1] and Sir John de Sudleye, kt.[2] He swore to reside. Coventry, 2 Feb. 1302.

> [1 *VCH Warwickshire*, v.72.
> 2 *Ibid.*, 70.]

122   Institution by M. Thomas de Abberbury, vicar-general, of Thomas de Herdwyk, priest, to Birdingbury church; patron, Sir John Paynel, kt. Steeple Aston (*Stepelaston*), 11 Feb. 1302.

123   Institution of Henry de Thurlaston, priest, to Wolvey (*Wolveye*) vicarage; patrons, abbot and convent of Combe (*Cumba*). Same day, year and place.

124   Institution by Thomas de Abberbury, vicar-general, of Henry de Cumpton, priest, to Whitnash (*Whytenassh*) church; patrons, prior and convent of Kenilworth. Lichfield, 3 Apr. 1302.

125   Institution by the [papal] administrators of the bishopric[1] of John de Lapwrth', priest, to Avon Dassett (*Avenederseth*) church; patron, Sir Walter de Campilupo. Lichfield, 13 Mar. 1303.

> [1 MS. *per administratores episcopatus*. See the introduction pp. xxx–xxxii.]

126   Note that the [papal] administrators have granted custody of Baxterley (*Baxterleye*) church to Thomas de Boudone, clerk, during pleasure; patron, Robert de Stoke. Southam, 12 Apr. 1303.

127   Note that William de Stretton, priest, has been admitted to the mastership (*regimen*) of Bretford (*Bretteford*) hospital[1] by the [papal] administrators; patron,

Sir Richard Turvile of Wolston (*Wlricheston*), kt. Abingdon (*Abindon*), 22 Apr. 1303.

[¹ *VCH Warwickshire*, ii.109.]

128 Institution of William de Daleby, priest, to Ladbroke church; patron, Sir John de Lodebrok'. Acomb, 29 Oct. 1303.

129 Institution of Geoffrey de Wenrich, priest, to the vicarage of Aston near Birmingham (*Aston juxta Burmingham*); patrons, prior and convent of [Tickford] Newport Pagnell (*Neuportpaynel*),¹ to whom the church is appropriated. Acomb, 31 Oct. 1303.

[¹ *VCH Buckinghamshire*, i.360–5 incorrectly states that the house was a Cluniac priory; it was a Benedictine house, dependent on Marmoutier, see D. Knowles, R.N. Hadcock, *Medieval religious houses: England and Wales* (London, 1953), 57, 78, 103.]

130 Institution of William de la Warde to Austrey (*Aldovestre*) church; patrons, abbot and convent of Burton upon Trent (*Burton*). Acomb, 23 Jan. 1304.
[Margin] He owes the fee.

[Fo. 7] COVEN'.

131 Note that on 28 Apr. 1304 Birmingham (*Bermyngham*) church was granted *in commendam* to M. Stephen de Segrave,¹ priest, for half a year; patron, Lady Isabella de Bermyngham. Dated at Stirling (*Stryvelyn*) as the bishop was then in Scotland with the king at Stirling.

[¹ *BRUC*, 516.]

132 Institution of Ellis de Staunford to Monks Kirby (*Kirkebi*) vicarage; patrons, prior and monks of Monks Kirby. Botolphs (*Sanctum Botulphum*), 16 July 1304.
[Margin] He owes the fee.

133 Institution of John de Chingunford, deacon, to Frankton (*Franketon*) church; patrons, Robert de Hokovere and Alice, his wife. York, 23 Sept. 1304.

134 Institution of John de Ailleston, priest, to Birmingham (*Burmyngham*) church; patron, Lady Isabella de Burmyngham. Acomb, 24 Oct. 1304.
[Margin] He owes the fee.

135 Institution of William de Brymesgrave, acolyte, to Seckington (*Sekkyndon*) church; patron, Guy de Beauchamp, earl of Warwick (*Warr'*), who has presented William to the church on account of his custody of Seckington manor and the advowson of the church by reason of the minority of the daughter and heir of Sir Gerard de Canvyll', deceased. London, 23 Mar. 1305.

136 Institution of Philip, son of John de Clynton of Coleshill (*Coleshull*) to Ratley (*Roctelegh*) church; patron Guy, earl of Warwick (*Warwik*). London, 5 Apr. 1305.

137   Institution of Robert de Valk, priest, to the vicarage of Grandborough (*Greneberewe*) church; patrons, prior and convent of St. Mary, Ranton (*Rainton*). London, 7 Apr. 1305.

138   Institution of M. William le Archer to Baddesley Clinton (*Baddesleye*) church; patron, James de Clinton. London, 11 May 1305.
[Margin] He owes the fee.

139   Institution of Robert de Farendon to Great Harborough (*Hardeborugh*) church; patron, Sir John de Langelegh, kt. Monks Kirby (*Kirkeby Monachorum*), 20 Dec. 1304.

140   Institution of Roger de Schustoce, priest, to the vicarage of Wormleighton (*Willmeleyhgton*) church; patrons, prior and convent of Kenilworth. He swore to reside. Packington (*Pakynton*), 17 Dec. 1304.
[Margin] He owes the fee.

141   Institution of John de Birhanger, deacon, to the vicarage of Curdworth (*Cruddeworth*) church; patrons, abbot and convent of St. Mary de Pratis, Leicester (*Leyc'*). He swore to reside. London, 23 June 1305.
[Margin] He paid the fee.

142   Institution of Nicholas de Bathekynton, priest, to the ¹perpetual¹ chantry ¹to be created by [the patron]¹ in the church of St. John the Baptist, Baginton (*Bathekynton*); patron, Sir Richard de Herthull, kt. London, 13 July 1305.
[Margin] He paid the fee.
     [¹⁻¹ Interlined together, MS. *perpetua facienda per ipsum*]

143   Institution of Geoffrey de Caldecote, chaplain, to the vicarage of Grandborough (*Greneberg'*) church; patrons, prior and convent of Ranton (*Ronton*). He swore on oath to reside. Coventry, 12 Aug. 1305.

144   Institution of Robert Achard, priest, to Honily (*Honyleye*) church; patron, Sir John Pecche, kt. Coventry, 12 Aug. 1305.

[Fo. 7v] COVEN'.

145   Institution of Conrad Howeschilt of Germany (*Alemannia*), clerk, to Fillongley (*Filungelegh*) church; patron, Sir John de Hastinges, kt. London, 16 Oct. 1305.

146   Institution by the vicar-general of Robert de Loggonere, clerk, to Southam (*Suham*) church; patrons, prior and convent of Coventry. He pledged on oath to pay an annual pension of 30 marks [£20] to the dean and chapter of Lichfield at the accustomed terms. London, 31 Oct. 1305.

147   Institution by the vicar-general of Robert de Beugrave, priest, to Bulkington (*Bulkynton*) vicarage; patrons, abbot and convent of Leicester. He swore to reside. Coventry, 9 Dec. 1305.

148 Institution of Nicholas de Castello to Wishaw (*Wyshawe*) church; patron, Sir William de Castello, kt. London, 9 Jan. 1307.

149 Sixteenth or seventeenth century copy of the charter of Bishop Alexander Stavensby appropriating High Ercall (*Ercalle*) church to the abbot and convent of Shrewsbury. Canterbury (*Cant'*), 22 Oct. 1228.

150 Sixteenth or seventeenth century copy of the confirmation of Bishop Stavensby's grant by the prior and convent of Coventry. 26 May 1229.

[Fo. 8] ARCHIDIACONATUS CESTRIE.

151 Institution of John de Middelton, clerk, to Middleton (*Middelton*) church; patron, Roger de Middelton, his father. 1297.

152 Institution of M. William de Bruera to Coddington (*Cotyndon*) church; patrons, abbot and convent of St. Werburgh, Chester. 5 Mar. 1297.

153 Note that John de Whalleye, priest, has had a letter addressed to the dean of Warrington and Robert, rector of Standish, to induct him to the vicarage of Whalley church (canonically ordained); patrons, abbot and convent of Whalley. York, 4 Oct. 1298.
   [See **7**.]

154 Institution of William de Lutton to Ormskirk (*Ormeschurche*) vicarage; patrons, prior and convent of Burscough. York, 15 Dec. 1298.
   [See **17**.]

155 Institution of William de Fuleburn, subdeacon, to Tarporley (*Torperleghe*) church; patron, Sir Reginald de Grey. Letters dimissory for the orders of deacon and priest. Coventry, 5 Jan. 1299.
   [See **20**.]

156 Collation to M. Walter de Thorp, the bishop's official, of Astbury (*Astbur'*) church, by lapse of time. Ind.: archd. of Chester. Coventry, 5 Jan. 1299.
   [See **22**.]

157 Institution of Richard de Citouns, clerk, to Warmingham (*Wermingham*) church; patron, the king[1]. Lichfield, 8 Jan. 1299.
   [See **28**.
   [1] *CPR 1292–1301*, 358.]

158 Institution of William le Duyn of Brickhill (*Brikehull*) to a moiety of Malpas church; patron, Sir Richard de Sutton, kt. London, 24 Mar. 1299.
   [See **35**.]

159 Institution of M. William de Lancastr' to Eccleston church; patrons, prior and convent of Lancaster. York, 18 May 1299.
   [See **47**.]

160 Institution of William de Mackeworth, deacon, to the vicarage of Weaverham church; patrons, abbot and convent of Vale Royal. York, 2 June 1299.
[See **51**.]

161 Institution of Adam de Kelsale [fo. 8v] to Mobberley church; patron, William de Madburleye. Acomb, 27 June 1299.
[See **54**.]

ARCHIDIACONATUS CESTRIE.

162 Institution of Otto de Grandisson, in the person of John Gusyn of Grandson, his proctor, to Manchester (*Mamecestre*) church; patron, the king. Licence to attend the schools for two years. [York] 18 Nov. 1299.
[See **82**.]

163 Institution of M. Henry de Hampton to North Meols church; patrons, abbot and convent of Evesham. London, 7 Mar. 1300.

ANNUS [M].CCC^{US}. INCIPIT.

164 Institution of Nicholas de Herty, clerk, to North Meols church; patrons, abbot and convent of Evesham. Lichfield, 13 May 1300.

165 Institution of M. Walter de Thorp, canon of Lichfield, to Astbury church; patrons, abbot and convent of St. Werburgh, Chester. Brewood (*Brewode*), 17 May 1300.

166 Institution of Stephen le Blund to Tarporley church; patron, Sir Reginald de Grey. Eccleshall (*Eccleshale*), 21 May 1300.

167 Institution of William de Fulburn, in the person of Adam de Kelsale, his proctor, to Heswall (*Haselwell*) church; patron, lord of Heswall. Same year, day and place.
[Margin] It is quit.[1]
    [[1] i.e. the fee.]

168 Institution of Walter de Norton, priest, to the vicarage of Prestbury (*Prestebur'*) church; patrons, abbot and convent of Chester. Lichfield, 27 May 1300.

169 Institution by Thomas de Abberbury, vicar-general, of Robert de Mackelesfeld, clerk, to St. Peter's church, Chester; patrons, abbot and convent of St. Werburgh, Chester. Ranton (*Ronton*), 30 June 1300.
[Margin] It is quit.

170 Institution by M. Thomas, vicar-general, of M. John de Havering[1] to Warmingham church; patron, the king, by reason of the minority of the heirs of

Warin de Maywaryn, deceased, tenant in chief.[2] Wellington under Wrockwardine (*Welynton subtus le Wrokene*), 29 June 1300.
[Margin] Nothing [for the fee] by the chancellor.
[[1] *BRUO*, iii.2181.]
[[2] *CPR 1292–1301*, 518.]

171 Institution of Thomas de Prestecote, deacon, to Acton vicarage; patrons, abbot and convent of Combermere (*Cumbermere*). York, 6 Oct. 1300.

172 Institution of Martin de Abington, priest, to the vicarage of Weaverham church; patrons, abbot and convent of Vale Royal. York, 27 Oct. 1300.

[Fo. 9] CESTRIE.

173 Institution of Robert de Basinges, clerk, in the person of his proctor, to Stockport (*Stokport*) church; patron, Sir William de Morleye, kt., [1]who has presented Robert[1] by reason of his custody of John, first-born heir of Sir Richard de Stokport, kt., deceased, who is under legal age. Acomb, 1 Dec. 1300.
[Margin] The instituted does not have the letter of his institution.
[[1-1] Interlined.]

174 Institution of M. Jordan de Maclesfeld to Mottram in Longdendale (*Mottrum*) church; patron, Thomas de Burgh, a layman. Burton upon Trent (*Burton super Trentam*), 17 Dec. 1300.
[Margin] Nothing [for the fee].
[Jordan apparently received a licence to study for seven years at about this time. On 10 May 1308 he had papal dispensation to study canon and civil law for a further three years without proceeding to higher orders, see *CPL*, ii.39, *BRUO*, ii.1200. He resigned his rectory before Feb. 1316 after Langton had begun proceedings to deprive him of his benefice, see **901***.]

175 Institution of M. Richard de Birchek to Tattenhall (*Tatenhale*) church; patrons, abbot and convent of St. Werburgh, Chester. Letters dimissory for all holy orders. [1]Licence to remain in the schools for three years under the terms of the statute.[1] Reepham, 12 Feb. 1301.
[Margin] Nothing [for the fee].
[Tattenhall church became vacant on 24 Jan. 1301. It was then placed under the bishop's sequestration and 3s. 2½d. was received from it, see **467**; Hughes, 'Account roll', n. 82.
[1-1] Added later. This licence is for one year in **430**, and dated 13 Feb. 1301.]

176 Institution of Henry le Waleys, priest, to Standish church; patron, William de Standissh. London, 25 May 1301.
[Standish church too had been placed under the bishop's sequestration prior to this institution and 38s. 4d. was received from it, see Hughes, 'Account roll', n. 87.]

177* Note that on Thurs. 7 Dec. 1301 at Chesterfield Robert de Askeby was instituted to Thornton le Moors church by M. Thomas de Abberbury, vicar-general; patron, the king, by reason of his custody of Peter, son and heir of Ranulph le Ruter, deceased, tenant in chief, a minor.[1]

Be it known that, with the counsel of the justices of both Benches and the barons of the Exchequer having been considered, J[ohn] de Drokenesford and J[ohn] de Langeton, the chancellor, have written by their letters, which are in John de Langeton's hand, to the vicar-general that, in order to avoid being in contempt of the king and of the king's son, the earl of Chester, who favoured that party, and in order to avoid loss to the bishop, the aforesaid clerk should be admitted without any difficulty. The vicar-general has had the king's letters close.[2]

> [Edward I had presented Robert to the church on 3 Jan. 1296 but he was unable to be instituted until 7 Dec. 1301 because of a 'lay force' and 'rebels in the church'. Thornton church had been placed under the bishop's sequestration for some time, and £22 4s. 2½d. was accounted for in the period Epiphany to Michaelmas 1301, see Hughes, 'Episcopate', i.144–6; Hughes, 'Account roll', n. 81.
> [1] *CPR 1292–1301*, 181.
> [2] *CCR 1296–1302*, 579.]

178   Institution by the vicar-general of Adam de Bunnebur', chaplain, to Rood chapel, Tarporley (*Roode in Torperlee*); patron, Sir Reginald de Grey. Lichfield. 26 Jan. 1302.

179   Institution by the vicar-general of Henry de Bletcheleye, clerk, to Tilston (*Tylstam*) church; patron, Urian de Sancto Petro, a layman. Same day, year and place.

180   Institution by the vicar-general of Simon de Radeswelle to West Kirby (*Kyrkeby in Wyrhale*) church; patrons, abbot and convent of Chester. Lichfield, 4 Mar. 1302.

181   Institution by the vicar-general of Henry de Walleton to Tattenhall (*Tatinhale*) church; patrons, abbot and convent of Chester. Lichfield, 4 Mar. 1302.

[Fo. 9v] CESTRIE.

182   Institution by the papal administrators[1] of M. Henry de Kanneleye to Haslington (*Heselurton*) chapel; patron, Sir Ralph de Vernoun. Banbury (*Bannebur'*), 26 July 1302.

> [[1] MS. *per custodes episcopatus deputatos per sedem apostolicam*
> Followed by three blank lines.]

183*   Note that on 9 Oct. 1301 at Acomb M. William de Rodyerd was instituted to Grappenhall church; patrons, prior and convent of Norton.[1] Note that William, coming in person to Steeple Aston on 17 Dec. 1302, sought letters dimissory for the order of priest from M. Thomas de Abberbury, who refused him the letter because a year had elapsed in which [William] ought to have been ordained priest, and because [Thomas's] colleagues,[2] whose presence he ought to have had more often, were not present; William appealed against this refusal.

[¹ For the priory see J. Patrick Greene, *Norton Priory: the archaeology of a medieval religious house* (Cambridge, 1989).

² i.e. the other papal administrators.]

184   Institution of Robert de Cliderow to Wigan (*Wygan*) church; patron, John de Langeton. Lichfield chapter-house, 22 Sept. 1303.

185   Institution of M. William de Cruce Roys¹ to Leyland (*Leylaunde*) church; patrons, abbot and convent of Evesham. Acomb, 15 Jan. 1304.

[¹ *BRUO*, i.523.]

186   Institution and induction by Philip de Everdon and Ellis de Napton, papal administrators,¹ of Thomas called le Waleys to Acton (*Acton Blundel*) church; patron, Richard Walensis. Lichfield, 16 June 1303.

[¹ MS. *Coventr' et Lich' episcopatus administratores per sedem apostolicam tunc temporis deputatos*]

187   Institution of Hugh de Masci, acolyte, to a moiety of Wallasey (*Kyrkebi in Waleya*) church;¹ patrons, abbot and convent of St. Werburgh, Chester. Muskham, 24 Feb. 1304.

[Margin] $\frac{1}{2}$ mark for the fee. It is quit.

[¹ *VCH Cheshire*, iii.131, 134.]

188   Institution of Robert de Chishulle, clerk, to Barthomley (*Bertumleye*) church; patron this turn, Edward, prince of Wales, earl of Chester, by reason of his custody of the lands of Richard de Praers, the patron of the church. Shrewsbury, 24 Mar. 1304.

189   Institution of John de Sancto Petro, subdeacon, to Bunbury (*Bunnebury*) church; patron, Urian de Sancto Petro. Lilleshall (*Lilleshull*), 31 Mar. 1304.

190   Institution of John Pupard, subdeacon, to Plemstall (*Pleymundestowe*) church; patrons, abbot and convent of Shrewsbury. Lenton Priory, 3 Apr. 1304.

191   Institution of Roger de Codyngton to Pulford (*Puleford*) church; patron, Robert de Puleford. Steeple Aston, 21 Aug. 1304.

[Fo. 10] CESTRIE.

192   Institution of Robert de Bruera to Pulford church; patron, Robert de Pulford. Acomb, 1 Nov. 1304.

193   Institution of Adam de Kelesale to Thornton le Moors (*Thornton*) church; patron, Peter de Thornton. Lichfield, 11 Dec. 1304.

[Margin] He owes the fee.

194 Institution of M. Richard Vernun[1] to Eccleston (*Ecleston*) church, vacant by the resignation of John de Venables; patron, Sir Hugh de Venables, kt. London, 19 Jan. 1305.

  [¹ *BRUO*, iii.1946.]

195 Institution of John de Modburlegh to Mobberley (*Modburlegh*) church, vacant[1] by the resignation of Adam de Kellesale; patron, William de Modburlegh. London, 27 Jan. 1305.

  [¹ MS. *vacabat* preceded by *resig'* deleted.]

196 Institution of Richard de Swetenham, clerk, to Swettenham (*Swetenham*) church; patron, Richard de Swetenham. London, 7 Feb. 1305.

197 Institution of Richard de Chaddisdene to the vicarage of Wynbunbury (*Wymburbur'*) church, belonging to the bishop's collation. He swore to reside. London, 17 Mar. 1305.

198 Institution of Henry de Blechelegh, clerk, to Northenden (*Norworthyn*) church; patrons, abbot and convent of St. Werburgh, Chester, saving an annual pension of 4s. due to them from of old. London, 11 Feb. 1305.
[Margin] He owes the fee.

199 Institution of Richard de Bletchele to Tilston (*Tylstan*) church; patron, Urian de Sancto Petro. London, 7 Feb. 1305.
[Margin] He owes the fee.

200 Institution of William de Bletcheleg' to Waverton church; patrons, abbot and convent of St. Werburgh, Chester. London, 19 June 1305.
[Margin] He owes the fee.

201 Institution of Walter de Coleshull to the vicarage of Weaverham church; patrons, abbot and convent of Vale Royal. London, 19 June 1305.

202 Institution of William de Bromyerd to Plemstall (*Pleymondestowe*) church; patrons, abbot and convent of Shrewsbury. Fulbrook (*Folbrok*), 4 Aug. 1305.
[Margin] He owes the fee.

203 Institution of William de Aston to the vicarage of Backford (*Bacford*) church; patrons, prior and convent of Birkenhead (*Byrkheved*). He swore to reside. London, 14 Oct. 1305.

204 Institution by the vicar-general of M. John Hurel[1] to Thurstaston (*Thurstanston*) church; patrons, abbot and convent of Chester, saving an annual pension due to them from of old. Steeple Aston, 23 Nov. 1305.

  [¹ *BRUO*, i.311 (Burleye).]

[Fo. 10v] CESTRIE.

205 Institution by the vicar-general of William de Scalariis to Ashton (*Asshton*) church; patron, Robert de Asshton. Steeple Aston, 7 Dec. 1305.

206 Institution by the vicar-general of Geoffrey de Meules to Coddington (*Codynton*) church; patrons, abbot and convent of St. Werburgh, Chester. Licence for non-residence until Assumption next. Coventry, 25 Dec. 1305.

207 Institution by the vicar-general of Nicholas de Arderna, clerk, to Ashton under Lyne (*Ashton*) church; patron, Thomas Grelle. Ind.: John Pupard.[1] Steeple Aston, 18 Mar. 1306.
[[1] The sequestrator-general.]

208 Note that M. Thomas, vicar-general, committed custody of the sequestration on Manchester (*Mamcestr'*) church to Geoffrey de Stokes, king's clerk, during pleasure. Steeple Aston, 31 Mar. 1306.
Afterwards, Geoffrey was instituted rector. Note of the letters patent of his institution, declaring that Geoffrey had been presented to Manchester church by Thomas de Grelly, saving in all things the right and possession of Nicholas de Ardena, clerk, of Ashton under Lyne church, which Nicholas acquired at the presentation of the same Thomas de Grelly, whose right and possession it is not intended to prejudice. London, 12 Apr. 1306.
Note of the letter of induction to the archdeacon of Chester, declaring [as above]. London, 12 Apr. 1306.

209 Institution of M. Richard de Vernoun to Stockport (*Stokeport*) church; patron, Nicholas, son of Nicholas de Eton. London, 15 Dec. 1306.

210 Institution of Robert de Farneworth, priest, to Ormskirk (*Ormeschirch*) vicarage; patrons, prior and convent of Burscough. He swore to reside. London, 30 Dec. 1306.
[Margin] He paid the fee.

211 Note that on 24 Jan. 1307 at Warmington (*Warmynton*) the election of Agatha de Dutton as prioress of St. Mary's, Chester, was confirmed. Note that a letter was sent to the justice of Chester that he should do those things which pertain to him concerning her election and confirmation.

[Fo. 11] CESTRIE.

212 Institution of William de Ravenesmoeles, clerk, to Lawton (*Lauton*) church; patrons, abbot and convent of St. Werburgh, Chester, saving an annual pension to Astbury church due from of old. Beningbrough (*Beningburg'*), 16 Jan. 1307.

213 Institution of Thomas Trussel, clerk, to Warmingham (*Wermyngham*) church; patron, Agnes de Maynwaring. 9 Jan. 1307.

214 Institution of John de Bambourg', priest, to Winwick (*Wynquik*) vicarage; patrons, prior and convent of St. Oswald, Nostell (*Nostel*). He swore to reside. After his admission and institution to the vicarage John swore on the holy gospels that he would pay the customary annual pension or payment (*prestacionem*) to the community of Lichfield church or their proctor in full forever at Winwick (*Wynnequik*); *viz.* 12 marks [£8] at Christmas and 12 marks on the Nativity of St. John the Baptist. He similarly swore to pay a pension of 24 marks [£16] each year to the prior and convent of St. Oswald at the same terms, in the same place. Carlisle (*Carleolum*), 8 Feb. 1307.

    [A hand drawn in the left-hand margin points to this entry in which the words *vicaria* and *vicariam* have been written over erasures.]

215 Note that proceedings were held concerning the restoration of the above erasures; *viz. vicaria, vicaria, vicar'* etc. 14 Dec. 1375.

[Margin] See the restoration in the register of Robert, bishop of Coventry.[1]

    [A hand drawn in the right-hand margin points to this entry.

    [1] Bishop Stretton's register notes that the text of **214** and other institutions to Winwick vicarage were inspected and evidence heard that the words *vicaria* and *vicariam* had been altered to *ecclesia* and *ecclesiam* by John de Leycester, chapter clerk of Lichfield. The commissary ordered the words *vicaria* and *vicariam* be restored in the text, see *The registers or act books of the bishops of Coventry and Lichfield. Book 5, being the second register of Bishop Robert de Stretton, A.D. 1360–1385: an abstract of the contents*, ed. R.A. Wilson (William Salt Archaeological Society, new series, 8, 1905), 127–9.

    The rest of the recto is blank.]

216 [Fo. 11v] Sixteenth or seventeenth century copy of the charter of Bishop Hugh Nonant (1188–1198) granting Baschurch church to the abbot and convent of Shrewsbury. n.d.

217 Sixteenth or seventeenth century copy of the confirmation of Bishop Nonant's grant by the prior and convent of Coventry. 16 Feb. 1224.

218 Sixteenth or seventeenth century copy of the confirmation to the abbot and convent of Shrewsbury of tithes by Bishop Roger. n.d.

[Fo. 12] ARCHIDIACONATUS DERBEYE.

219 Institution of Eudes de Derby, priest, to Heanor church; patron, Sir Henry de Grey, kt. He resigned the church and received the same *in commendam*, as is clear below.[1] 1298.

    [[1] See **8, 237**.]

220 Institution of John de Whalleye, priest, to Crich (*Cruch*) vicarage; patrons, abbot and convent of Darley (*Derley*). 1298.

221 Institution of John Torkard, deacon, to Ault Hucknall (*Alto Hokenhale*) vicarage; patrons, prior and convent of Newstead in Sherwood (*Novi loci in Shirewode*). Littleborough (*Lutleburgh*), 18 June 1298.

222 Institution of Thomas de Welton, priest, to Chesterfield (*Cestrefeud*) vicarage; patron, P[hilip] de Willughby, dean of Lincoln. Ely, 19 Apr. 1298.

223 Institution of Robert de Mar to a moiety of Eckington church; patron, the king.[1] York, 24 Sept. 1298.
[Margin] Nothing [for the fee][2].
　[[1] *CPR 1292–1301*, 145.
　[2] **1** notes he owed $\frac{1}{2}$ mark.]

224 Note that Alexander de Wighton, priest, having been presented to the vicarage of Hartington parish church (canonically ordained) by the abbess and convent of B.V.M. without the walls of London, of the order of St. Clare, has had a letter addressed to the archdeacon of Coventry and M. W[alter] de Thorp, the bishop's official, to institute him. Acomb, 4 Oct. 1298.
[Margin] Nothing [for the fee].
　[See **6**.]

225 Institution of Henry Berchelmen, subdeacon, to Barlborough church; patron, Sir Walter de Goushull, kt. Afterwards the date of institution was changed to 19 July 1299, and he then had letters dimissory for the orders of deacon and priest. York, 21 Nov. 1298.
[Margin] Nothing [for the fee].
　[See **11**.]

226 Institution of Br. Simon de Radeford, canon of Dale, to Kirkhallam vicarage; patrons, abbot and convent of Dale. York, 9 Dec. 1298.
[Margin] It is quit.
　[See **16**.]

227 Institution of Br. Godman, canon of Shelford, to Alvaston vicarage; patrons, prior and convent of Shelford. Lichfield, 12 Jan. 1299.
[Margin] It is quit.
　[See **26**.]

228 Institution of Simon de Hegham, subdeacon, to Barton Blount (*Barton Bagepuz*) church; [fo. 12v] patron, John Baggepuz. Licence to attend the schools for three years, paying 1 mark (13s. 4d.) each year to the bishop for his alms on the Nativity of St. John the Baptist. He paid for the first year. London, 26 Mar. 1299.
[Margin] Nothing [for the fee].
　[See **37, 79**.]

229 Institution of Geoffrey de Merston, canon of Dunstable, to the vicarage of Bradbourne church, without any inquiry. London, 28 Mar. 1299.
　[See **38**.]

230 Institution of Richard de Hereford, subdeacon, to Pinxton (*Pengeston*) church; patron, Denise le Wyne. London, 30 Mar. 1299.
　[See **42**.]

231   Institution of Thomas de Sadington, clerk, in the person of William de Sadington, his brother and proctor, to Duffield church; patron, Roger le Brabazoun, proctor or deputy of Lady Blanche, widow of Edmund, earl of Lancaster, son of King Henry [III]. London, 18 Apr. 1299.
[Margin] Nothing [for the fee].
   [See **43**.]

232   Institution of Ralph de Cressi to Thorp church; patron, P[hilip] de Willugby, dean of Lincoln. York, 18 May 1299.
[Margin] Nothing [for the fee].
   [See **46**.]

233   Institution by Walter de Thorp, vicar-general, of John de Leges to Dalbury (*Dalbur'*) church; patron, Sir Giles de Meigniel, kt. Lichfield, 24 Sept. 1297.
[Margin] He was not ordained within time.
   [John was ordained subdeacon on 21 Sept. 1297 at Leicester by letters dimissory issued by the vicar-general when it was noted that he had been presented to Dalbury church; his name does not appear in Langton's ordination lists, see *Reg. Sutton*, vii.94–5; Hughes, 'Episcopate', i.137–8.]

234   Institution of John Mauclerk of Leicester to Clowne (*Clune*) church; patrons, prior and convent of Worksop (*Wirsop*). Lichfield, 25 Feb. 1300.
[Margin] *ab'*

235   Institution of Alexander de Kyngeston, subdeacon, to Duffield church; patron, Lady Blanche, queen of Navarre, countess palatine of Champagne (*Campagn'*) and Brie. London, 17 Mar. 1300.
   [See **53**.]

236   Note that the bishop has delivered custody of the moiety of Eckington (*Ekinton*) church which was M. Peter de Pratellis's to Theobald de Beaumont until 1 Aug. next; patron, the king.[1] Acomb, 17 May 1299. Afterwards, Theobald was instituted to the moiety, and he had letters to attend the schools for five years under the terms of the statute that he shall be ordained subdeacon within a year. London, 23 Mar. 1300.[2]
[Margin] Nothing [for the fee].
   [[1] *CPR 1292–1301*, 408.
   [2] The date here is *eodem anno x kal. Aprilis* (23 Mar. 1300), but see **45** where the date is 24 Mar. 1300.]

[Fo. 13] DERBEI.

INCIPIT ANNUS [M].CCC^{us}.

237   Institution of Eudes de Derb', priest, to Heanor church; patron, Sir Henry de Grey, kt. London, 30 Mar. 1300.

238 Institution by Thomas de Abberbury, vicar-general, of Robert de Chaundys, acolyte, to Radbourne (*Rodburn*) church; patron, John de Chaundys. Lichfield, 7 June 1300.

239 Institution of M. Walter de Fodringeye, priest, to Matlock (*Matlok*) church; patron, Philip, dean of Lincoln. York, 27 Aug. 1300.

240 Institution of Thomas de Welleton, priest, to Ashbourne (*Assheburn*) vicarage; patron, Philip de Willughby, dean of Lincoln. Marr (*Marre*), 13 Dec. 1300.

241 Institution of John de Brentingham, subdeacon, to the portion of Darley church which was M. Walter de Fodringeye's; patron, Philip de Willugby, dean of Lincoln. Lichfield, 18 Dec. 1300.

242 Institution of Walter de Suthleyrton, priest, to Chesterfield (*Cesterfeld*) vicarage; patron, dean of Lincoln. Reepham, 3 Feb. 1301.

243 Institution of Thomas de Querle, clerk, to a moiety of Staveley (*Stavele*) church; patron, the king, by reason of his custody of the land and heir of Nicholas Musard, the last rector of the moiety.[1] Reepham, 9 Feb. 1301.
[Margin] It became vacant on [2][Thurs.] before Christmas [22 Dec. 1300].[2]
  [The moiety was placed under the bishop's sequestration during the vacancy and 21s. 4½ d. was received from it, see Hughes, 'Account roll', n. 61.
  [1] *CPR 1292–1301*, 560.
  [2–2] Abraded, see **468**.]

244 Institution of M. Robert de Bromlegh to Shirley (*Shirlegh'*) vicarage; patrons, abbot and convent of Darley. Lincoln, 21 Feb. 1301.

245 Institution of M. Walter de Lega to Boylestone (*Boyleston'*) church; patron, John de Basinges, a layman. Same day, year and place.

246 Institution of Alexander de Breton', priest, to Steetley (*Stivetelay*) church; patron, Alice, widow of James le Bretoun. Stock Wood (*Stok'*), 2 Apr. 1301.

247 Institution of William de Weston, clerk, to Tibshelf (*Tippeshulf*) church; patrons, prioress and convent of Brewood White Ladies (*albarum monialum de Brewod*). Woodstock (*Wodestok*), 9 July 1301.
  [Tibshelf church had been placed under the bishop's sequestration prior to this institution and £8 was received from it, see Hughes, 'Account roll', n. 69.]

248 Institution of Br. Robert de Sutton, canon of Welbeck (*Wellebek*), of the Premonstratensian (*Premonstrn'*) order, to Etwall (*Ettewell*) vicarage; patrons, abbot and convent of Welbeck, by authority of a privilege they have to present any of their canons to such vacant vicarages.[1] Woodstock, 5 Aug. 1301.
  [Etwall vicarage also had been placed under the bishop's sequestration prior to this institution and 32s. 11½ d. was received from it, see Hughes, 'Account roll', n. 64.

[1] The privilege enabling the order to present canons as vicars of their appropriated churches was granted by Pope Clement III in 1188, see D. Knowles, *The religious orders in England* (Cambridge, 1961–2), ii.139. See also A. Hamilton Thompson, *The Premonstratensian Abbey of Welbeck* (London, 1938).]

249	Institution by the vicar-general of M. Richard de Wermington to North Wingfield (*Wynefeld*) church; patron, John Deyncourt.[1] Coventry, 12 Nov. 1301.
[[1] For John Deyncourt's biography see Foulds, *Thurgarton Cartulary*, pp. cxiv–cxv.]

250	[Fo. 13v] Institution by the vicar-general of Adam de Novo Castro subtus Lymam, priest, to Sutton-on-the-Hill vicarage; patrons, prior and convent of Trentham. Repton (*Repindon*), 1 Dec. 1301.
[The vicarage had been placed under the bishop's sequestration and 38s. 8d. was received from it during the period Epiphany to Michaelmas 1301, see Hughes, 'Account roll', n. 66.]

251	Institution by the [papal] administrators[1] of Roger de Malberthorp, deacon, to Whittington (*Whytington*) church; patron, Philip de Willugby, dean of Lincoln. York, 3 Oct. 1302.
[[1] MS. *per administratores episcopatus*]

252	Institution by the [papal] administrators of Reginald de Cusaunce,[1] in the person of M. John de Cusaunce, his proctor, to a moiety of Eckington church; patron, the king, by reason of the lands of Robert de Stotevill', an alien, being in his hands.[2] Haughmond (*Haghemon'*), 19 Mar. 1303.
[[1] Perhaps brother of Gerard de Cusaunce, see *BRUO*, i.530.
[2] *CPR 1301–7*, 118.]

253	Institution of William de Eyncourt to Morton church; patron, John de Eyncourt. Lichfield chapter-house, 22 Sept. 1303.

254	Institution of Henry de Coleshull, priest, to Boylestone church; patron, John Seuch. Acomb, 15 Jan. 1304.

255	Institution of Henry Sauvage of Lichfield to Hartshorne (*Herteshorn'*) church; patron, Robert de la Warde. Acomb, 23 Jan. 1304.
[Margin] He owes the fee.

256	Institution of Stephen de Brawode, acolyte, to Tibshelf (*Tibbeshulf in E*) church; patrons, prioress and convent of Brewood White Ladies. York, 6 Feb. 1304.

257	Institution of Jordan de Sutton, priest, to Longford (*Langeford*) vicarage; patron, M. John de Cressi, rector of Longford. Acomb, 28 June 1304.
[Margin] He owes the fee.

258	Institution of William le Palmere of Nottingham (*Notingham*) to the vicarage of Horsley (*Horseleg'*) church; patrons, prior and convent of Lenton. Same day.

259 Institution of John de Cindeford, clerk, to Sutton Scarsdale (*Sutton in Dale*) church; patron, Thomas, earl of Lancaster (*Langcastr'*), by reason of his custody of the heir of Richard de Grey, a minor, and his lands. York, 23 Sept. 1304.

260 Institution of Roger de Shulton, priest, to Heanor church; patron, Sir Henry de Gray, kt. Acomb, 3 Oct. 1304.

[Fo. 14] DERBEI.

261 Note that custody of Aston upon Trent (*Aston super Trent*) church was delivered to John de Sandales, king's clerk,[1] during pleasure. 3 Nov. 1304.
[2]Afterwards John was instituted rector of Aston upon Trent.[3] London, 1 Oct. 1305.
[Margin] He owes the fee.[2]
[[1] *DNB*, xvii.739–40.
[2-2] Added later at the top of the folio, before the grant of custody.
[3] By papal dispensation for plurality, non-residence, and orders, see *CPL*, ii.9, 27, 88; *Reg. Winchelsey*, ii.1192–5.]

262 Institution of John de Brentingham, clerk, to Bonsall (*Bontesal*) church; patron, Philip de Wylugby, dean of Lincoln. Acomb, 11 Nov. 1304.
[Margin] He owes the fee.

263 Institution of Nicholas de Kinelworth, clerk, to the portion in Darley church which was John de Brentingham's; patron, Philip, dean of Lincoln. Same day, year and place.
[Margin] He owes the fee. He paid.

264 Institution of Robert de Notingham, clerk, to Bradley (*Bradeleye*) church, vacant by the resignation of Hugh de Hengham, the former rector, whose resignation the bishop has. London, 23 Jan. 1305.
[Margin] He paid.

265 Institution of Robert de Felkirk, priest, to the vicarage of Shirley (*Shirlegh*) church; patrons, abbot and convent of Darley (*Derlegh*), at the bishop's nomination. London, 4 Apr. 1305.

266 Institution of Richard de Novo Castro to the vicarage of Stapenhill (*Stapenhull*) church; patrons, abbot and convent of Burton upon Trent. London, 28 May 1305.
[Margin] He owes [the fee].

267 Institution of Richard Cursoun, clerk, to Breadsall (*Breydeshale*) church; patron, Richard Cursoun. London, 16 Sept. 1305.

268 Note that in Bishop Langton's chapel, London, immediately after mass, M. Gocelin, dean of Lincoln,[1] in the person of M. Walter de Foderyngeye, his proctor, swore canonical obedience to the bishop, his successors, officials, and ministers with regard to the churches of Ashbourne (*Essebourne*), Wirksworth, and Chesterfield. As an act of grace, the bishop has deferred receiving the dean's obedience in respect of the church of All Saints, Derby, which was omitted from the proxy through negligence, during pleasure. The bishop has relaxed his sequestration on the fruits of the above three churches. 1 Oct. 1305.

[¹ Jocelin Kirmington elected 27 Sept. 1305, see *Fasti*, i.3.]

269 Institution of Robert de Alsop, deacon, to St. Peter's vicarage, Derby; patrons, abbot and convent of Darley. He swore to reside. London, 1 Oct. 1305.

270 Institution of William de Barthon, clerk, to Sutton Scarsdale church; patron, Thomas, earl of Lancaster. London, 30 May 1306.

271 [Fo. 14v] Note that Br. Hugh de Macworth has been admitted to the care and rule of the house of Holy Trinity, Breadsall (*de parco de Breydeshale*), and instituted prior of the same; patron, Richard le Corzoun of Breadsall. London, 7 June 1306.

272 Institution of Richard, son of Hugh Waleys of Walton upon Trent (*Walton*), to Walton upon Trent (*Walton super Trentam*) church; patron, Robert de Montalt, steward of Chester. Northampton, 3 July 1306.

273 Institution of Gilbert de Bruera, priest, to Hathersage (*Haversegh'*) church, vacant by the resignation of Thomas de Billesdon; patrons, prior and convent of Launde. London, 12 Nov. 1306.

274 Collation to Thomas de Nevill' of the treasurership of Lichfield church,¹ vacant by the death of M. Alan le Bretoun. London, 12 Nov. 1306.
[Recorded in a Derby archdeaconry section in error.
¹ *Fasti*, x.11; see **689, 690**.]

275 Sixteenth or seventeenth century copy of the charter of Bishop Alexander Stavensby (1224–1238) granting the tithes of Wellington (*Welynton*) church to the abbot and convent of Shrewsbury. 1232–3.

276 Sixteenth or seventeenth century copy of the confirmation of Bishop Stavensby's grant by the prior and convent of Coventry. n.d.

[Fo. 15] ARCHIDIACONATUS STAFFORD'.

277 Institution of Richard de Camera, clerk, to Leigh (*Leye*) church; patron, Philip de Draicote. Lichfield, 9 Jan. 1299.

278 Institution of Simon de Wykeford to the prebend of Wilnecote in Tamworth church; patron, Sir Ralph Basset, kt. Ind.: archd. of Stafford. York [1298].
[See **10**.]

279 Institution of Robert de Kenilleworth, chaplain, to Ellastone vicarage; patrons, prior and convent of Kenilworth. Coventry, 6 Jan. 1299.
[See **21**.]

280 Institution of Nicholas de Aylesbur', clerk, to Pattingham (*Patingham*) church; patrons, prior and convent of Launde. Lichfield, 8 Jan. 1299.
[See **24**.]

281 Institution of Roger de Bowode to Wombourn vicarage; patrons, prior and convent of Dudley (*Duddeleye*). Lichfield, 8 Jan. 1299.
[See **29**.]

282 Institution of Roger de Gretewych to Kingswinford church; patron, Lady Agnes de Somery. York, 23 Jan. 1299.
[See **30, 41**.]

ANNUS DOMINI M.CCC^{us}. INCIPIT.

283 Institution by Thomas de Abberbury, vicar-general, of William de Pulesdon, acolyte, to Gratwich (*Gretewych*) church; patron, Philip de Chetewynd. Lichfield, 7 June 1300.

284 Institution by the same M. Thomas of Nicholas de Verdoun, acolyte, to Stoke upon Tern (*Stok super Tyrne*) church; patron, Sir Theobald de Verdoun. Same year, day and place.
[Margin] Shrewsbury.[1]
 [[1] In a contemporary hand. Stoke upon Tern (in Shropshire) was listed under Shrewsbury archdeaconry in 1304 and 1312, see **341, 578**.]

285 Institution by M. Thomas of M. Alexander de Verdoun, subdeacon, to Biddulph (*Bydulf*) church; patron, Henry de Verdoun. Stone, 2 July 1300.
[Margin] It is quit.

286 Institution by the vicar-general of John de Hales, priest, to Drayton Bassett (*Drayton Basset*) chapel; patrons, dean and chapter of Tamworth. Lichfield, 30 July 1300.
[Margin] It is quit.

287 Institution of M. Thomas de Thorp, clerk, in the person of M. Simon de Shirleye, his proctor, to Kingswinford church; patron, Lady Agnes, widow of Sir Roger de Somery, kt. Coventry, 16 Jan. 1301.

288 [Fo. 15v] Institution of John de Brikehull, clerk, to Standon (*Staundon*) church; patron, Sir Robert de Staundon, kt. Stock Wood (*Stok'*), 2 Apr. 1301.

289 Institution of M. Peter de Askam to Checkley (*Checkele*) church; patron, Richard de Draycote. Acomb, 4 May 1301.

290   Institution of Roger de Clungunford to the prebend of Coton (*Cotes*) in Tamworth church; patron, Ralph Basse[t] of Drayton Bassett (*Drayton*). Thorpe Waterville (*Thorp Watervill'*), 21 June 1301.
[Margin] It is quit.[1]
  [See Hughes, 'Clergy list', 8, 16.
  [1] Followed by *nota ut ponitur in T* by the hand that made marginal notes for the index compiled in the seventeenth century, see LJRO, *Seventeenth century index to Lichfield bishop's register B/A/1/1*, no. 71, p. 29.]

291   Institution of William de Neuton, acolyte, to Thorpe Constantine (*Thorp'*) church; patron, Richard Constantyn, lord of Thorpe Constantine. London, 28 Oct. 1301.
[Margin] It is quit.
  [See Hughes, 'Clergy list', 9, 17.]

292   Institution by the papal administrators[1] of Roger, son of Roger de Aston to Weston upon Trent (*Weston super Trentam*) church; patron, Robert de Bures. Banbury, 26 July 1302.
  [[1] MS. *per custodes episcopatus deputatos per sedem apostolicam*]

293   Institution of Richard de Tettebur' to the prebend of Syerscote (*Shyrescote*) in Tamworth (*Tameworth*) collegiate church; patron, Thomas de Lodelowe, presenting by reason of Joan, his wife. York, 12 Oct. 1303.
  [See Hughes, 'Clergy list', 8, 16.]

294   Institution of Thomas le Hunte to Madeley (*Madeleye*) church; patrons, prior and convent of Stone (*Stanes*).[1] Acomb, 25 Oct. 1303.
  [[1] *VCH Staffordshire*, iii.241.]

295   Institution of Richard de Bristoll, clerk, to Quatt (*Quatte*) church; patrons, prior and convent of Great Malvern (*Majoris Malverne*). Acomb, 28 June 1304.

296   Institution of William de Pecco to Brewood vicarage; patron, dean of Lichfield. Acomb, 8 July 1304.
[Margin] He owes the fee.

297   Note that custody of the sequestration on Tatenhill (*Tatenhulle*) church has been committed to John de Kynardeseie, clerk, until 1 Feb. [1305], having been presented to the same church on the first day of the vacancy. He is to receive all things. 18 Oct. 1304.
  [Instituted 18 Apr. 1305, see **300**.]

298   Note that the bishop has committed custody of the sequestration on Stoke upon Trent (*Stokes subtus Limam*) church to John de Sandale, king's clerk, during pleasure, having been presented to the church by the earl of Lancaster. London, 20 Jan. 1305.
  [Instituted 20 Apr. 1305, see **302**.]

299 Institution of Hugh de Hotoft, clerk, to Water Eaton (*Eyton*) church; patrons, abbess and convent of Polesworth, at the nomination of Sir Adam de Brympton, kt., saving an annual pension of 20 marks [£13 6s. 8d.] due to the nuns from of old. London, 30 Mar. 1305.
[Margin] He owes the fee.

300 Note that on 18 Apr. 1305 at Coventry John de Kynardeseye, clerk, was instituted to Tatenhill (*Tatynhull*) church; patron, Thomas, earl of Lancaster. However, the letter of induction was given at London on 8 Apr. as the induction was made at the special command of the bishop by his sequestrator, and not the archdeacon or official, by whom he should have been inducted, and on that date the bishop was in London.
[See Hughes, 'Clergy list', 10, 18.]

301 Note that Richard de Bristoll, rector of Quatt, freely gave 5 marks [£3 6s. 8d.] to the bishop for the first fruits which the bishop assigned to be paid to Richard de Lympodeseye, who received the 5 marks at Oxford from M. William de Glovernia, the rector's uncle. n.d.

[Fo. 16] STAFFORD'.

302 Institution of John de Sandale to Stoke upon Trent (*Stok' underlym*) church;[1] patron, Thomas, earl of Lancaster. 20 Apr. 1305.
[Margin] He owes the fee.
[[1] By papal dispensation, see **261**, n. 3.]

303 Institution of Alan de Asshebourne, priest, to the vicarage of Mayfield (*Madderfeld*) church; patrons, prior and convent of Tutbury (*Tuttebur'*). Kenilworth, 18 Dec. 1304.

304 Institution of Hugh de Bisshebur', clerk, to Bushbury (*Bysshebur'*) church; patron, Henry de Bisshebur'. 31 May 1305.

305 Institution of M. Andrew de Janna to Forton church; patron, Sir John de Someri, kt. London, 18 June 1305.

306 Note that Br. Ralph de Quertu, monk of Saint-Rémy, Reims (*Sancti Remigii, Remen'*), proctor of his abbot, has been deputed by the abbot's letters patent to present to the priorate of Lapley (*Lappele*) by the same [letter] if it happens to be vacant.[1] The said priorate was vacant by the free resignation of the former prior, Br. Peter de Passiaco, made to the bishop, and he presented Br. John de Tannione, monk of Saint-Rémy, who was admitted prior. Brewood, 26 Mar. 1305.
[Margin] He owes a 40s. fee.
[*VCH Staffordshire*, iii.343.
[1] Followed by a drawn line measuring 2cm.]

307 Note that Br. Thomas de Boweles was admitted to the keepership or rule of the cell of Calwich (*Calewych*) and instituted prior of the same; patrons, prior and convent of Kenilworth. London, 14 Oct. 1305.

   [*VCH Staffordshire*, iii.239.]

308 Institution by the vicar-general of Br. William de Beulu, monk of Great Malvern (*Magna Malverna*), as prior of Alvecote (*Avecote*); patrons, prior and convent of Great Malvern. London, 29 Oct. 1305.

309 Institution by the vicar-general of Walter de Bedewynde[1] to the deanery of Tamworth collegiate church; patron, Sir Alexander de Fryvyll, kt. London, 29 Oct. 1305.

   [[1] *CPL*, ii.41.]

310 Note that the election of Br. John de Burton, prior of the same place [Burton upon Trent], as abbot was confirmed, and a letter [was sent] to the king that he should deign do those things which pertain to him concerning the election and confirmation.[1] 30 Oct. 1305.

   [[1] *CPR 1301–7*, 392.]

311 Institution by the vicar-general of Robert de Ingwerby to Kingsley (*Kyngeslegh*) church; patron, Sir Robert de la Warde, kt. Steeple Aston, 7 Nov. 1305.

312 Institution by the vicar-general of John Tok, clerk, to Blore church; patron, Alan de Audelegh. Steeple Aston, 22 Dec. 1305.
[Margin] He paid the fee.

313 Institution by the vicar-general, the bishop being outside the realm, of Hugh de Bampton to Gratwich (*Gretewich*) church; patron, Philip de Chete-wynde. Bishops Itchington (*Ichinton*), 24 Mar. 1306.
[Margin] He paid the fee.

314 Institution by the vicar-general of Thomas de Aula, priest, to the vicarage of Leek church; patrons, abbot and convent of Dieulacres (*Deulacreste*). He swore to reside. Hailes Abbey (*abathia de Hales*), 26 Mar. 1306.
[Margin] He paid the fee.

[Fo. 16v] STAFFORD'.

315 Institution of Peter de Brembre to Norbury (*Northbiri*) church; patron, the king, by reason of the lands and tenements of John Walrand, an idiot, being in his hands.[1] London, 16 Apr. 1306.

   [[1] *CPR 1301–7*, 370–1.]

316 Institution of John de Tamworth to Haughton (*Halughton*) church; patrons, the canons of Gnosall (*Gnoushale*), at the nomination of Edmund, baron of Stafford, keeper of the heir, lands, and tenements formerly held by

Robert de Halughton, deceased, saving a pension to the canons due from of old. London, 7 Nov. 1306.

317 Institution of John de Hungeford, clerk, to Uttoxeter (*Uttoxhather*) church; patron, Thomas, earl of Lancaster, saving an annual pension to the abbot and convent of Darley due from of old. London, 13 Nov. 1306.
[Margin] He owes $\frac{1}{2}$ mark for the bishop's fee.

318 Institution of Walter Reginaldi to Mucclestone (*Mukeleston'*) church; patron, Adam de Mukeleston'. London, 30 Dec. 1306.

319 Institution of Thomas de Leyes, clerk, to Blithfield (*Blithefeld*) church; patron, Richard, lord of Blithfield. Carlisle (*Carleolum*), 9 Apr. 1307.
[Margin] He paid the fee.

320 [Fos. 16v–17] Sixteenth or seventeenth century copy of the ordination of Lapley vicarage by Bishop Roger Meuland. Brewood, 19 Mar. 1266.

321 [Fo. 17v] Sixteenth or seventeenth century copy of the charter of Abbot N.[1] of Lilleshall (*Lillyshull*) inspecting Bishop Meuland's ordination of Lilleshall vicarage dated 5 Mar. 1286. Lilleshall, 16 Aug. 1315.
    [[1] *Sic.* The abbot of Lilleshall 1308–30 was John de Chetewynd, see **519***; *VCH Shropshire*, ii.79.]

Note that the register was inspected in the Exchequer on 15 Apr. 1782.

[Fo. 18] ARCHIDIACONATUS SALOP'.

322 Institution of Richard de Hatton, priest, to Leighton vicarage. 2 Mar. 1298.

323 Institution of Thomas de Acton Reyners, priest, to Cound (*Conede*) church; patron, Lady Matilda Burnel. Ashley (*Asshelegh*), 19 May 1298.

324 Institution of Richard de Morton, chaplain, to Buildwas chapel; patrons, abbot and convent of Buildwas. York, 28 Nov. 1298.
    [See **12**.]

325 Institution of John de Morton, chaplain, to Baschurch (*Baschurche*) vicarage; patrons, abbot and convent of Shrewsbury. Lichfield, 10 Jan. 1299.
    [See **23**.]

326 Institution of William de Clif, subdeacon, to Acton Burnell church; patron, King E[dward I].[1] York, 30 June 1299.
    [[1] *CPR 1292–1301*, 395; see **44**.]

327 Institution of Thomas de Charnes to the portion of Condover church which was William de Wesenham's; patrons, abbot and convent of Shrewsbury. York, 31 Jan. 1300.

[Margin] It is quit.

328   Institution of Walter de Petling, priest, to the vicarage of Drayton in Hales church; patron, Br. Ralph, prior of Ware, proctor of the abbot and convent of Saint-Evroul, Normandy (*Sancto Ebrulpho in Normannia*). Lichfield, 25 Feb. 1300.
[Margin] The official received. Nothing.[1]
     [[1] Added later.]

ANNUS [M].CCC[us]. INCIPIT.

329   Institution of Richard de Aston, clerk, to Albright Hussy (*Atbrighton Husee*) chapel; patron, John Husee. Lichfield, 13 May 1300.

330   Institution by Thomas de Abberbury, vicar-general, of Richard, son of John de Abberbury, acolyte, to Rodington church; patrons, abbot and convent of Shrewsbury. Lichfield, 7 June 1300.

331   Collation to William de Piccheford, priest, of Albrighton church, the advowson of which the bishop has acquired. Ind.: archd. of Shrewsbury. Eckington, 4 June 1300.

332   [Fo. 18v] Institution of Hugh de Peppelowe, deacon, to Moreton Corbet (*Morton Corbet*) vicarage; patrons, abbot and convent of Haughmond (*Haghmoun'*). Letters dimissory for the order of priest. York, 20 Oct. 1300.
[Margin] It is quit.

333   Institution of John de Foresta, acolyte, to Longford (*Longeford*) church; patron, Sir Adam de Brimpton, kt. Reepham, 29 Jan. 1301.
[Margin] It is quit.
     [Longford church had been placed under the bishop's sequestration prior to this institution, and 2s. 6d. was received from it, see Hughes, 'Account roll', n. 78.]

334   Institution of Richard de Kynredeleye, clerk, to Harley (*Harle*) church; patron, Sir Richard de Harle, kt. Evesham, 24 Mar. 1301.
[Margin] He owes [the fee].
     [Harley church too had been under the bishop's sequestration prior to this institution, and 13d. was received from it, see Hughes, 'Account roll', n. 77.]

335   Institution of Roland de Viquiria, acolyte, to the portion of Wroxeter (*Wroxcestr'*) church which was Belingar de Quiliano's; patron, Richard, earl of Arundel (*Arundell*). Kenilworth, 31 May 1301.
[Margin] He owes the fee.

336   Institution of Thomas de Hales', clerk, to Wednesbury (*Wednesbur'*) church;[1] patrons, abbot and convent of Halesowen (*Hales'*). Kenilworth, [?1] June 1301.[2]
[Margin] He owes [the fee].
     [[1] MS. *ecclesia* over *capella* partially erased. Wednesbury church, in Stafford archdeaconry, was listed as a parish church by the *Taxatio* in 1291, but it was apparently

a chapelry of Walsall church at that date and it gradually acquired the status of a parish church thereafter; Wednesbury was, however, recorded as being a chapelry of Walsall again in 1319, see *Taxatio*, 243; *VCH Staffordshire*, iii.93, n. 11; Hughes, 'Clergy list', 14.

² This letter and **449** have been dated *v non. Junii* in error; *iv non. Junii* is 2 June.]

337 Institution by the papal administrators[1] of Philip de Byrton, priest, to Wellington (*Welinton*) vicarage; patrons, abbot and convent of Shrewsbury. Lichfield, 26 July 1302.

[¹ MS. *per custodes episcopatus deputatos per sedem apostolicam*]

338 Institution of John de Sheynton, subdeacon, to Sheinton (*Sheynton*) church; patron, Hugh de Sheynton. Lichfield chapter-house. 22 Sept. 1303.

339 Collation to Roger de Bisshopeston, clerk, of Kemberton (*Kembrighton*) church, which has devolved to the bishop's collation by lapse of time. Ind.: John Pupard, then keeper of the archdeaconry of Shrewsbury. Acomb, 26 Jan. 1304.

340 Institution of Thomas de Bredewell, clerk, to Colton church;[1] patron, Lady Hawise la Mareschale. Acomb, 30 Jan. 1304.
[Margin] He owes.

[¹ In Stafford archdeaconry, see *VCH Staffordshire*, iii.93, n. 12.]

341 Institution of M. Henry de Bray to Stoke upon Tern (*Stok super Tyrne*) church; patron, Sir Theobald de Verdoun, senior Ind.: archd. of Shrewsbury. Shrewsbury, 24 Mar. 1304.

342 Collation to M. Richard Bernard[1] of the archdeaconry of Shrewsbury. Ind.: John Pupard, the sequestrator, keeper of the archdeaconry. Shrewsbury, 24 Mar. 1304.

[¹ *BRUO*, i.178.]

343 Collation to William de Thorpwatervill of Prees (*Preez*) vicarage. Ind.: John,[1] vicar of Baschurch. Lilleshall, 28 Mar. 1304.

[¹ De Morton, see **23, 325**.
Followed by five blank lines.]

344 Note that Thomas de Bradewell, rector of Colton, freely gave 5 marks [£3 6s. 8d.] to the bishop for the first fruits at the request of Sir William de Carleton. The payment is assigned to John Pupard's keeping. York, 28 June 1304.

[Fo. 19] SALOP'.

345 Institution of John de Biriton, acolyte, to West Felton (*Felton*) church; patrons, Thomas de Lee, Hugh, son of Philip, and Stephen, son of Thomas de Felton. London, 7 Feb. 1305.

346   Institution of M. Richard de Norhampton, priest, to Adderley (*Addirdele*) church; patron, John de la Mare. London, 8 Mar. 1305.
[Margin] He owes the fee.

347   Institution of Edmund de Portlaunde, clerk, to Berrington (*Biriton*) church; patrons, abbot and convent of Shrewsbury, saving an annual pension of 10 marks [£6 13s. 4d.] to the dean and chapter of Lichfield, and an annual pension of 24s. to the abbot and convent of Shrewsbury due from of old. London, 30 Mar. 1305.

348   Institution of John de Clone to the third part of Wroxeter church which M. Walter de Clone held when rector; patron, King E[dward I], by reason of the lands and heir of Richard Fitzalan, earl of Arundel, deceased, tenant in chief, being in his hands.[1] 25 May 1305.
   [1 *CPR 1301–7*, 331.]

349   Institution of Thomas de Langeton, clerk, to Harley church; patron, Sir Richard de Harle, kt. London, 10 July 1305.

350   Institution of Ralph de la Bolde, clerk, to Edgmond (*Egemundon*) church; patrons, abbot and convent of Shrewsbury. London, 25 July 1305.

351   Institution of Richard de Lilleshull, priest, to the vicarage of Attingham church; patrons, abbot and convent of Lilleshall. He swore to reside. Burton upon Trent (*Burtonam supra Trentam*), 20 Aug. 1305.

352   Institution of John de Morton, priest, to High Ercall (*Ercalewe*) vicarage; patrons, abbot and convent of Shrewsbury. He swore to reside. London, 16 Sept. 1305.

353   Institution [1]by the vicar-general[1] of Richard de Rodynton, priest, to the vicarage of Baschurch church; patrons, abbot and convent of Shrewsbury. He swore to reside. London, 28 Oct. 1305.
   [[1–1] Interlined.
   Followed by three blank lines.]

354   [A cancelled copy of **349** with this additional information.] Ind.: archd. Thomas [de Langeton] has the letter of his institution.
   [A hand drawn in the left-hand margin points to this entry.]

355   [Fo. 19v] Institution by the vicar-general of John de Petton, clerk, to Petton chapel; patron, Richard, lord of Petton. Bishops Itchington, 12 Feb. 1306.
[Margin] He paid the fee.

356   Institution by M. Thomas de Eadburbury, vicar-general, of John de Torrynton, clerk, to Acton Burnell church, vacant by the resignation of William de Clyf; patron this turn, the king, by reason of [his] custody of the land and heir of Philip Burnel, deceased, tenant in chief.[1] Steeple Aston, 31 Mar. 1306.
   [1 *CPR 1301–7*, 417.]

357 Institution of Adam de Neweporte, priest, to Roden (*Rodene*) chapel; patron, Thomas de Lee. London, 11 July 1306.

358 Institution of Simon de Cotenham, priest, to Berrington church; patrons, abbot and convent of Shrewsbury, saving pensions of 10 marks [£6 13s. 4d.] to Lichfield cathedral, and of 24s. to St. Peter's monastery, Shrewsbury, due from of old. 14 Aug. 1306.

359 Note that custody of Frodesley (*Frodeslegh*) chapel and of Hugh de Aldenham who has been presented to it was committed to Thomas,[1] rector of Cound, during pleasure, at the request of Lady Matilda Burnel, the patron, and Hugh le Despenser, beseeching by letter for the presentee. London, 29 Nov. 1306.

[1 De Acton Reyners, see **323**.]

360 Institution of Alan de Neweton, clerk, to Buildwas (*Boulewas*) church; patron, King Edward, by reason of [his] custody of the land and heir of Roger, son of John, deceased, tenant in chief.[1] Carlisle, 9 Feb. 1307.

[1 *CPR 1301–7*, 425.

The rest of the folio is blank.]

[Fo. 20] NEGOCIA FORINSECA QUE NON CONTINGUNT JURISDICTIONEM EPISCOPI.

361 Letters patent. Sir Henry de Maul and Anne, his wife, were once bound to Bishop Langton for £102 13s. 4d. by their recognizance made before the mayor of York and Robert de Sex Vallibus on 13 Dec. 1298,[1] and to make the said payment faithfully to him before the same mayor and Robert, having been deputed to receive such recognizances and obligations, according to the form of the statute proclaimed at Acton Burnell.[2] The bishop wholly acquits them of the said money. He wills that if the said letter is found it shall be entirely of no consequence. York, 13 Nov. 1299.

[1 Henry de Maul made six recognizances to Langton at York between 1297 and 1302 totalling £388 6s. 8d., and another recognizance at Lincoln for £110 on 10 Oct. 1299 by which Langton held the manor of Colly Weston, Northamptonshire, see Beardwood, *Records*, 76–7, 295; Beardwood, 'Trial', 33; A. Beardwood, 'Bishop Langton's use of statute merchant recognizances', *Medievalia et Humanistica*, 9 (1955), 63.

2 The statute of merchants was enacted at the parliament held at Acton Burnell from 12 Oct. 1283, see *Statutes of the Realm*, i.53–4; T.F.T. Plucknett, *Legislation of Edward I* (Oxford, 1970), 138–43.]

362 LITTERA ABBATIS WESTM' DIRECTA FUIT REGI PRO RESTITUCIONE TERRARUM TENEMENTORUM ET BONORUM W[ILLELMI] DE ASSHINDON. Letters supplicatory of Walter,[1] abbot of Westminster, to King Edward. William de Asshindon, clerk, has recently been arrested, imprisoned, and impeached before the justices of King's Bench, Westminster, for the homicide of Hugh Mulgar and for robbery at, or near, Hugh's manor at Littlebury (*Litlebur'*), Essex, and at his houses without Bishopsgate (*Bisshopesgate*), London.[2] The abbot is his lawful judge and ordinary because he was, and is, a freed clerk (*clericus liberatus*), to be judged of all the crimes of which he has been impeached according to the liberties of the church and canon law. He has canonically purged himself of all the crimes of which he has been charged by a sufficient and fitting number of wise and honest compurgators before the abbot; he is finally pronounced guiltless and absolved from the infamy which has sprung up against him, and his good name restored. The abbot requests the restitution of the clerk's lands, tenements, goods and chattels which have been taken into the king's hands. Westminster, 4 Nov. 1299.

[¹ De Wenlock, see *VCH London*, i.455; *Documents illustrating the rule of Walter de Wenlock, abbot of Westminster, 1283–1307*, ed. B.F. Harvey (Camden, 4th series, 2, 1965).
² Alice, widow of Hugh le Taillur (?*alias* Mulgar), brought an appeal against William for the death of her husband, and for robbery, see *CPR 1297–1301*, 319.
This may be connected with the case cited in L.C. Gabel, *Benefit of clergy in England in the later Middle Ages* (New York, 1969), 66; PRO Gaol delivery (Just.3) 38/7, m. 7d. If so, William said he was a clerk, but he was without clerical habit or tonsure, and he was unable to read. When asked to plead as a layman he initially refused to put himself on the country; when he did, he was convicted and sentenced to hang. He was hanged for felony, see *CCR 1302–7*, 60. William was probably not the principal in these crimes: Guy de Shenefeld, kt., received a royal pardon in Sept. 1298 for robbery committed against Hugh Mulgar, see *CPR 1297–1301*, 363.]

363 Copy of the indenture of M. Philip Martel,¹ advocate of the court of Canterbury, witnessing his appointment to deal with all causes and business in that court in London or elsewhere for Walter, bishop of Coventry and Lichfield, his official, and ministers [fo. 20v] for an annual fee of 5 marks [£3 6s. 8d.], to be paid in equal parts at Easter and Michaelmas. In witness of which his seal has been affixed to both parts of the indenture. London, 5 Nov. 1299.

[¹ *BRUO*, iii.2196; Churchill, *Canterbury administration*, i.562 note; ii.121.]

364* [Fo. 20]¹ Note that at the bishop's command T[homas] de Eadburbury has paid 10 marks [£6 13s. 4d.] from the bishop's hanaper to Galhard de Pursato and John de Corbino, papal nuncios, for the creation of the same [bishop], and afterwards, 40s. to Lady Lucy . . .² Devorcis. [1306–7.]³

[A hand drawn in the right-hand margin points to this entry.
¹ This entry and **365** have been added at the foot of fo. 20 and cut in two **363**.
² MS. one word erased and illegible.
³ Pursato and Corbino were in England in 1306–7, see Lunt, *Financial relations*, 461, 467, 557, app. ix. Eadburbury (M. Thomas de Abberbury) died in May 1307, see *BRUO*, i.2.
This entry is a record of one of the instalments of the common service tax Langton would have paid to the pope for his confirmation as bishop, see W.E. Lunt, *Papal revenues in the Middle Ages*, 2 vols. (Columbia University Press, 1934), i, 82–7. Thanks are due to Professor D.M. Smith for his advice.]

365 Note that at the request of Alexander, nuncio of the archbishop of Canterbury, the bishop has commanded that letters dimissory be issued to John de Perewyche, a clerk of Coventry and Lichfield diocese, who has no title, for all orders which John has not yet received. n.d.

366 [Fo. 20v] Note that on 18 Mar. 1300 Eudes de Derb', clerk, acknowledged his seal before M. Thomas de Abberbury, the bishop's chancellor, which seal he had put on a bond the same day whereby he was bound to the bishop for 50 marks [£33 6s. 8d.] for the fruits of Heanor church which he had received for the said year, to be paid in equal parts on [the Nativity of] St. John the Baptist and at Michaelmas next following. W[illiam] de Eston has the letter. London.

367 Resignation (by letter) of Thomas de Cantebr', the bishop's devoted clerk, of Gratwich rectory, as he is unable to devote himself to the rule of the church. He has not received the fruits of the church he has held for five years and more, except 6 marks [£4], or thereabouts. He wishes and grants that all the rest of the same fruits for that time, if it shall please the bishop to make diligent inquiry thereon as to whom they have gone to, to be used for the repair of the houses and other needs of the church at the bishop's discretion. London, 26 Mar. 1300.

368 Note that M. Thomas de Abberbury paid 100s. 5d. in crocard to William de Eston, clerk, to be reckoned as 1 crocard for 1d., and he paid 5s. in sterling to the same [William], all from the bishop's hanaper. London, 7 Apr. 1300.

369 CONDEMPNACIO PARSONE DE LODBROK'. Note that John de Pavely, rector of Ladbroke, personally acknowledged before the bishop at his visitation made at Grandborough (*Grenebur'*) that he was bound to Adam Absolon, a citizen of London, for 12 marks [£8], of which he should pay him 4 marks [£2 13s. 4d.] immediately, 3 marks [£2] at Michaelmas, 3 marks at Purification, and 2 marks [£1 6s. 8d.] on 3 May. Following his confession, [John] was condemned to pay all the money to Adam at the said terms. n.d.

370 Note that M. Thomas de Abberbury paid 6 marks 9s. [£4 9s.] to John de Chageley, bishop's clerk, from the bishop's hanaper at Martinmas. Acomb.

371 Note that Henry le Waleys, rector of Standish, is bound to the bishop for 20 marks [£13 6s. 8d.] to be paid at Michaelmas 1301 by a letter which was delivered to W[illiam] de Eston. n.d.
[Henry was bound to the bishop for the fruits of Acton church in 1302, see **373**. His obligation here may have been for the fruits of Acton church in 1301; this was the same sum (£13 6s. 8d.) accounted for by the sequestrator-general for the autumn fruits of that church in 1301, see Hughes, 'Account roll', n. 85.]

372 Note that Robert, vicar of Wybunbury (*Wibenbur'*), is bound to the bishop for £10 to be paid on the Nativity of St. John the Baptist and at Assumption in the said year by a similar bond which was delivered to W[illiam] de Eston. n.d.

373 Note that Henry le Waleys, rector of Standish, is bound to the bishop by a bond for £20 for the fruits of Acton church for the year 1302, peacably and without diminution. n.d.

374   Letters patent to the bishop's friends and well-wishers. After many requests he has thought fit to ask them that if they are asked by Chyne, son of Nonch de San Gimignano they shall take care to treat him kindly, not causing him trouble or undue harm. York, 1 Dec. 1304.

[Fo. 21] COLLACIONES PREBENDARUM.

375   Collation to John de Benstede[1] of the prebend of Sandiacre,[2] vacant by the bishop's consecration. Walsingham, 3 Feb. 1297.
    [1 *DNB*, ii.261–2; C.L. Kingsford, 'John de Benstede and his missions for Edward I',
      in *Essays in history presented to R.L. Poole*, ed. H.W.C. Davis (Oxford, 1927), 332–59.
    2 *Fasti*, x.53.]

376   Collation to John Picard of the prebend in St. John's collegiate church, Chester, which was M. William Pikerel's.[1] 18 Oct. 1297.
    [1 *BRUO*, iii.1480.]

377   Collation to Nicholas called le Mareschal, clerk, of the prebend in St. Chad's collegiate church, Shrewsbury, which was Gilbert de Roff's. 18 Oct. 1297.

378   Collation to M. W[alter] de Thorp of the prebend [of Darnford][1] in Lichfield church which was M. H[enry de Newark]'s,[2] the elect of York. 24 May 1298.
    [1 See **3**.
    2 *HBC*, 282; *BRUO*, iii.2200.]

379   Collation to William de Scalariis, priest, of the prebend in St. John's collegiate church, Chester, vacant by the resignation of William de Weseham. 5 June 1298.
    [See **61**.]

380   Collation to Nicholas called le Mareschal of the prebend in Gnosall (*Gnousale*) [church] vacant by the death of M. William de Abyndon. 26 June 1298.

381   Collation to M. Hugh de Mouselee[1] of the prebend in St. Chad's collegiate church, Shrewsbury, which was Nicholas called le Mareschal's. 26 June 1298.
    [1 *BRUO*, ii.1330.]

382   Collation to M. W[alter] de Thorp of the prebend of Weeford in Lichfield church. Lead Grange, 16 June 1298.
    [See **4**.]

383   Collation to John de Drokenesford of the prebend [of Darnford] in Lichfield church which was M. W[alter] de Thorp's. York, 24 Sept. 1298.
    [See **3**.]

384 Collation to M. Thomas de Eadberbur', the bishop's clerk, of the prebend of Whittington and Berkswich in Lichfield church which was M. John de Monte Majori's. Ind.: dean and chapter of Lichfield. York, 17 Dec. 1298.
[See **18**.]

385 Collation to Philip de Everdon of the prebend of Wellington in Lichfield church which was M. Thomas de Abberbury's. York, 15 Feb. 1299.
[See **31**.]

386 Collation to M. William called le Conestable of the prebend in St. John's collegiate church, Chester, which was John Picard's. London, 18 Oct. 1299.
[See **78**.]

387 [Fo. 21v] Collation to M. Peter de Insula of the archdeaconry of Coventry. Acomb, 14 Nov. 1299.
[See **60**.]

388 Collation to Philip de Willugby, dean of Lincoln, of the prebend [of Bubbenhall][1] in Lichfield church which was John de Silveston's. Ind.: dean and chapter of Lichfield. Eccleshall, 28 Feb. 1300.
[[1] *Fasti*, x.22.]

ANNUS [M]CCC[us].

389 Collation to William de Retford, priest, of Longford vicarage, devolved to the bishop [by lapse of time] by authority of the [Lateran] Council. Acomb, 18 Apr. 1301.
[Longford vicarage had been placed under the bishop's sequestration prior to this collation and 23s. was received from it, see Hughes, 'Account roll', n. 60.]

390 Note that the bishop has granted a letter to William de Newerk concerning the first two prebends to become vacant in Chester collegiate church and in Gnosall church, which William has accepted. Acomb, 1 July 1301.

391 Note that the [papal] administrators have collated to Richard Abel[1] the prebend in [St. Chad's] church, Shrewsbury, which was Thomas de Denton's. Lichfield, 15 Aug. 1302.
[[1] *BRUO*, i.3.]

392 COLLACIO PRECENTORIE ECCLESIE LYCH'. Note that the bishop has collated the precentorship of Lichfield church, vacant by the death of M. Adam de Waleton, to M. Thomas de Abberbury, which Thomas has accepted. London, 1 Sept. 1303. The bishop repeated and performed his collation at York on 13 Oct. 1303. Ind.: dean and chapter [following this last collation.][1]
[The prebend of Bishops Itchington was attached to the precentorship: *Fasti*, x.7.
[1-1] Interlined.]

393 Collation to William de Style of the prebend in St. John's church, Chester, which was Ralph de Hengham's. York, 19 Oct. 1303.

394 Collation to Ralph de Hengham of the prebend in St. John's church, Chester, which was William de Style's. York, 22 Oct. 1303.

395 Collation to M. Philip de Cornwall of the archdeaconry of Shrewsbury. Ind.: either M. Geoffrey de Blaston or John Pupard. Acomb, 15 Jan. 1304.

396 Collation to Walter de Clipston,[1] clerk, of the prebend of Tarvin (*Tervenn*)[2] in Lichfield church, vacant by the death of M. William de Sarden.[3] Acomb near York, 21 Jan. 1304.
   [[1] One of Bishop Langton's two clerical nephews, see Hughes, 'Family' 73–4.
   [2] *Fasti*, x.59.
   [3] *BRUO*, iii.1641–2.]

397 Collation to John de Drokenesford, king's clerk, of the prebend of Whittington and Berkswich (*Berkeswiz*) in Lichfield church, vacant by the admission of M. Thomas de Eadberbur' to the precentorship of Lichfield.[1] [Same date and place.]
   [[1] See **392**.]

398 Collation to Philip de Willugby, dean of Lincoln, of the prebend of Ryton (*Ruton*)[1] in Lichfield church, vacant by the death of M. Philip de Cornwall, canon of Lichfield. [Same date, and place.]
   [[1] *Fasti*, x.51.]

[Fo. 22] CUSTODIE FACTE PER EPISCOPUM IN SINGULIS ARCHIDIACONATIBUS.

399 Note that the bishop has delivered custody of his sequestration on Rodington church to Richard, son of John de Abberbury until the next holy orders. Acomb near York, 26 Dec. 1299.

400 Note of similar custody of the sequestration on Biddulf (*Bidulf*) church to M. Alexander de Verdoun. York, 31 Dec. 1299.

401 Note of similar custody of the sequestration on Tibshelf (*Typpeshulf*) church to Robert de Cotingham, clerk. Letters dimissory for all orders, except the order of priest. York, 13 Jan. 1300.

402 Licence to Robert de Bredbur', vicar of Wirksworth, to be absent from his vicarage to go to and remain at the Curia, returning by Michaelmas next. York, 15 Jan. 1300.

403 Licence to John de Leyc[ester], rector of Clowne, to study for one year. London, 14 Apr. 1300.
[Margin] Derby.

404 Note that the bishop has delivered custody of his sequestration on the fruits of Kinglsey (*Kingesleghe*) church to William de la Warde, and authority to dispose of the fruits, as is clear in the following letter. Letter to William de la Warde, rector of Hartshorne (*Herteshorne*) . . .[1] Lichfield, 26 Feb. 1300.
[Margin] Letter of custody to a third party (*extraneo*), not the parson.
  [[1] Unfinished; followed by four blank lines.]

405 Note that the bishop has delivered custody of his sequestration on Wolfhamcote church to Peter de Leycester, during pleasure. Ind.: archd. of Coventry. Kenilworth, 1 Mar. 1300.
[Margin] Coventry.

406 Licence to M. Robert Tankard, parson of Withybrook (*Wythebrok*), to study for one year from 2 Mar. [1300].

407 Grant *in commendam* to M. Walter de Fodringeye of Matlock church for half a year. London, 15 Mar. 1300.
[Margin] Derby.

408* Letter to M. A[lan] de Britonii, treasurer of Lichfield church. The bishop has inspected the letter [quoted] of his predecessor, R[oger Meuland], bishop of Coventry and Lichfield (dated Brewood, 12 Apr. 1266), granting Prescot church *in commendam* to Alan when he was rector of Coddington on account of his many perilous services to the bishop and his church. The grant is ratified on condition that [Alan] takes care to restore the rights, liberties, and goods of the church which were damaged and alienated by the negligence of his predecessors [fo. 22v]. Lichfield, 26 Feb. 1300.

ANNUS [M]CCC^{us}.

409 Note that the bishop has delivered custody of his sequestration on the portion of Darley (*Derle*) church which was M. Walter de Fodringeye's to John de Brentingham, clerk; patron, Philip, dean of Lincoln. Worksop, 5 May 1300.

410 Grant *in commendam* to M. Robert de Sileby of Checkley (*Checkelee*) church, in accordance with the statute of commendation. Ind.: archd. of Stafford. Eccleshall, 18 May 1300.

411 Licence to Hugh de Uppewell, subdeacon, rector of Brinklow, to study for two years. He shall not be compelled to further orders for that period. Eccleshall, 21 May 1300.

412 Grant to Philip de Everdon of those houses within Lichfield close which were M. William de Wymundham's. Great Haywood (*Heywode*), 24 May 1300.

413 Note that the bishop has committed custody of his sequestration on Tibshelf church to William de Weston, during pleasure. York, 18 Oct. 1300.

414   Licence to Belingar,[1] portioner of Wroxeter, to go to the Curia and to be absent from his church until Easter next. York, 18 Oct. 1300.

[1 De Quiliano, see **335**.]

415   Note that the bishop has committed custody of his sequestration on Standon church to William de Brikehull, during pleasure, to which W[illiam] has been presented by Sir Robert de Staundon, kt. Burton upon Trent (*Burtonie*), 17 Dec. 1300.

416   Licence to Thomas de Charnes, rector of a moiety of Condover, to study for one year. Same day, place and year.

417   Licence to Richard de Abberbury, subdeacon,[1] rector of Rodington, to study for seven years according to the terms of the statute, and that for the said seven years he shall not be compelled to further orders. Same day, place and year.

[1 Interlined. Ordained subdeacon the same day, see **1286**. Ordained deacon in 1305, and priest in 1307, see **1295, 1298**.]

418   Note that the bishop has committed custody of his sequestration on Rugby chapel to Robert de Halughton, during pleasure; patron, Sir Peter de Leyc[ester]. Leicester, 20 Dec. 1300.

[Instituted 2 July 1301, see **115**.]

419   Note that the bishop has delivered custody of his sequestration on Swarkeston (*Swerkeston*) church to M. Simon de Shirlegh, during pleasure, because John de Becco, clerk, who has been presented by John de Becco, the patron, is under age and he is unable to commit the cure of souls to him. M. Simon is to support the presentee in the schools during the custody. Northampton (*Northt'*), 26 Dec. 1300.

420   Note that the bishop has committed custody of his sequestration on Eaton Constantine (*Eton Constantyn*) chapel to Richard, son of William le Despenser of Eaton Constantine (*Eton*) until Michaelmas next. Mandate to the archdeacon to deliver custody. Reepham near Lincoln, 31 Jan. 1301.

421   Licence to M. Alexander de Verdoun, rector of Biddulph, to study for one year. Reepham, 1 Feb. 1301.

422   Note that the bishop has relaxed the sequestration on Stapleton (*Stepelton*) [church] until Easter. Same day, year and place.

[Fo. 23] STAFFORD'.
   [*Sic*]

423   Licence to Robert Bagod, rector of Alrewas (*Alrewych*), to study for one year. Reepham, 4 Feb. 1301.

424   Note of similar licence for Nicholas de Aillesbur', rector of Pattingham. Same year, day and place.

425   Note of like licence for Richard Tuchet, rector of Middlewich (*Medii Wyci*), for two years. Reepham, 6 Feb. 1301.

426   Note of like licence for Roger Fitzherbert, rector of Norbury (*Northbur'*), for one year from Easter 1301. Reepham, 4 Feb. 1301.

427   Licence to M. Walter de Fodringeye, rector of Matlock, to study for five years in England or overseas.[1] Reepham, 9 Feb. 1301.
   [[1] *BRUO*, ii.703.]

428   Licence to M. Matthew de Sholure, rector of Prestwich (*Prestewych*), to be in the service of Roger de Pilkinton until Whitsun next. Same day, year and place.

429   Licence to Simon Tuchet, rector of Mackworth, to study for two years. Same place, 8 Feb. 1301.

430   Note of like licence for M. Richard de Birchek, rector of Tattenhall, for one year. Reepham, 13 Feb. 1301.

431   Collation to William de Cornwall of the chantry of the Blessed Mary in Lichfield cathedral. Rickling (*Rikeling*), 6 Mar. 1301.

432   Licence to John Mauclerk of Leicester, rector of Clowne (*Cloune*), to study for one year. Evesham, 24 Mar. 1301.

433   Note that the bishop has delivered and granted custody of his sequestration on the fruits of Ashover (*Eshovere*) church to Roger Deyncurt, rector of North Wingfield (*Hallewynefeud*), during pleasure, having been presented to Ashover (*Esshovere*) church by Margery de Rerisby and Simon de Rerisby. Evesham, 31 Mar. 1301.
   [Roger Deyncurt was subsequently granted Ashover church *in commendam* for half a year on 26 Apr. 1301. He had vacated North Wingfield church by 12 Nov. 1301 and although there is no record of his institution to Ashover church in the register it is probable that he became its rector at about that time; an incumbent of the same name is recorded witnessing a charter in Jan. 1303, and again in 1337. The sequestrator-general's account roll for Epiphany to Michaelmas 1301 records that the bishop received 9s. from Ashover church, see **442, 249**; I.H. Jeayes, *Descriptive catalogue of Derbyshire charters in public and private libraries and muniment rooms* (London, 1906), nos. 115, 123; Foulds, *Thurgarton Cartulary*, pp. cxiii–cxiv, table 2 (p. cxvii); Hughes, 'Account roll', n. 62.]

434   Licence to M. Jordan de Caunvill', rector of Clifton Campville (*Clifton*), to study for two years. Feckenham, 4 Apr. 1301.

435   Note of like licence for Robert Chaundeis, rector of Radbourne (*Rodeburn*), for three years. Same year, day, and place.

436   Note of similar licence for Nicholas de Aillesbur', rector of Pattingham. Offenham (*Uffenham*), c. 25 Mar. 1301.[1]

[[1] MS. *circiter viij kal. Aprilis*]

437   Note that the bishop has committed custody of his sequestration on the portion of Wroxeter [church] which was Belingar Quiliano's to Roland de Vinquiria until the next holy orders. Acomb, 18 Apr. 1301.

[The bishop received 37s. 1d. from this sequestration, see Hughes, 'Account roll', n. 76. Vinquiria was instituted 31 May 1301, see **335**.]

438   Note that the bishop has delivered and demised custody of Eyam (*Eyom*) church and its rector to Roger le Wyne, dean of Tamworth, because of the rector's incapacity (*insufficientiam*). He is to cause the church to be served by suitable ministers, support and maintain the rector, and distribute, or cause to be distributed by another person to be named or assigned by the bishop, 100s. among the poor of the parish each year. Acomb, 21 Apr. 1301.

[See **36**.]

439   [Fo. 23v] To Br. Walter, prior of Tutbury. The bishop grants him licence to visit the monastery of St. Mary, Saint-Pierre-sur-Dives, Séez (*Cagyen'*) dioc., to make his profession,[1] on condition that he will return to his monastery on, or before, the octave of the Nativity of St. John the Baptist. York, 22 Apr. 1301.

[[1] The prior may have been elected by the monks of Tutbury in 1297 without reference to the rights of the mother house, a time when Edward I had seized the property of alien priories because of his war with France; the prior's visit may have been made to regularize his position, see *VCH Staffordshire*, iii.334–5, 339; Matthew, *Monasteries*, 47–8, 81–5.]

440   Licence to Thomas le Bretoun, rector of Church Lawford, to study for one year. Acomb (*Akum*), 22 Apr. 1301.

441   Letters patent to the archdeacon of Chester. He is to deliver custody of the sequestration on Bangor church to Walter Reginaldi, priest, to whom the bishop has granted it, during pleasure. William, son of Sir John de St. John has been presented to the church and the bishop is unable to admit him because he is under age. The bishop wishes the priest to support suitably the presentee in study from the revenues of the church according to its resources, and cause the church to be served by suitable ministers so that the cure of souls is not neglected. York, 25 Apr. 1301.

[The bishop received 2 marks [£1 6s. 8d.] from this sequestration, see Hughes, 'Account roll', n. 84.]

442   Grant *in commendam* to Roger de Eyncourt of Ashover church for half a year. York, 26 Apr. 1301.

443 Note of similar grant to M. William de Marklau[1] of Prestwich church, who has been presented to the same by Adam de Prestewych. Acomb, 4 May 1301.

[Prestwich church became vacant after 9 Feb. 1301. It was then placed under the bishop's sequestration and he received 79s. from it, see **428**; Hughes, 'Account roll', n. 88; see also **461**.
[1] *BRUO*, iii.2195.]

444 Note that the bishop has committed custody of his sequestration on the fruits of the portion which was Nicholas de Troughford's in Wroxeter church to M. Walter de Clune, during pleasure; patron, Richard, earl of Arundel. York, 29 June 1301.

[The sequestrator-general's account roll for Epiphany to Michaelmas 1301 records that the bishop received 40s. 6d. from the sequestered portion of Nicholas de Troughford, but that this portion was in St. Chad's church, Shrewsbury, not Wroxeter. St. Chad's was a secular college, and no other record has been found that Nicholas held a prebend there; it seems that the wrong church was recorded on the account roll, see Hughes, 'Account roll', n. 75.]

445 Licence to M. Philip de Turvill',[1] rector of Bedworth, to attend the schools for three years. Acomb, 1 July 1301.

[[1] *BRUO*, iii.1918.]

446 Licence to Hugh de Hotot, rector of Berrington (*Byrington*), to attend the schools for five years in the order of subdeacon according to the terms of the statute. Acomb, 30 June 1301.

447 Note that the bishop has committed custody of his sequestration on Sheinton church to [1]the archdeacon of Shrewsbury,[1] during pleasure, because the presentee, John de Sheynton,[2] clerk, is under age, on condition that the archdeacon will suitably support the presentee in the schools. Woodstock, 18 July 1301.

[The bishop received 11d. from this sequestration in the period Epiphany to Michaelmas 1301, see Hughes, 'Account roll', n. 79.
[1–1] Interlined.
[2] Instituted 22 Sept. 1303, see **338**.]

448 Licence to Robert de Basinges,[1] rector of Stockport, to study for seven years in the order of subdeacon. London, 19 May 1301.

[[1] *BRUO*, i.128.]

449 Licence to the rector of Acton Burnell,[1] to study for one year. Kenilworth, [?1] June 1301.[2]

[[1] William de Clif, see **326, 356**.
[2] This letter and **336** have been dated *v non. Junii* in error; *iv non. Junii* is 2 June.]

450 Note that the bishop has committed custody of his sequestration on Tilston (*Tilstan*) church to John de Sancto Petro, during pleasure; patron, Urian de Sancto Petro. Hinton Waldrist (*Heenton*), 10 July 1301.

[The bishop received 18s. 2½ d. from this sequestration, see Hughes, 'Account roll', n. 89.]

451 Note of similar grant of the bishop's sequestration on St. Nicholas's church, Birdingbury (*Burthingbur*') to Ingram de Yerdele, having been presented to the church by Sir John Paynel, kt. York, 23 Aug. 1301.

[Instituted 31 Aug. 1301, see **116**. The bishop received 5½ marks [£3 13s. 4d.] for the autumn fruits of Birdingbury church, see Hughes, 'Account roll', n. 72.]

452 Note that the bishop has committed custody of his sequestration on Pulford church to M. Simon de Schirleye, during pleasure, because the presentee is under age and he is unable to commit the cure of souls to him. Simon is to be answerable to the bishop for the revenues of the church, and to support the presentee. Same year, day and place.

453 Note that the bishop has committed custody of his sequestration on the church of . . .¹ York, 30 Aug. 1301.

[¹ Unfinished.]

454 Letter to the archdeacon of Stafford, or his lieutenant. The bishop has caused the custody of Swynnerton church and of Richard de Swynnerton, clerk, who has been presented to the church, to be committed to M. John Pupard, canon of Lichfield, for some time. The archdeacon is to induct the presentee into the church, with all its rights and appurtenances, in accordance with what the bishop has previously declared. London, 18 Nov. 1306.

[Fo. 24] STAFFORD'.
  [*Sic*]

455 Note that the bishop has put in respite those 200 marks [£67 6s. 8d.] which he has demanded from the prioress and convent of the order of St. Clare without the walls of London, their rent in England till now. London, 28 Oct. 1301.

456 Note that M. Thomas de Abberbury, vicar-general, has committed custody of the sequestration on Bunbury (*Bunnebur*') church to William de Brikhull, during pleasure, because the presentee, John de Sancto Petro, is under age and he is unable to commit the cure of souls to him. William is to answer to the bishop and the archdeacon of the place for 60 [marks (£40)] and 10 marks [£6 13s. 4d. (respectively)] each year during the sequestration, and he is to support the presentee in the schools. 28 Jan. 1302.

457 Note that M. Thomas de Abberbury, vicar-general, has committed custody of the sequestration on Wappenbury (*Wappenbur*') church to Robert de Halughton, priest, during pleasure; patrons, prior and convent of Monks

Kirby. Steeple Aston, 12 Feb. 1302. ¹Note of Robert's institution by the vicar-general. Monks Kirby, 1 Mar. 1302.¹

[¹⁻¹ Interlined later.]

458 Note that the vicar-general has committed similar custody of Rugby chapel to William de Leone; patrons, abbot and convent of [St. Mary] de Pratis, Leicester, at the nomination of Peter de Leyc[ester], by reason of his custody of Annabel, daughter and heir of Ranulph de Rokeby, deceased. n.d.

459 Note that on Thurs. 12 Apr. 1301 the vicar-general sequestered Sutton vicarage in the archdeaconry of Shrewsbury and he has written to the [rural] dean of Newport (*Neuport*) that he should keep this sequestration well and cause the vicarage to be served properly¹ from its revenues.

[¹ Interlined.]

460 Note that the [papal] administrators have collated M. Simon de Schirele to the mastership of Denhall (*Danewell*) hospital, with the church appropriated to it, and with all its other appurtenances, to be held for all his life. Lichfield, 15 Aug. 1302.

[The hospital was in the bishop's collation. Burton in Wirral church was appropriated to the hospital, which was built by Bishop Stavensby in the 1230s, see *VCH Cheshire*, iii.184, 185. Simon was still master of the hospital in 1310, see *CPL*, ii.70.]

461 Note that the [papal] administrators have committed custody of Prestwich (*Prestewich*) church to M. William de Markislau, during pleasure; patron, Adam de Prestewych. York, 23 Oct. 1302.

462 Note that the bishop has committed custody of Solihull church to Ralph de Hengham, during pleasure; patron, Sir John de Grey. Acomb, 27 Oct. 1303.

463 Note that M. Thomas de Abberbury has written under his own seal, but with the bishop's knowledge, to John Pupard, his sequestrator, to keep Mobberley (*Modburleye*) church, in the archdeaconry of Chester, under the bishop's sequestration until Richard de Modbur' attains full age and will be able to receive institution; he has been presented by his father, William de Modburleye, and an inquiry made, but he is under 21 years of age. 30 Apr. 1306.

464 Note that custody of Buildwas church has been committed to Alan de Neweton, clerk, until Annunciation; patron, King Edward, by reason of [his] custody of the lands and heir of Roger, son of John, tenant in chief.¹ Day was given to Alan to come before the bishop to receive institution.² London, 10 Nov. 1306.

Note that on 16 Dec. 1306, the custody having been revoked, the bishop committed the same custody to William de Chene, priest, during pleasure.

[¹ *CPR 1301–7*, 425.
² Instituted 9 Feb. 1307, see **360**.]

465 [Fo. 24v] Note that Chesterfield vicarage became vacant on Sun. 18 Dec. 1300. On 3 Feb. following Walter de Suthleyrton was instituted vicar.[1]
[The vicarage was placed under the bishop's sequestration during the vacancy and 27s. 10d. was received from it, see Hughes, 'Account roll', n. 63.
[1] See **242**.]

466 Note that Birmingham church became vacant on Sun. 4 Dec. 1300.

467 Note that Tattenhall church became vacant on Tues. 24 Jan. 1301.

468 Note that a moiety of Staveley (*Stavelegh*) church became vacant on Thurs. 22 Dec. 1300.

469 Note that Stockport (*Stocport*) church became vacant on Thurs. 10 Nov. 1300.

470* Copy of a bull of Pope Boniface VIII to the bishops of Salisbury, London, and Lincoln concerning the appeal between R[obert Winchelsey], archbishop of Canterbury, and M. Ralph de Mallingges, who calls himself rector of Pagham, Chichester dioc., on the one part, and Theobald de Barroducis, treasurer of York, on the other part, regarding Theobald's claim to have been provided to Pagham church by papal authority, and of certain processes by the abbot of St. Michael, Verdun dioc., who asserts he was Theobald's executor as regards this provision in opposition to the archbishop and Ralph. The pope appointed M. Humphrey de Trebis, dean of Meaux, his chaplain and auditor of causes of his palace, as auditor to the parties with power to absolve provisionally the archbishop and Ralph from the sentences of excommunication, suspension, and interdict which the abbot had issued. The parties presented petitions to the auditor by M. Andrew de Piperno, proctor of Theobald, and M. George de Interampne, proctor of the archbishop and Ralph. Having heard the evidence, the auditor has provisionally absolved the arch- bishop and Ralph from the sentences, and the pope orders the bishops to publish the absolution. Lateran, 9 Feb. 1302.
    Notarial certificate of Hugh Hugonis of Mursley, clerk of Lincoln dioc., notary public by papal authority.

471* Copy of a bull of Pope Boniface VIII to the bishops of Salisbury, Lincoln, and London concerning the appeal between the archbishop of Canter- bury and M. Ralph de Mallingges, clerk of Canterbury dioc., on the one part, and Theobald de Barroducis, clerk, on the other part, regarding Pagham church which has been directed to M. Humphrey de Trebis, dean of Meaux, papal chaplain and auditor of causes of the papal palace, before whom petitions were presented between M. George de Interampne, proctor of the archbishop and Ralph, and M. Andrew de Piperno, proctor of Theobald. The auditor has favourably considered a petition from M. George for the other party to be inhibited, and the pope orders the bishops to publish the inhibition. Lateran, 9 Feb. 1302.
    Notarial certificate of Hugh Hugonis of Mursley [as in **470***].
    [For an outline of this case see *Reg. Winchelsey*, i.xvii, 346, 362–3, 416; ii.539–42,

602–12, 748–9, 754–5, 763–5; Denton, *Winchelsey*, 273–4. For a calendar of the same papal bulls see *The register of the diocese of Worcester during the vacancy of the see, usually called Registrum Sede Vacante, 1301–1435*, ed. J.W. Willis Bund (Worcestershire Historical Society, 8, 1897), 60–1.]

472 Copy of letters dimissory issued by J[ohn le Romeyn, archbishop of York] to Th[eobald de Bar], a clerk of his diocese, for all minor and holy orders which he has not yet received. n.d.

[Theobald was a kinsman of the count of Bar (the king's son-in-law). He held the prebend of Masham, York dioc., from 31 May 1295, and was treasurer of York cathedral from 1297 until he became bishop of Liège in 1303, see *CPL*, i.591; *Reg. Romeyn*, i.xxvii, 24–5; ii.219; *Fasti*, vi.12, 66, 92.]

473* Commission to M. G[eoffrey] de Blaston, commissary-general, and M. R[ichard Bernard], archdeacon of Shrewsbury. By visitations made of the monastery of Haughmond the bishop has ascertained that although John de Sarum, Peter de Sumerford, Richard de Peppelawe, William de Leghton, and Thomas de Bruges, canons of Haughmond, wear the regular habit, they live irregularly and contrary to the rule, and show themselves incorrigibly determined in their wickedness. They are to go immediately to Haughmond in person and send the brethren to various houses: John de Sarum to Kenilworth, Peter de Sumerford to Repton, Richard de Peppelawe to Darley, William de Leghton to Stone, and Thomas de Bruges to Norton. The heads of those monasteries are to be enjoined by letter to admit and hold the brethren until the bishop thinks fit to ordain, ordering that they should attend divine services in the church with the other brethren at the accustomed hours, both day and night; be last both in choir and in refectory, being content with bread, weak ale, and vegetables only; fast with bread and water only in each quarter and sext; [and] busy themselves in the church, close, dormitory, and refectory at the accustomed hours, with other places being entirely prohibited to them. If any of the rebels presume to go against these decrees he is to be held in a secure place under strict custody, and have only bread and water, until the bishop shall ordain otherwise. London, 23 Jan. 1305.

474 [Fo. 25v] Licence to John de Weston to build an oratory and to cause divine service to be celebrated in the same for three years. Reepham, 4 Feb. 1301.

475 Note that M. Thomas de Abberbury, vicar-general, sealed thirteen charters delivered to him by William de Brikhull, steward, recording 16 acres and $1\frac{1}{2}$ roods of land given to several men in exchange for as much land which the bishop holds of them in his park of Beaudesert. Lichfield, 5 Feb. 1302.

476* Letters patent of Thomas de Abberbury, canon of Lichfield, vicar-general, ordaining the vicarage of Castleton in the Peak. The abbot and convent of Vale Royal claim to have Castleton in the Peak parish church appropriated to them. They have presented William Notekyn, priest, to the vicarage of the church, canonically ordained. An inquiry has been made of the portions and revenues of the church both by neighbouring rectors and vicars, and trustworthy

men. The inquiry has been returned to the vicar-general under their seals.
Having had full deliberation thereon, he has summoned the religious and the
presentee to hear and receive his decree concerning the portion of the church,
and the charges incumbent to the vicar and his vicarage, and all other things.
With the bishop's authority the vicar-general ordains the vicarage:

Half the manse, which had been the rector's by custom, *viz.* half the manse in
which the barn is situated, with the benefits and profits of the moiety, will
pertain to the religious and their successors by right of appropriation, which
they claim to have. They will also receive the tithe of corn of the entire parish
from lands now cultivated, and the tithe of hay of all the parishioners, without
diminution; also the mortuary animals, the tithe of the mine, the tithe of the
foals from the king's stud, the tithe of the king's water mill.

The other half of the rector's manse will pertain to the vicar, and his
successors, because he is bound to reside in person, together with the demesne
land and demesne park of the church, the tithes of lambs, wool, milk, and other
small tithes, and the revenues, oblations, and income of the church, except the
tithes and revenues assigned above to the religious. The vicars and other
ministers will first serve Castleton church. Besides the charge of hospitality to
be exercised, which their personal residence requires, which is expensive where
Castleton church is situated, they will bear archidiaconal synodalia, and
maintain the books, vestments, and ornaments of the church, and all ordinary
charges for all time, saving only the charge of building a new chancel, which
charge, if necessary, will pertain to the religious and their successors forever. Of
the extraordinary charges, two parts will pertain to the religious, and a third part
to the vicars forever.

Full power is reserved to the bishop and his successors to augment, diminish,
change, correct, and pronounce concerning the foregoing. Lichfield, 6 Apr.
1302.

Note of William Notekyn's institution to the vicarage.

477 [Fo. 26] Collation to W[illiam] de Chadleshont of the prebend of
Bubbenhall (*Bobenhull*)[1] which was Philip de Willugby's, the dean of
Lincoln. Lilleshall, 28 Mar. 1304.

    [[1] *Fasti*, x.22.]

478 Collation to M. G[eoffrey] de Blaston of the prebend of Bishopshull
(*Bisshopishull*)[1] which was Peter de Leycester's. Same year, day and place.

    [[1] *Fasti*, x.20.]

479 Collation to[1] William de Brikhull of the prebend of Darnford (*Derneford*),[2]
which was vacant because John de Drokenesford has been admitted to the
prebend of Whittington and Berkswich in Lichfield church.[3] York, 8 Nov. 1304.
[Margin] He owes the fee.

    [[1] Followed by 'M. Richard de Abendon of the prebend of Wellington in Lichfield
      church, vacant by the death of Philip de Everdon' deleted.
    [2] *Fasti*, x.32.
    [3] See **397**.]

480 Collation to M. Richard de Abendon of the prebend of Wellington in Lichfield church,[1] vacant by the death of Philip de Everdon. Note that Richard was inducted by the chapter the same day. Lichfield, 11 Dec. 1304.
[Margin] He owes the fee.
[[1] *Fasti*, x.65.]

481 Collation to M. Rhys ab Howel of the prebend which was Thomas called Jotro's in St. Chad's church, Shrewsbury. London, 20 Mar. 1305.

482 Collation to Robert de Clipston,[1] the bishop's familiar clerk, of the prebend of Flixton,[2] vacant by the death of M. William Burnel. Ind.: dean and chapter of Lichfield. London, 20 June 1305.
[[1] Bishop Langton's other clerical nephew, see Hughes, 'Family', 73–4.
[2] *Fasti*, x.36.]

483 Collation to M. John Pupard of the prebend of Curborough (*Coreburgh*)[1] in Lichfield church, vacant by the resignation of William de Bromyerd. Ind.: dean and chapter of Lichfield. London, 26 July 1305.
[[1] *Fasti*, x.27.]

484 Collation to M. Thomas de Goldbourgh, nephew of A[ntony Bek], bishop of Durham,[1] of the prebend of Ryton in Lichfield church,[2] vacant by the death of Philip de Wyloby. London, 20 Sept. 1305.
[[1] *HBC*, 242.
[2] *Fasti*, x.51.]

485 Collation to Robert de Klipston, the bishop's nephew, of the prebend which was John de Langeton's in Lichfield church,[1] vacant by his consecration as bishop of Chichester, which consecration was celebrated at Canterbury on Sun. 19 Sept. 1305. Same day.
[[1] Unidentified, see *Fasti*, x.70.]

486 Note that M. Thomas de Eadburbury, vicar-general, by command of [1]the bishop, who was then in Lyon (*Lugdun*')[2] on the king's business[1] with the other king's nuncios, sent by letter from Lyon, collated to M. Roger de Martival,[3] archdeacon of Leicester, the vacant prebend of Flixton,[4] which was Robert de Klipston's, the bishop's nephew, because Robert has received another prebend in Lichfield church, that which was J[ohn] de Langeton's, the bishop of Chichester. Steeple Aston, 15 Jan. 1306.
[[1–1] Underlined.
[2] He had travelled there for the coronation of Pope Clement V on 14 Nov. 1305, see Hughes, 'Episcopate', i.236–8.
[3] *BRUO*, ii.1232–3.
[4] *Fasti*, x.36.
The rest of the recto is blank.]

487 [Fo. 26v] Sixteenth or seventeenth century copy of Bishop Langton's ratification of the appropriation of Kingstone (*Kyngeston*') church, valued at 100s. a year, to the abbot and convent of Rocester (*Roucester*), of the Augustinian order, by his predecessor Bishop Roger [Meuland (1258–95)] during a visitation of the house, because they exercise hospitality and charity in receiving a great number of poor and travellers in their monastery. Brewood, 14 Aug. 1305.

488 Sixteenth or seventeenth century copy of the royal licence to the abbot and convent of Rocester (*Roucestr'*) to hold Kingstone church, notwithstanding the Statute of Mortmain. Witnessed the king, Westminster, 4 Mar. 1280.

[Fo. 27] REGISTRUM SUB DISCRETO VIRO MAGISTRO ROBERTO DE REDESWELL', ARCHIDIACONO CESTRIE, VENERABILIS PATRIS DOMINI WALTERI DEI GRACIA COVENTR' ET LICH' EPISCOPI ¹EO IN REMOTIS AGENTE¹ VICARIO A XVI KAL. MENSIS OCTOBRIS ANNO DOMINI MILLESIMO .CCC^mo. SEPTIMO [16 SEPT. 1307] USQUE . . .²
   [¹⁻¹ Underlined.
   ² Unfinished.]

489 Institution of Roger Illari, clerk, to Aldridge (*Alrewych*) church; patron, Robert de Barre Magna. He said [the vow of] canonical obedience. Packington (*Pakynton Prioris*), 6 Oct. 1307.
   [See Hughes, 'Clergy list', 7, 14.]

490 Institution of John de Wylmeleghton, deacon, to Stoneleigh (*Stonleg'*) vicarage; patrons, prior and convent of Kenilworth. He swore [the oath to reside], etc. Packington, 7 Oct. 1307.

491 Institution of Robert de Munsterton, deacon, to the vicarage of Leighton (*Leghton*) church; patrons, abbot and convent of Buildwas. He swore the oath of canonical obedience, and personal and continual residence. Lichfield, 14 Oct. 1307.

492 Institution of Hugh de Audele, acolyte, to Blore church; patron, Alan de Audele. He swore, etc. Lichfield, 18 Oct. 1307.

493 Licence to M. John de Byryton, rector of West Felton, to study for one year in any established school. Lichfield, same day.

494 Note that at the presentation of Sir Hugh de Venables, kt., Robert de Dutton, a minor, has been admitted to Eccleston (*Eccleston ultra Dee*) church as an act of special grace and in charity, on condition that he shall attend to letters and learning until [he attains] full age;¹ a fixed portion from the church shall be provided to him in the schools, with the support of his parents (*subsidio parentum sui²*), otherwise this grace will be of no account. Lichfield, 23 Oct. 1307.
[Margin] He is to be given a curate.
   [¹ Instituted rector 16 Dec. 1310, see **849**.
   ² Originally *sibi*]

495 Note that Richard de Adbaston, priest, has been admitted to the rectory of Stapleton (*Stepelton*) chapel, in charity; patron, Sir Robert de Stepelton, kt. He swore, etc. Lichfield, 26 Oct. 1307.

496   Institution of William de Essheborn, priest, to the vicarage of Castleton in the Peak church; patrons, abbot and convent of Vale Royal. He swore [etc.]. It was maintained at the inquiry that the vicarage had been vacant for three years, in consequence of which the collation was thought to have devolved to the bishop at first sight. It was found however that the priest had been presented by the religious within time; there had been no disregard for the law. Lichfield, 2 Nov. 1307.

497   Institution of Henry de Lee, acolyte, to Halsall (*Halsale*) church, according to the constitution of Pope Boniface [VIII]; patron, Gilbert de Halsale. He swore, etc. 7 Nov. 1307.
   [The rest of the recto is blank.]

498   [Fo. 27v] Licence to M. Alexander de Verdoun, rector of Biddulph (*Bydolf*), to study from Christmas next for one year in any established school, provided the church meanwhile is not defrauded of duties, etc. Lichfield, 12 Nov. 1307.

499   Institution of William de Walingford, a suitable and well-learned clerk, to Willey (*Wylye*) church; patron, Br. Nicholas,[1] prior of Warmington (*Warmynton*), proctor-general in England of Préaux (*Pratell'*) church,[2] Lucon (*Lexen'*) dioc. He swore [etc.]. Letters dimissory for all minor and subdeacon's orders. Lichfield, 11 Nov. 1307.
   [[1] De Canpyngnio, see **635**.
   [2] The monastery of Saint-Pierre, Préaux, Normandy, see Matthew, *Monasteries*, 41, 53.]

500   Institution of Henry de Buniburw, priest, to the vicarage of Neston church; patrons, abbot and convent of St. Werburgh, Chester. He swore [etc.]. Lichfield, 13 Nov. 1307.

501   Institution of Roger le Wyne, clerk, to Normanton (*Normunton*) church; patron, Lady Denise called le Wyne. He swore, etc. Letters dimissory for all minor and subdeacon's orders. Licence to study for one year in any established school. Lichfield, same day.

502   Institution of Thomas de Poule, subdeacon, to Newton Regis (*Neuton Regis*) church; patron, Sir Richard de Herthull, kt. He swore, etc. Lichfield, 15 Nov. 1307.

503   Licence of the vicar-general to Nicholas de Castro, having been admitted to Wishaw (*Wyshawe*) church, to study for four years according to the constitution of [Pope] Boniface, provided that the church is not defrauded of duties, etc. Lichfield, 25 Nov. 1307.

504   Institution of Philip de Harle, acolyte, [1][to Ness church][1] in the person of Richard de Laverden', chaplain, [his] proctor, who has sufficient [mandate] for this which remains in the chancellor's letter-chest (*in scrinio cancellarii*); patrons,

abbot and convent of Shrewsbury. The proctor swore obedience, etc., for his
principal. Lichfield, 27 Nov. 1307.

[¹⁻¹ Omitted, see **922**.]

505 Grant *in commendam* to Ingelard de Warleye, a priest so it is said, of
Albrighton (*Albriston*) church; patron, Sir John de la Warre, kt. Lichfield, 30 Nov.
1307.

506 Licence to Richard de Bristoll, subdeacon, rector of Quatt, to study for
two years from 22 Feb. 1308. He shall not be compelled to receive further orders
meanwhile, according to the tenor of the constitution of Pope Boniface, etc.
Lichfield, 13 Nov. 1307.

507 Institution of Richard de Modberleg', acolyte, to Mobberley (*Modberleye*)
church; patron, William de Modberleye. He swore, etc. Lichfield, 14 Dec. 1307.

508 William de Hodynet, a priest of good character, is appointed coadjutor to
the blind and infirm vicar of Lapley. He swore to protect the vicar and his
possessions, and to render a faithful account. The bishop is advised of this grant
because [fo.28] the said priest is a kinsman of the vicar, and it is presumed he
will act better for that master than a stranger. Lichfield, same day.

509 Institution of Henry de Waverton, priest, to the vicarage of Childwall
(*Childewell*) church; patron, John de Drokenesford, rector of Childwall. The
vicar-general has determined and ordained that the vicar now admitted and his
successors shall receive and have for their support three chaplains and a deacon,
all kinds of oblations, the Lenten tithes of merchants and servants, and the tithes
of linen, hemp, geese, calves, piglets, eggs, cheese, and milk, together with the
principal mortuary payments, but not [those] of livestock. They will also have
the manse in the grounds of the church called 'Grenebond', which is next to the
church, on condition that the present vicar and his successors will sustain and
support all ordinary charges incumbent on the church. Saving the right of the
churches of Coventry and Lichfield, etc. Lichfield, 17 Dec. 1307.

510 Institution of John de Dunclent, clerk, in the person of M. Richard called
le Bachiler, his proctor, to Berkswell (*Berkeswell*) church; patron, Guy, earl of
Warwick. The proctor swore, etc. for his principal by virtue of his proxy, which
remains in chancery. Lichfield, same day.

511 At the nomination and special mandate of the bishop the vicar-general
has collated the vicarage of Prees to Thomas Crok', in the person of M. Richard
de Norhampton, his lawful proctor, and granted him possession of the same,
enjoining him to warn Thomas to come in person to Lichfield before
Purification to receive institution. Lichfield, 30 Dec. 1307. Thomas did not
come, nor received institution, and the vicarage was collated to another.[1]

[¹ See **531**.]

512 Licence to Thomas Trussel, subdeacon, rector of Warmingham, to study for two years under the terms of the constitution of [Pope] Boniface. Lichfield, 5 Jan. 1308.

513 Licence to Henry de Lee, rector of Halsall, to study for two years in any established school, on condition that the church etc. Lichfield, 14 Jan. 1308.

514 Note of similar licence for William de Meles, rector of Lawton. Same day.

515 Thomas de Osmundeston called Bercar' has died intestate. Wishing to provide for the salvation of his soul from the goods of the same, administration of the deceased's goods is granted to Richard, vicar of Spondon, then dean of Derby, the vicar of Alvaston, and Thomas Pouchier, on condition that they will render a faithful account of the same. Lichfield, 18 Jan. 1308.

516 [Fo. 28v] Institution of Richard de Cavereswell, deacon, to the vicarage of Caverswall (*Cavereswell*) church; patrons, abbot and convent of St. Thomas by Stafford. He swore, etc. Lichfield, 19 Jan. 1308.

517 By special command of the bishop, licence is granted to William de Walingford, rector of Willey (*Wylie*), subdeacon, to study for two years in any established school, on condition that the church, etc. He shall not be compelled to further [orders] meanwhile. Lichfield, 28 Jan. 1308.

518 Licence to Henry called Sawvag', rector of Hartshorne (*Herteshorn'*), to study for three years in any established school, on condition that the church, etc. Lichfield, 30 Jan. 1308.

519* John de Chetewynd, canon of Lilleshall church, which is vacant [and] deprived of solace by the retirement of Br. William de Brugges, the pastor, has been unanimously elected. The election has been quashed because of its very many defects. Wishing to provide for the house lest it should come to ruin, or suffer harm in some way by escheators or others, the elect has been provided to the church and appointed abbot and pastor. Lichfield, 29 Feb. 1308.

[A mandate to restore the temporalities of the abbey to Chetewynd was issued on 13 Mar. 1308, see *CPR 1307–13*, 58.]

ANNO DOMINI MILLESIMO .CCC^mo. OCTAVO INCIPIENTE.

520 Licence to Hugh de Byshbury, rector of the same [Bushbury], being suitable and fit to study, that he may absent himself lawfully from his cure from Easter next, and farm the church to an ecclesiastical person, [provided] that the church, etc. Lichfield, 1 Apr. 1308.

521 Institution of Adam de Leghton of Arden (*Arderne*), priest, to Ashton under Lyne (*Ashton subtus Lymam*) church; patron, Sir Thomas Grelle, kt. He swore, etc. Lichfield, 4 Apr. 1308.

522   Licence to Henry de Berleston, portioner of Darley church, [to be absent] for one year from Michaelmas next.[1] Lichfield, same day.

[[1] No reason is given, but see **1040, 1053**.]

523   Note that custody of the sequestration on the vacant vicarage of Tarvin (*Terveyn*) has been granted until 9 June to Nicholas de Blaston, clerk, who has been presented to it, on condition that he causes himself to be qualified. 14 Apr. 1308.

524   Commission and injunction to M. Adam Byron to sequestrate all spiritualities of Tutbury (*Tottebury*) Priory in the diocese, and to cause them to be kept under his most firm sequestration, at his peril, and to be answerable for them. Lichfield, 7 May 1308.

525   Grant *in commendam* to William called Selet of Coventry, priest, of Brinklow (*Brynkelowe*) church, on condition that the church, etc. Lichfield, 18 May 1308.

526   Institution of Ingelard de Warle to Albrighton church,[1] in the person of Adam de la More, his proctor, who has sufficient mandate for this and whose proxy remains in chancery. He swore for his principal, etc. 26 May 1308.

[The patron, Sir John de la Warre, is not recorded, see **505**. In 1317 there was a question whether this presentation was void because Bishop Langton was in prison at the time. It was adjudged lawful however, and Warre recovered his presentation from the bishop. See *Year Book 11 Edward II, 1317–18* (Selden Society, 61, 1942), 309–17. (Thanks are due to Dr A.K. McHardy for this reference). Although this subsequent presentation has not been recorded, the church had a new incumbent, Robert, by 1 July 1319, see **1006**.
[1] By papal dispensation for plurality, see *CPL*, ii.23, 39, 72. Keeper of the king's wardrobe in 1312, see *HBC*, 80.]

527   [Fo. 29] Institution of John Libener', chaplain, to the vicarage of Harbury (*Herberbury*) church; patrons, prior and convent of Kenilworth. He swore, etc. Lichfield, 1 June 1308.

528   In continuance of grace,[1] custody of the sequestration on the vacant vicarage of Tarvin is granted to Nicholas de Blaston, subdeacon, until Michaelmas next, on condition that the church, etc. Lichfield, 3 June 1308.

[[1] See **523**.]

529   Grant *in commendam* to Ingelard de Warle, priest, of Mucklestone (*Mukleston'*) church, in accordance with the constitution of [Pope] Gregory [X], on condition that the church, etc. Lichfield, 10 June 1308.

530   Br. Gilbert called Putok', canon of Norton monastery, has been elected prior of the said house, which is vacant by the death of Br. Roger de Buddeworth. Following lawful confirmation, he is honorably installed prior by the vicar-general. He swore obedience to the bishop. Norton, 29 June 1308.

531 With the bishop's authority, the archdeacon of Chester, vicar-general, has collated and instituted John de Pritewell, priest, to the vacant vicarage of Prees church, according to the constitution of Ottobon, sometime legate in England. He swore [etc.]. Huyton, 1 July 1308.

532 Institution of M. Thomas de Pontesbury, acolyte, to Trusley (*Trussele*) church; patrons, prior and convent of Trentham. He swore, etc. Lichfield, 14 July 1308.

533 Tutbury Priory is vacant by lapse of time because to date no-one has been presented to the bishop or to his vicar-general for the priorate since the death of Br. Walter, the late prior. The vicar-general has collated Br. Robert de Longedon, monk of Burton upon Trent (*Burton super Trente*), to the priorate with its rights, etc. 20 July 1308.

On the Sunday following [21 July], by the vicar-general's authority, he was honourably installed at Lichfield by John de Sutham[1] for the rector of Morton, in the presence of many great men.

[[1] Perhaps prebendary of St Chad's church, Shrewsbury, see **982**; also **612**.]

534 Institution of Robert de Ashton, clerk, to Ashton on Mersey (*Ashton*) church; patron, Robert de Ashton super Merse. Lichfield, 22 July 1308.

535 Grant *in commendam* to Robert de Chaundoys of a moiety of Mugginton (*Mogynton*) church according to the constitution of Pope Gregory X, provided that the church, etc; patron, Sir John de Chaundoys, kt. Lichfield, same day.

536 Licence to William Pentyn, rector of Handley (*Haneleye*), to study for one year from Michaelmas next, provided that the church, etc. Lichfield, same day.

537 Note that the mastership of Bretford hospital is committed to Thomas de Olughton, priest; patron, Sir Richard de Turville, kt. He swore, etc. Lichfield, 26 July 1308.

538 Institution of James de Tifford, priest, to the third portion of Wroxeter church; patron, Edmund, earl of Arundel. He swore, etc. Lichfield, 2 Aug. 1308.

539 [Fo. 29v] At the command and mandate of the bishop the vicar-general has collated to William de Eston, clerk, the prebend which was M. Andrew de Eshebourn's in Gnosall (*Gnousale*) collegiate church, in charity. He has written to W[illiam] de Seukesworth and G. de Stotwell, canons of the said church, to induct him or J., his lawful proctor, whose proxy remains in chancery, in corporal possession of the prebend, [assigning] the stall in choir and place in chapter, etc. Lichfield, 1 Sept. 1308.

540 Licence to M. Thomas de Pontesbury, rector of Trusley (*Trusseleye*), to be absent for two years from Michaelmas next [to study][1], on condition that the church, etc. Lichfield, 2 Sept. 1308.

[[1] See **1031**; *BRUO*, iii.1497–8.]

541   In continuance of grace,[1] licence is granted to M. William de Bletchesle, rector of Waverton, to study for one year in any established school, and for the same time he shall not be compelled to further orders, provided that the church, etc. Lichfield, 28 Aug. 1308.

[1 See **819**.]

542   John de Dunklent, deacon, rector of Berkswell, has had letters dimissory so that he may be ordained priest lawfully by any bishop of the province of Canterbury, on condition that he will show the letters of the orders thus received within a year from the time the rule [of the church] was committed to him.[1] Lichfield, 5 Sept. 1308.

[1 17 Dec. 1307, see **510**.]

543   Institution of Richard de Paylyngton, priest, to Monks Kirby (*Kirkeby*) vicarage; patrons, abbot and convent of Monks Kirby. He swore [etc.]. Lichfield, 6 Sept. 1308.

544   Institution of Ingelard de Warle to Mucklestone church in the person of his proctor who has sufficient mandate, a copy of whose proxy remains in chancery. The proctor swore obedience, etc. The vicar-general has declared that, by such an admission, he does not intend to approve fully the privileges which I[ngelard] claims himself to have.[1] Lichfield, 12 Sept. 1308.

[1 He had papal dispensations for plurality in 1307, 1308, and 1310, see *CPL*, ii.23, 39, 72.]

545   At the presentation of Sir John de Orreby, kt., Adam, son of William de Donecastr', subdeacon, is admitted to the chantry of the Blessed Virgin in St. John's church, Chester, by special grace, in this form: he shall be ordained to the next successive orders without any interruption; then, he shall serve in person at the same altar as is customary, otherwise this grace will be of no consequence. Lichfield, 9 Oct. 1308.

546   Institution of John called Lob, deacon, to Lillington (*Lyllyngton*) vicarage; patrons, prior and convent of Kenilworth. He swore, etc. Lichfield, same day.

547   Institution of Nicholas de Blaston, deacon, to the vicarage of Tarvin (*Terven*) church; patron, Walter de Klypeston, canon of Lichfield, prebendary of Tarvin. He swore obedience, etc. Lichfield, 22 Sept. 1308.

548   Institution of William de Prayers, acolyte, to Childs Ercall (*Erkalwe Parva*) church; patrons, abbot and convent of Combermere. He swore, etc. Lichfield, 27 Oct. 1308.

549   [Fo. 30] Institution of Thomas de Pyctesleye, priest, to Harthill (*Herthull*) chapel; patron, Sir Urian de Sancto Petro, kt. He swore, etc. Lichfield, 30 Oct. 1308.

550 Licence to Richard de Modberleye, rector of the same [Mobberley], to study for two years in any established school, provided that the church, etc. Lichfield, 9 Nov. 1308.

551 Grant *in commendam* to John de Borne, priest, of Leyland (*Laylond*) church, according to the constitution of Pope Gregory X, provided that the church, etc.; patrons, abbot and convent of Evesham (*Eveshaune*). Lichfield, 9 Nov. 1308.

[The rest of the folio is blank.]

[Fo. 31] REGISTRUM VENERABILIS PATRIS DOMINI .W[ALTERI]. DEI GRACIA COVENTR' ET LYCH' EPISCOPI DE TEMPORE MAGISTRI RADULPHI DE LEYCESTRIA EJUSDEM PATRIS [1]IPSO IN REMOTIS AGENTE[1] VICARIUS[2] IN SPIRITUALIBUS GENERALIS A DIE LUNE .IIII^{TO}. IDUS MAII ANNO DOMINI .M^{o}.CCC^{mo}. DUODECIMO ET CONSECRACIONIS DICTI PATRIS .XVI^{mo}. [12 MAY 1312].

[1-1] Underlined.
[2] Recte *vicarii*]

DERB'.
[Underlined.]

552 Institution of M. Henry Byran, acolyte, to Weston upon Trent (*Westone super Trentam*) church; patrons, abbot and convent of St. Werburgh, Chester. 12 May 1312.

553 Institution of Robert de Deneford, chaplain, to Shirland (*Schirlond*) church; patron, Sir John de Grey, kt., lord of Dyffryn, Clwyd (*Deffreyncloyth*). 9 June 1312.

554 Institution of William de Billesdon, chaplain, to Youlgreave (*Ʒelgreve*) vicarage; patrons, abbot and convent of St. Mary de Pratis, Leicester. 7 July 1312.

555 Grant *in commendam* to M. Harvey de Luda, priest, of Kirk Ireton chapel near Wirksworth (*Hyrton juxta Workeswode*). The commendation was afterwards changed to sequestration in response to the bishop's [command], etc. 4 Aug. 1312.

556 Institution of Walter de London, priest, to St. Werburgh's vicarage, Derby; patron, prioress of King's Mead by Derby (*de Pratis juxta Derbeyam*). 30 Aug. 1312.

557 Institution of Robert de Frodesham, chaplain, to Aston upon Trent (*Aston super Trentham*) church; patrons, abbot and convent of Chester. 22 Sept. 1312.

558 Institution of Adam de Pontefracto to a moiety of Eckington (*Egynton*) church; patron, John de Stodevyll', 20 Sept. 1312.

[Margin] It is void ¹because Reginald de Cusaunce,² who was rector of the said church, is alive (*qui fuit rectore ecclesie predicte est in rerum natura*).¹

> [¹⁻¹ Added later to the main entry after the name of the patron by the same hand which wrote *vacat* in the margin.
> ² Instituted 19 Mar. 1303, still rector 21 Feb. 1309, see **252, 1024**; also *CPL*, ii.41.]

559 Institution of John de Stotevyle to the moiety of Eckington church which was Robert de Ma's; patron, John de Stotevyl'. 5 Dec. 1312.

560 Institution of Br. William de Calverton, chaplain, canon of Thurgarton, to Blackwell (*Blacwell*) vicarage¹ after the resignation of Br. Henry de Northwell, fellow-canon of the priory, and vicar of Blackwell; patrons, prior and convent of the same. 16 Dec. 1312.

> [¹ See Foulds, *Thurgarton Cartulary*, no. 1150; also nos. 967, 1014, 1015, 1017, 1018, 1148, 1151.]

561 Institution of Thomas de Pakinton, deacon, to Stapenhill vicarage; patrons, abbot and convent of Burton upon Trent. 5 Jan. 1313.

562 Institution of John de Baliiden, deacon, to Bolsover vicarage; patrons, abbot and convent of Darley. 15 Jan. 1313.

563 Licence to Richard Waleys, rector of Walton upon Trent (*Walton super Trentham*), to study for two years. 15 Jan. 1313.

564 Note that Nicholas de Derleye, chaplain, has been inducted to Haversage (*Haversegge*) church by papal authority directed to the bishop by M. William de Testa.¹ 26 Jan. 1313.

> [¹ Papal collector, see Lunt, *Financial relations*, 165–6, 488–93, 584–8.]

565 Institution of Hugh de Lekebourne, chaplain, to Youlgreave (*3olgrave*) vicarage, [vacant] by the resignation of William de Billesdon; patrons, abbot and convent of Leicester. 10 Mar. 1313.

566 Institution of Walter de Coleshull, chaplain, to Castleton [in the Peak] (*Castro* ¹ . . .) vicarage . . .¹. 11 Mar. 1313.

> [¹⁻¹ Abraded.]

[Fo. 31v] DERB'.

567 Institution of Henry de Longedon, chaplain, to Shirley (*Schirle*) vicarage; patrons, abbot and convent of Darley, at the bishop's nomination. 28 Mar. 1313.

568 Institution of Henry Pouger, chaplain, to Horsley (*Horsele*) vicarage; patrons, prior and convent of Lenton. 29 Mar. 1313.

569 Institution of Richard de Wamberg', acolyte, to a moiety of Mugginton (*Mogintone*) church; patron, Thomas, earl of Lancaster. 1 Apr. 1313.

570 Institution of John de Kaynes, clerk, to Whittington (*Wytinton*) church; patron, M. Roger de Martivall, [dean] of Lincoln. 10 Apr. 1313.

571 Institution of Robert de Chaundoys, chaplain, to Radbourne (*Rodbourne*) church; patron, Lady Elizabeth de Chaundoys. Same day.

572 Institution of Miles de Leicester, chaplain, to Wirksworth (*Wyrkesworth*) vicarage; patron, M. Roger de Martivall, dean of Lincoln. 20 May 1313.

573 Institution of John de Lely, chaplain, to the vicarage of St. Michael's church, Derby; patrons, abbot and convent of Darley. 21 July 1313.
[The rest of the folio is blank.]

[Fo. 32] SALOP'.

574 Institution of Robert de Egliton, priest, to the chantry or vicarage of Moreton Corbet (*Mortone Corbet*) chapel; patrons, abbot and convent of Haughmond (*Hagmon'*). 26 May 1312.

575 Institution of John de Wonbourne, priest, to Ellesmere vicarage; patron, Br. William de Tothale, prior of the hospital of St. John of Jerusalem in England. 4 June 1312.

576 Institution of William Pope, chaplain, to St. Alkmund's vicarage, Shrewsbury; patrons, abbot and convent of Lilleshall. [?8] July 1312.[1]
[[1] Dated *viij non. Julii* in error.]

577 Note that custody[1] of the sequestration on Hordley (*Hordel'*) chapel has been granted to Robert de Marchumle until Michaelmas, and then for one year, having been presented to the chapel. 2 Aug. 1312.
[[1] Interlined.]

578 Institution of Geoffrey de Thyrneby, chaplain, to Stoke upon Tern (*Stoke super Tyrnam*) church [which] became vacant on Tues. 21 Mar. 1312; patron, Sir Theobald de Verdoun, kt. 4 Oct. 1312.
[Margin] [1]Note, another institution of a previous date [is] in the archdaeaconry of Stafford.[1]
[A hand drawn in the left-hand margin points to this entry.
[1–1] In a later hand. See **284**.]

579 Licence to Thomas [de Cheynee],[1] subdeacon, rector of West Felton, to study for two years. 17 Jan. 1313.
[[1] See **976**.]

580 Note of similar licence for Roger de Smethecote, rector of the same [Smethcott]. 1 Jan. 1313.
[The rest of the recto is blank.]

[Fo. 32v] CESTR'.
[Underlined.]

581 Note that Alice de Alderdelegh, a nun of St. Mary's, Chester, has been instituted prioress, having been lawfully elected by the convent. 16 Oct. 1312.
[Royal mandate to restore the temporalities followed on 30 Oct. 1312, see *CPR 1307–13*, 503, 507.]

582 Institution of Richard de Perebald, chaplain, to Rochdale (*Racchesdal'*) vicarage; patrons, abbot and convent of Whalley (*Walleye*). 9 Dec. 1312.

583 Institution of William de Snayth, chaplain, Nicholas de Berghton, William de Castello, Robert de Acton, Walter de Derb', Thomas de Sutton, and William de Walton, chaplains, to prebends in Upholland (*Houland*) chapel; patron, Sir Robert de Holand.[1] 9 Jan. 1313.
   [1 A retainer of Thomas, earl of Lancaster, see J.R. Maddicott, 'Thomas of Lancaster and Sir Robert Holland: a study in noble patronage', *EHR*, lxxxvi (1971), 449–72. Holland founded a secular college at Upholland for a dean and twelve priests in 1310, which was refounded as a Benedictine monastery at the patron's request in 1319, see *MRA*, nos. 328–33, 369–71, 373, 375; D. Knowles, R.N. Hadcock, *Medieval religious houses: England and Wales* (London, 1953), 57, 79; *CPL*, ii.188; *VCH Lancashire*, ii.111–12.]

584 Institution of Benedict de Wodeford, chaplain, to Frodsham (*Frodesham*) vicarage; patrons, abbot and convent of Vale Royal. 24 Jan. 1313.

585 Institution of Robert de Aula, chaplain, to Weaverham vicarage; patrons, abbot and convent of Vale Royal. 19 Mar. 1313.

586 Institution of Thomas de Duttone, chaplain, to Over (*Overe*) vicarage; patrons, prioress and convent of St. Mary, Chester. 31 Mar. 1313.

587 Institution of Osbert Giffard, acolyte, to Barrow (*Barwe*) chapel, in the jurisdiction of the prebend of Tarvin (*Tereven*); patron, Hugh le Despencer. 14 May 1313.

STAFFORD'.
[Underlined.]

588 Note that Ralph de Longedon has had his letters of holy orders examined by suitable witnesses. 7 June 1312.
   [Ordained priest 22 Sept. 1302, see **1288**.
   588–593 are subsequently duplicated and cancelled on fo. 116, see **1308**.]

589 Institution of Philip de Cotes, chaplain, to Ilam (*Ylom*) vicarage, by the bishop's mandate. 30 Oct. 1312.

590 Institution of John de Codeshale, chaplain, to Dilhorne (*Dulverne*) vicarage; patrons, dean and chapter of Lichfield. 13 Feb. 1313.

INCIPT ANNUS DOMINI .M^{US}.CCC^{US}.XIII^{US}.

591 Institution of Thomas de Blaston, deacon, to Sandon (*Sondone*) vicarage; patrons, abbot and convent of Combermere. 10 Apr. 1313.

592 Institution of Br. Walter de Aston, canon of Rocester, to the vicarage of St. Michael's church, Rocester; patrons, abbot and convent of the same. Note that the vicar is to be removed by the abbot and convent at will, according to the terms of their privileges. 11 Apr. 1313.

593 Institution of Br. John de Leicestr', canon of Kenilworth, to the priorate of Calwich; patrons, prior and convent of Kenilworth. 17 May 1313.

[Fo. 33] COVENTR'.
  [Underlined.]

594 Institution of Hugh de Wytacre, priest, to the perpetual chantry of St. Alphegus, in the parish of Solihull (*Solyhul*), [vacant] by the resignation of William de Bockemor, chaplain; patrons, Ralph de Perham and Alice de Cauntone. 6 June 1312.

595 Institution of Geoffrey Marmyon, priest, to the perpetual vicarage of the mother church of Kenilworth; patrons, prior and convent of the same. 17 June 1312.

596 Institution of John de Kyrby, chaplain, to Alspath (*Alspathe*) vicarage; patrons, prior and convent of Coventry. 5 Sept. 1312.

597 Institution of William de Alspathe, chaplain, to Willoughby (*Wyleby*) vicarage; patrons, Br. Nicholas, master of St. John's hospital without the east gate of Oxford, and the fellow-brethren of the same. 21 Aug. 1312.

598 Institution of Geoffrey de Sutton, chaplain, to Weddington (*Wedyndon*) church; patron, Sir Nicholas de Asteley, kt. 3 Nov. 1312.

599 Institution of Geoffrey Marmyon to Packington (*Paginton Prioris*) vicarage; patrons, prior and convent of Kenilworth. 6 Mar. 1313.

600 Institution of Roger Boyvill', chaplain, to the vicarage of Kenilworth (*Kennelworth*) church; patrons, prior and convent of the same. 14 Mar. 1313.

601 Licence to William de Clinton, rector of Ratley (*Rocteleye*), to study for three years. 6 May 1313.
  [Followed by six blank lines.]

602 Copy of an indenture (sixteenth or seventeenth century hand). The bishop has recently exercised the office of visitation in the archdeaconry of Chester. He has received the petition of the abbot and convent of Dieulacres (*Deulacres*) containing, etc.: whereas they have recently demised newly to local tenants or farmers there lands which pertain to their manor or grange of Pulton in the archdeaconry of Chester, which lie outside the boundaries and limits of any parish, [and] which are known to have been exempt from the levy on church lands since time immemorial; which tenants, villeins, or farmers have not received certain ecclesiastical sacraments or sacramentals in any parish church hitherto since they do not have their own priest. In order to remove the uncertainty and the litigation which might arise [between] the said tenants and neighbouring rectors in future, and also for the salvation of the said tenants' souls, the religious have asked the bishop that he might deign to ordain thereon, and if he would confirm any composition they make on the foregoing with any neighbouring rector. The bishop has commissioned his official Philip de Turvill', canon of Lichfield, his lieutenant in this regard, having summoned all persons whom it concerns, or might concern, to inquire on the business and to ordain thereon, for the honour of God and the salvation of the said tenants' souls, and, having examined the form and manner of any composition the said religious make with any neighbouring [fo. 33v] rector, to confirm it as his lieutenant, if it is just and lawful. Whereupon Philip de Turvill', the aforesaid commissary in this regard, with diligent inquiry having been made in lawful form on all and each and of the circumstances of the foregoing, by certificate of the archdeacon of Chester's official summoned the neighbouring rectors of Eccleston and of Pulford, and all other persons whom it concerns, or might concern, together with Lady Joan, widow of Robert de Pulford, the patron, before a tribunal in Lichfield cathedral on Wed. 27 Jan. [1316]. Having studied the composition or covenant made between the religious and the rector of Pulford, and having carefully considered the inquiry and composition, and certain other documents presented by the religious, [the commissary] has ordained and decreed with the express consent of Br. Peter de Petristall, prior of Dieulacres, proctor of the said religious, who has sufficient authority in this regard, and also of Robert,[1] rector of Pulford, who were then present:

The rector, at his expense, will minister all sacraments and sacramentals to all the tenants or farmers of the manor or grange of Pulton of the said abbot and convent of Dieulacres in Pulford church or Pulton chapel by a suitable and capable priest before August, or a suitable time.

With the agreement of the abbot and convent, the rector of Pulford and his successors will receive the following portions from the tenants of the said religious without any opposition: from the tenants who hold ecclesiastical property on tithable land in Pulford marked by the bounds and limits from 'Hervesheved' to 'le Gredeneburgge' extending to 'Tunpirisdale' and 'le Pull' de Alinore' in length, and from 'le Gradenebrugg'' to the new ditch which extends as far as the metes and bounds between Pulton and Pulford or the watercourse (*cissaturam*) in breadth, all the predial tithes of Cistercian lands and all personal tithes of the said tenants in peace and forever, except for the progeny of animals (*de nutrimentis animalium*), of which the said abbot and convent and Robert, the rector, and his successors, will receive milk, calves, wool, lambs, foals, and goats divided equally between them.

From all the tenants who hold ecclesiastical property or dwell anywhere in Pulton on untithed land in the other part of the said bounds up to the grange, *viz.* up to their own fields in Pulton, Robert, the rector, and his successors will receive all oblations from the tenants at the four principal feasts, mortuary dues in Lent, money for marriage dues, half of all mortuary payments due to the church, and half the oblations on the day of burial without any diminution, and the religious will receive all others without any challenge from the rector or his successors.

If it happens that the tenants, villeins, or farmers on that part of the untithed land towards Pulton subsequently do not abide by this agreement with the said religious, [the commissary] does not wish to prejudice the previous agreement. Sealed with the seals of the official, the religious, and Robert, the rector. Lichfield, 27 Jan. 1316.

[¹ De Bruera, see **192**.]

[Fo. 34] COVENTR'.
[Underlined.]

REGISTRUM ARCHIDIACONATUS COVENTR' A FESTO SANCTE TRINITATIS ANNO GRACIE .M°.CCC^mo. SEPTIMO ET CONSECRACIONIS .W[ALTERI]. DE LANGETON COVENTR' EPISCOPI XI°.

603 Note that custody of the sequestration on Stoneleigh (*Stonleye*) vicarage has been committed to John de Wylmeleghton, subdeacon, during pleasure; patrons, prior and convent of Kenilworth. The vicarage became vacant on Mon. 13 Mar. by the death of William de Merston, the last vicar. Letters dimissory for the order of deacon. Bowes, 19 May 1307. ¹Look in the vicar-general's register.¹
[Margin] To be answerable for lambs and wool for the time of the sequestration.
[¹⁻¹ Added later and referring to his institution on 7 Oct. 1307, see **490**.]

604* Letters patent to Conrad Howeschilt of Germany, rector of Fillongley. Since he has a mind to study, so that he will bear seasonable fruit in God's church, the bishop grants that he may study at university for one year, meanwhile receiving wholly the fruits of his church. He will not be bound to receive further orders, except the order of subdeacon, which he is obliged to receive within one year from the time the rule [of the church] was committed to him,¹ by authority of the constitution of Pope Boniface VIII,² provided that he employs a good and reliable vicar in his church. The vicar is to be provided for from the revenues of the church, as the constitution requires. London, 17 Oct. 1305.
[¹ Instituted 16 Oct. 1305, see **145**.
² The constitution *Cum ex eo*, see **45**, n. 4.]

605 Letters patent to Conrad Howeschilt of Germany, rector of Fillongley. The bishop grants him licence to study at university for one year only [as in **604***], provided that his church will not be defrauded of duties. London, 13 Nov. 1306.

606 Note that the same Conrad has now obtained a third licence to study for three years from Michaelmas 1307 by letters of the first kind,[1] at the request of Raymond [de Got], cardinal-deacon of St. Maria Nova.[2] London, 17 June 1306.

[[1] See **604***.
[2] *Fasti*, x.7.]

607 Letters patent to William [fo. 34v] de Picheford, priest. Farnborough (*Farneberghe*) church has devolved to the bishop's collation this turn by lapse of time by authority of the General Council.[1] Wishing to provide beneficially for the church and the cure of souls which he strives for, the bishop collates the church to him in charity, with all its rights and appurtenances. London, 30 June 1307.

[[1] The Third Lateran Council, 1179, see **22**, note.]

[1]QUERERE SUPRA[2] REGISTRUM .. ARCHIDIACONI VICARII EPISCOPI[1] DE ANNO DOMINI .M°.CCC^mo. OCTAVO.

[See the vicar-greneral's register **489–551** for business between 16 Sept. 1307 and 9 Nov. 1308; also **1027**.
[1-1] Added later.
[2] Interlined.]

REGISTRUM [1]POST EGRESSUM EPISCOPI A CARCERE[1].

[[1-1] Underlined.]

608 Note that the bishop has instituted William de Knychtecot', priest,[1] to Chilvers Coton (*Chelvercote*) vicarage, which was then vacant by the death of M. Roger, the last vicar, on Tues. 22 Oct.; patrons, prior and convent of Arbury (*Ordbur'*). Ind.: archd. of Coventry. Theydon Mount, Essex (*Theydene Mountfichet in Essex*), 20 Dec. 1308.

[[1] Interlined.]

609* Commission to the archdeacon of Coventry, or his official. Br. Thomas, prior of Arbury, and the convent of the same have presented William de Knyghtecote, clerk, to the vacant vicarage of Chilvers Coton, which they say belongs to their presentation. He is commanded to inquire in a full chapter of the place by rectors and vicars summoned [there] concerning the circumstances of the vicarage, is it vacant, or not, and if it is vacant when the vacancy began, and how; who the true patron is, who last presented to [the vicarage], at whose presentation the last vicar was admitted, or is it disputed, charged with a pension, or not and, if it is, to who or to whom, for how much, and at whose valuation it is; the suitability of the presented, [his] good repute, learning, age, orders, whether he is free, [of] legitimate birth, beneficed elsewhere, or not, and other customary points. His findings are to be notified to the bishop. London, 1 Dec. 1308.

[Common form for such a commission, see J.W. Gray, '*Ius praesentandi* in England', *EHR*, 67 (1952), 508–9.]

610 Institution of Thomas de Harewell, priest, to Cubbington (*Cobynton*) church, vacant by the resignation of Henry de Sondwych, the last rector, on

Tues. 4 Mar. last; patrons, prior and convent of Kenilworth. Ind.: archd. Theydon Mount (*Theyden*), 22 Mar. 1309.

[Margin] Nothing for the fee.

INCIPIT ANNUS DOMINI .M.CCC^{US}. NONUS.

611 Letters dimissory to Richard de Solihull, deacon of Coventry and Lichfield dioc., for the order of priest, in common form, with the addition of this clause: provided that he will have shown sufficient title to his ordainer. London, 30 Apr. 1309.

612 Letters dimissory to John de Suham, acolyte, for all holy orders, with the addition of this clause [as in **611**]. London, 30 Apr. 1309.

613 [Fo. 35] Institution of John Dod of Henley (*Henleye*), priest, to Berkswell church, vacant by the death of John de Dunclen[t], the last rector, on Mon. 4 Nov. last; patron, Guy de Beauchamp, earl of Warwick. Ind.: archd. of Coventry. London, 2 May 1309.

614 To the archdeacon of Coventry or his official. At the presentation of the prior and convent of Kenilworth the bishop has admitted John de Peperinge, clerk, to the custody of Brinklow church and of his sequestration placed on its fruits and revenues until, having been ordained acolyte, he will return to the bishop without delay to receive institution in the same.[1] Mandate to ind. him or his proctor. London, 1 May 1309.

> [Entry deleted by two crossed lines with *va . . .cat* marginated down the length of the entry.
> [1] Ordained acolyte before his institution on 9 May 1309, see **615, 616**; also **617, 632, 665**.]

615 ITEM, DIMISSORIAS PRO EODEM. Faculty to John de Pepering, who has been presented to Brinklow church. He may be promoted to all minor and subdeacon's orders by any Catholic bishop of England. He will not acquire another title except only custody of the bishop's sequestration on the said benefice, provided that there is no other canonical impediment. Dated as above.

616 Institution of John de Peperinge, acolyte, to Brinklow church, vacant by the resignation of M. William Celet, the last rector, on Fri. 1 Nov. last; patrons, prior and convent of Kenilworth. Ind.: archd. of Coventry. Letters dimissory for the order of subdeacon. London, 9 May 1309.

[Margin] $\frac{1}{2}$ mark for the fee.

617 Licence to John de Peperinge, rector of Brinklow, to study for two years under the terms of the constitution of Pope Boniface VIII. Solihull, 27 Mar. 1310.

618 Note that on 4 July 1309 M. John Popard was instituted to Bedworth church in the person of his proctor in this form. Letters patent of R[obert] de

Redeswelle, archdeacon of Chester, vicar-general. At the presentation of Henry de Cherneles of Bedworth he has admitted and instituted M. John Popard, priest, rector of Bedworth. Davenham, 4 [fo. 35v] July 1309. The church was vacant by the resignation of M. Philip de Turville, the last rector. Ind.: archd.

619 Institution of Richard de Kereseye, acolyte, to Willey church, vacant by the resignation of William de Walingford, the last rector; patron, Br. Nicholas, prior of Warmington (*Warmyncton*). Ind.: archd. 12 Sept. 1309.

620 Licence to Richard de Kerseye, acolyte, to study for one year under the terms of the constitution of Pope Boniface VIII. Letters dimissory for all holy orders. London, 20 Feb. 1310.

621 Institution of William de Clynton, acolyte, to Ratley (*Rotteleye*) church, vacant by the death of Philip de Clynton, the last rector, on [1] . . .day near . . . the feast . . .;[1] patron, Guy de Beauchamp, earl of Warwick. Ind.: archd. Merevale (*Mirevall'*), 6 Mar. 1310.

    [1–1 Blank spaces.]

ANNUS [M].CCC[us].X[us]. INCIPIT.

622* Note that after the resignation of Lady Katherine Boydin, the former prioress of Henwood, made freely [and] purely to the bishop at Lichfield on 8 Apr. 1310, the bishop wrote to the subprioress and convent to elect a new prioress; he gave them licence for this. He wrote to the abbess and convent of Polesworth to receive Katherine and [for her] to remain there for some time. Having sought a licence to elect from Ralph de Perham, the abbot of Westminster's deputy, their patron,[1] the subprioress and convent unanimously elected or nominated Margaret le Corzon their prioress, and presented the same election or nomination to the bishop by their letters sealed with the common seal by Millicent de Fokerham, subprioress, Margery atte Barre, and Agnes de Wyveleston, nuns of the house, and they offered a letter patent with the agreement of their patron at Lichfield on 15 Apr. 1310. [fo. 36] The letters were received and examined by the bishop and his council, with M. Robert de Radeswelle, archdeacon of Chester, M. Luke de Ely, chancellor of Lichfield church,[2] and M. Geoffrey de Blaston, canon of the same, being present. Because the subprioress and convent had observed no formula propounded by the rule in electing or nominating the prioress, the bishop quashed the election and pronounced [it] invalid. As an act of special grace, he provided the said Margaret prioress, and she sang the canticle *Te Deum* well. He wrote to the subprioress and convent to receive her and obey her as prioress, and to the rector of Maxstoke to install her.

    [1 The election of a prioress required only the abbot's confirmation according to *VCH Warwickshire*, ii.66.
    2 *BRUO*, i.637; *Fasti*, x. 9.]

623 Faculty to the prior of Coventry to receive the probate of the will of Cecilia, widow of Adam des Okes, deceased, and to do all that is required in this matter. Eccleshall, 28 Apr. 1310.

624 Institution of William de Muneworth, acolyte, to the moiety of Kingsbury (*Kynesbury*) church vacant by the death of Gilbert,[1] the last rector, on Mon. 26 Oct. last; patrons, prioress and convent of Holy Trinity of the wood, Markyate. Note that the moiety pays a pension of 40s. to the religious. Ind.: archd. Bishops Itchington, 16 Nov. 1310.
[Margin] He paid the fee.
  [1 De Kynesbur', see **103**.]

ANNO CONSECRACIONIS W[ALTERI] EPISCOPI QUINTO DECIMO.

625 Licence to William de Clynton, subdeacon, rector of Ratley, to study from the time of his institution[1] until Michaelmas next under the terms of the constitution of Pope Boniface. 7 Jan. 1311.
  [1 6 Mar. 1310, see **621**.]

626 Note that custody of the sequestration placed on the fruits and revenues of Wishaw (*Wishawe*) church has been committed to M. Thomas de Weston, during pleasure. Lichfield, 16 Jan. 1311.

627 Institution of William de Laberton, acolyte, to Wishaw church, vacant by the death of Nicholas,[1] the last rector, on Sun. 15 Nov. last; patron, Sir George de Castello, kt. Ind.: archd. Letters dimissory for all holy orders. Lichfield, 23 Jan. 1311.
  [1 De Castello or de Castro, see **148, 503**.]

628* [Fo. 36v] Letters patent to William de Bulkenior, priest. According to the Apostle, it is granted to the pastoral office incumbent on the bishop's shoulders [that] he is bound to assist by suitable support those seen to be wanting and with debility. Peter,[1] rector of Maxstoke, is known to labour with very severe infirmity. He requires the care of another, as established by an inquiry held by the archdeacon of Coventry's official. Having faith in [William's] industry and circumspection, he appoints him keeper of the rector, his church, and his things, and also curate, provided that he faithfully makes an inventory of the rector's extant goods and he will render an account of these and other things in future to him or to [commissaries]. Lichfield [1311].
  [1 De Ilmendon, see **87**.]

629 Licence, in common form, to Thomas de Napton, rector of Napton on the Hill (*Napton*) to study for one year. London, 18 Feb. 1311.

630* Institution of Geoffrey de Vylers to Nuneaton vicarage, vacant by the death of M. John de Hinkele, the last vicar, on Tues. 10 Nov. last; patron, Br.

Peter de Criketot, proctor-general in England and Wales of the abbot and convent of Lire.[1] Ind.: archd. Eccleshall, 19 Mar. 1311.

[Margin] Nothing [for the fee].

[[1] Matthew, *Monasteries*, 194.]

INCIPIT ANNUS DOMINI .M^{us}.CCC. UNDECIMUS.

631 Institution of Ralph de Redale, priest, to the vacant chantry of Kinwalsey (*Kynebaldesleye*); patron, Sir John de Bractbrugg', kt. Ind.: archd. York, 24 May 1311.

632 Licence to John de Poperinge, subdeacon, rector of Brinklow, to study for four years from the date of his institution[1] under the terms of the constitution of Pope Boniface. York, 10 June 1311.

[[1] 9 May 1309, see **616**.]

633* Letters patent. As each statute with constraints always excuses a lawful impediment, it is fitting for the pastoral office to admit the lawful excuses of the flock and to grant compurgation concerning them. Having been presented to the bishop for the vicarage of Nuneaton by the patrons, and afterwards having been canonically instituted in it by him,[1] with due order having been observed in all things, Geoffrey de Vilers, deacon, had agreed to go in person to the bishop to receive the priestly order at York at the next fixed term for holy orders to be conferred according to canon law. Having been detained by great personal indisposition at that time, the bishop was unable to promote the same to the priestly order without physical danger;[2] lest the said vicar falls into danger of the canon published concerning this,[3] or incurs some risk of the same by this, as testimony to the truth of the matter the bishop declares the same vicar to have been reasonably impeded from accepting the priesthood at the said term, and having sufficient excuse, provided that he will be ordained to the priesthood at the next orders after the date of these letters.[4] York, 5 June 1311.

[[1] Instituted 19 Mar. 1311, see **630***.
[2] Langton had faculty on 24 May 1311 to ordain in the diocese of York but he was then detained in prison there, see the introduction pp. xxi, xxxiv.
[3] See **118**, n. 2.
[4] Ordained subdeacon Dec. 1310 by letters dimissory of Rouen dioc., and subdeacon on 6 Mar. 1311, see **1306, 1307**. No record of his ordination to the priesthood has been found.]

634 [Fo. 37] Note that custody of the sequestration on Solihull church has been committed to John de Sandale, subdeacon, [1]the king's treasurer,[1] during pleasure. Mandate to the archd. of Coventry, or his official, or M. Richard de Norhampton, the bishop's sequestrator, to deliver the said custody to John, or his proctor. York, 5 Aug. 1311.

[Instituted 29 Oct. 1311, see **638**.
[1-1] Interlined.]

635 Institution of M. William de Bokstanes, subdeacon, to Warmington (*Wermynton*) church, vacant by the death of M. Ellis de Napton, the last rector, on Mon. 12 July last; patron, Br. Nicholas de Canpyngnio, proctor-general in England and fellow-monk of the abbot and convent of [Saint-Pierre] Préaux. [The church] pays an annual pension of 2 marks [£1 6s. 8d.] to Br. Nicholas. Ind.: archd. London, 17 Sept. 1311.
[Margin] He owes the fee.

636 Grant *in commendam* to William de Welesbur', priest, of the vacant church of Compton Verney (*Compton Murdak*), according to the form of the statute of commendation. Ind.: archd. of Coventry. London, 30 Sept. 1311.

637 Note that on 29 Oct. 1311 Henry de Nouton, priest, was admitted [1]and instituted[1] to Seckington (*Sekyndon*) church; patron, Henry de Campvill'. The church became vacant[2] on the said day by the resignation of William de Brimesgrave at London. Ind.: archd.
[Margin] He owes the fee.
  [[1-1] Interlined.
  [2] Interlined.]

638 Institution of John de Sandale, subdeacon, to Solihull church,[1] vacant by the death of Ralph de Hemgham, the last incumbent, on Tues. 18 May; patron, Lady Alice de Caunton, lady of Pyrton (*Pyriton*). Ind. him [2]or his proctor:[2] archd. [London] 29 Oct. 1311.
[Margin] Nothing for the fee.
  [[1] By papal dispensation, see *CPL*, ii.119–20.
  [2-2] Interlined.]

639 Institution of William de Knistecote, priest, to the vacant vicarage of Burton Dassett (*Magna Derset*); patrons, prior and convent of Arbury (*Erdbury*), to whom the church of Burton Dassett is appropriated, and Sir John de Sudleye, kt. The vicarage became vacant on Sun. 26 Sept. last by the admission (*per admissionem*) of another benefice with a similar cure of souls, which Ralph,[1] the last vicar of the same, accepted, and he was instituted in the same.[2] Ind.: archd. of Coventry. London, 18 Nov. 1311.
[Margin] He paid the fee.
  [[1] De Derset, see **121**.
  [2] There is no record of his institution to this benefice, but he appears to have been re-instituted vicar of Burton Dassett on 8 July 1314, see **655**.]

640 Licence to William de [Muneworth][1], rector of a moiety of Kingsbury church, to study for one year or to be[2] in the service of his lord, Henry de Spigornel, the king's justice,[3] at the justice's request. London, 22 Nov. 1311.
  [[1] Blank space, see **624**.
  [2] Interlined.
  [3] Justice of King's Bench, 1307, and justice of Common Pleas, see Foss, *Judges*, 301–3; *DNB*, xviii.809–10.]

641 [Fo. 37v] Note that custody of the sequestration on the fruits and revenues of Compton Verney church has been committed to Thomas de Hamslape, clerk, during pleasure, having been presented to the same church by Guy, earl of Warwick. London, 6 Dec. 1311.

642 Institution of Robert de Hordewyk, priest, to Chilvers Coton vicarage, vacant by the resignation of William de Knystecote, the last vicar, on Fri. 19 Nov. last; patrons, prior and convent of Arbury. Ind.: archd. Daventry (*Daventr'*), 22 Dec. 1311.
[Margin] He owes the fee.
[Followed by a line drawn across the folio.]

ANNUS CONSECRACIONIS DOMINI .W[ALTERI]. EPISCOPI COVENTR' ET LICH' .XVI^us.
INCIPIT.

643 Institution of William de Bockemor', priest, to Arley (*Arleye*) church, vacant by the death of Nicholas de Byrmyngham, the last rector, on Fri. 21 July last; patron, Lady Ela de Oddingeseles. Ind.: archd. Lichfield, 7 Jan. 1312.

644 Institution of Henry called[1] Trunket of Wolston, priest, to Willoughby vicarage, vacant by the death of Nicholas called Benet, the last vicar, on Sun. 5 Mar. last; patrons, Br. Nicholas, master, and the fellow-brethren of the hospital [of St. John the Baptist] without the east gate of Oxford. He swore to reside.[2] Lichfield, 24 Mar. 1312.
[1 Interlined.
2 No mandate to induct.]

REQUIRE REGISTRUM MAGISTRI RADULPHI DE LEICESTR' VICARII GENERALI DOMINO EPISCOPO EXISTENTE IN CURIA ROMANA.
[Underlined. See **552–601** for the vicar-general's register.]

ANNUS DOMINI MILLESIMUS .CCC^mus. TERTIUS DECIMUS INCIPIT.

645 Note that custody of the sequestration placed on the fruits and revenues of Rugby church has been committed to . . .[1] London, 18 Nov. 1313.
[1 Unfinished. Entry deleted.]

646 Institution of William de Leone, priest, to Withybrook (*Wythibrok*) church, vacant by the death of M. Robert Tankard, the last rector, on Wed. 17 Oct. last; patrons, prior and fellow monks of Monks Kirby. Ind.: archd. London, 18 Nov. 1313.
[Margin] He paid the fee.

647 Institution of Richard de Touecestr', acolyte, in the person of Richard de Norton, clerk, his proctor, who has sufficient mandate for this, to Rugby church, vacant by the resignation of William de Leone, the last rector, . . .[1] [in] Nov.;

patron, Annabel de Mundevill', lady of Rugby. Ind. him or his proctor: archd. London, 20 Nov. 1313.
[Margin] He owes the fee.
  [¹ Blank space, but on or before 18 Nov., see **645, 646**.]

648 [Fo. 38] Collation to Thomas de Langeton, priest, of Southam church, which has devolved to the bishop this turn by authority of the Lateran Council.¹ He swore obedience, etc. Ind. him or his proctor: archd., or his official and the vicar of Bishops Tachbrook (*Tachebrok*). [London] 27 Nov. 1313.
[Margin] He owes [the fee].
  [See **654** which duplicates this entry. Southam church was vacant because the previous rector, Robert de Loggonere, had been deprived of his living after his conviction for perjury in the court of Canterbury in June 1312 following a suit brought against him by the dean and chapter of Lichfield concerning his withholding of a pension due to them: see **146**; *MRA*, nos. 478–80, 482, 484.
  ¹ By lapse of time.]

649 Institution of Thomas called Legat, priest, to the chantry chapel of William de Copston, vacant by the death of Maurice, the last [chantry] priest, at Martinmas last; patron, prior of Coventry. Ind.: archd. London, 15 Dec. 1313.
[Margin] Nothing [for the fee].

650 Institution of M. John de Shotteswell, acolyte, ¹in the person of John de Chelvescote, clerk, his proctor,¹ to Cubbington church, vacant by the death of Thomas,² the last rector, on Fri. 12 Oct. last; patrons, prior and convent of Kenilworth. Ind. him or his proctor: archd. Grove near Stevenage (*La Grave juxta Stevenasche*), 3 Jan. 1314.
[Margin] Nothing [for the fee].
  [¹⁻¹ Interlined.
  ² De Harewell, see **610**.]

651 Institution of M. William de Bourton, priest, to Priors Hardwick (*Herdewyk*) vicarage near Priors Marston (*Merston Prioris*), vacant by the death of Roger Bacoun, the last vicar, on Thurs. 17 Jan. last; patrons, prior and convent of Coventry. Ind. him or his proctor: archd. London, 1 Feb. 1314.
[Margin] He paid the fee.
  [The church had been appropriated to the prior and convent of Coventry by Bishop Meuland in 1260, and a vicarage ordained. The prior and convent exercised a peculiar jurisdiction in this parish and, although the bishop retained the right of institution, it apparently fell to the official of the peculiar to induct. The copy of this letter, and several others in the mid-fifteenth century, addressed the mandate to induct to the archdeacon of Coventry or his official, see R.N.Swanson, 'The priory in the later Middle Ages' in *Coventry's first cathedral. The cathedral and priory of St. Mary, Coventry: papers from the 1993 anniversary conference*, ed. G. Demidowicz (Stamford, 1994), 150–1; Hughes, 'Account roll', n. 23.]

652 Institution of Thomas de la Grave, priest, to the vicarage of Kingsbury church, vacant by the resignation of Nicholas, the last vicar, on Sun. 27 Jan. last; patrons, prioress and convent of Holy Trinity of the wood, Markyate. Ind.: archd. London, 8 Feb. 1314.
[Margin] He paid the fee.

653   Commission to M. Philip de Turvill', the bishop's official. From the report of trustworthy men it is evident that the rector of Baginton (*Bathekinton*)[1] labours with a grave illness and physical infirmity so that he requires the care of another person. The bishop wishes to provide suitable relief for the same and for his church. He is to summon the neighbouring clerks and laity before him to inquire into the circumstances of the same. If the inquiry and physical inspection find the rector inadequate for the rule of his church, he is to assign another suitable and circumspect man, of whom he has full trust, as his coadjutor. Eccleshall (*Eclishale*), 5 Mar. 1314.

[1 *e* interlined.]

654   [Fo. 38v] Letters patent to Thomas de Langeton, priest. Southam church has devolved to the bishop's collation this turn by lapse of time by the authority of the Lateran Council. Wishing to provide beneficially for the church and the cure of souls in it, the bishop collates him to the church, saving an annual pension of 30 marks [£20] to the dean and chapter of Lichfield due from of old, which [Thomas] has sworn to pay each year at the accustomed terms. Saving the right [etc.] of the churches of Coventry and Lichfield. London, 27 Nov. 1313.

[Duplication of **648**.]

655   Institution of Ralph de Derset, priest, to the vacant vicarage of Burton Dassett; patrons, prior and convent of Arbury and Sir John de Sudleye, kt. Ind.: archd. of Coventry. Grove (*La Grave*), 8 July 1314.

656   Licence, in common form, to Thomas de Napton, rector of Napton on the Hill, to study for one year from Michaelmas next. London, 8 July 1314.

657   Letters patent to M. Philip de Turvill', the bishop's official. He is to examine the business of the presentation of Stephen de Stocton, priest, to the vicarage of Chilvers Coton (*Chelverescote*) parish church by the prior and convent of St. Mary, Arbury, which is said to be vacant, and the presentee. If it was lawful, he is to admit and institute the same, receive [his] oath of residence and obedience in the bishop's name, issue letters of institution and induction, and do all other things which the business demands and requires, with power of coercion. York, 10 Sept. 1314. [1]The presentee has had the letter of inquiry under the same date.[1]

[1-1 Added later at the end of the entry by the hand which recorded the next two entries.]

658   Note that William de Shulton, clerk, presented to Baginton church by the prior and convent of Kenilworth, has had the letter of inquiry. The bishop has commissioned the prior of Arbury, his lieutenant, to admit and institute William[1] in the form noted above. Same place, day, and year.

[1 Instituted 20 Sept. 1314, see **660**.]

659   Licence to Conrad de Almania, rector of Fillongley (*Fylongelegh*), to be in the bishop of Worcester's service for two years. York, 25 Sept. 1314.

660 Licence to William de Shulton, acolyte, to study for two years from the date of his institution to Baginton church, *viz.* from 20 Sept., under the terms of the constitution of Pope Boniface VIII. York, 25 Sept. 1314.

661 [Fo. 39] Institution of William Wiltons, priest, to the vacant chapel of St. Alphegus of Solihull; patron, Ralph de Pepham. Ind.: archd. London, 22 Jan. 1315.

662 Institution of William de Wellesbourn', ¹in the person of Edmund de Gnousale, his proctor,¹ to Berkswell church, vacant by the resignation of John Dod, the last rector, on Fri. 3 Jan. last; patron, Guy de Beauchamp, earl of Warwick. Ind.: archd. London, 25 Jan. 1315.
   [¹⁻¹ Interlined.]

663 Note that letters [quoted] of Abbot William and the convent of St. Nicholas, Angers, were delivered to the bishop at London on 6 Feb. [1315] presenting Br. Peter Franciscus, their fellow-monk, to the bishop for the priorate and rule of Monks Kirby, which is free and vacant by the death of John, the late prior, supplicating humbly and devotedly that he might admit him to the same (dated and sealed at their monastery, Sat. 18 Jan. 1315). Having deliberated with his clerks, the bishop has admitted, instituted, and appointed Br. Peter prior of Monks Kirby, with no inquiry or any other process [having been made]. Ind.: Robert,¹ rector of Wappenbury.
   Note of letters patent [quoted] to Br. Peter Franciscus. He has been presented to the bishop for the vacant priorate of Monks Kirby by Br. William, the abbot, and the convent of St. Nicholas, Angers. The bishop admits and institutes him in the same, appointing him prior of the house with all its members, rights, and appurtenances. Saving the honour [etc.]. n.d.
   [¹ De Halughton, see **457**.]

664 Commission by letter [quoted] to Robert, rector of Wappenbury, to induct Br. Peter Franciscus prior of Monks Kirby, with all its members, rights, and appurtenances, declaring that the monks shall obey and be attentive to Br. Peter as prior. London, 7 Feb. 1315.

665 Note that [John]¹ de Pepering, subdeacon,² rector of Brinklow, has had a licence to study for one year under the terms of the constitution of [Pope] Boniface. Peterborough (*Burgum Sancti Petri*), 25 Feb. 1315.
   [¹ MS. *Willelmus*, see **614–617, 632**.
   ² Interlined.]

666 [Fo. 39v] Note of similar licence to William,¹ subdeacon, rector of Ratley (*Rottelegh*). Castle Ashby (*Ashebi David*), ²2 Mar.² 1315.
   [¹ De Clynton, see **621, 625**.
   ²⁻² Interlined.]

667 CONFIRMACIO PRIORIS DE ORDEBUR'. Letters patent to Br. William de Bloxham, prior of the conventual church of Arbury. Having considered his probity, and the fervour of his religion, for which the bishop has learnt he is remarkable in many ways, and wishing to make special grace to him because of this, he has ratified, as well as approved and confirmed his appointment to the priorate which M. Ralph de Leicestr', the bishop's former vicar-general, had made, which was then vacant and belonging to the bishop's provision, having devolved that turn by right. Brewood, 27 Mar. 1315.

668   Note that custody of the sequestration on Compton Verney (*Cumpton*) church has been committed to Adam de Herwynton, clerk, during pleasure. Mandate to the dean of Stoneleigh (*Stonlegh'*) or M. Richard de Norhampton, the bishop's sequestrator, to deliver custody to Adam or his proctor. Castle Ashby (*Assheby David*), 2 Aug. 1315.

669   Institution of Adam de Herwinton, priest, to Compton Verney church, vacant by the resignation of Thomas de Hamslepe, the [last] rector; patron, Guy de Beauchamp. Ind.: dean of Stoneleigh (*Stonleigh*). 7 Aug. 1315.
   [1]Note that this was registered according to the tenor of a schedule delivered to Robert de Weston at Coldham by Sir R. de Kembr'.[1]
   [[1-1] Added later.]

670   Institution of Henry de Keten', chaplain, to Leamington Priors (*Lemignton*) vicarage, vacant by the death of Roger de Wolwardinton on Sat. 16 Aug. last; patrons, prior and convent of Kenilworth. He swore to reside [etc.]. Coldham, 5 Sept. 1315.

671   Institution of Nicholas de Bredon, chaplain, to Clifton on Dunsmore (*Clifton super Donnesmor*) vicarage, vacant by the resignation of Simon Swift, the last vicar, on Thurs. 25 Sept. last; patrons, abbot and convent of [St. Mary] de Pratis, Leicester. He swore [etc.]. Ind.: dean of Marton (*Merton*). Grove (*Le Grove*), 17 Oct. 1315.

672   Commission to Abbot W[illiam][1] and John, the prior of Darley, jointly or separately. Thomas de Leycester has been presented to Clowne (*Cloune*) church[2] by the prior and convent of Worksop (*Wyrsop*), York dioc., the preferment of whom pleases the bishop. They are to admit and institute Thomas, or his proctor, to Clowne church, provided that the inquiry to be made with the bishop's authority concerning the vacancy shall decide sufficiently for the presenting and the said presentee, and nothing from the canons shall prevent his institution, doing all things required, with power of coercion. Penwortham, 8 Nov. 1315.
   [[1] William de Alsop, abbot 1287–1330, see *VCH Derbyshire*, ii.53.
   [2] In Derby archdeaconry.]

673   [Fo. 40] Institution of M. Henry de Kirkeby to Wappenbury church, vacant by the death of Robert de Halugton, the last rector, on Tues. 4 Nov.; patrons, prior and convent of Monks Kirby (*Kyrkeby Monachorum*). Ind.: archd. of Coventry. Wybunbury (*Wybbenbury*), 13 Dec 1315.

674   Institution of John, son of Richard de Pollesworth to Ansley (*Ansteleye*) vicarage, vacant by the death of Roger de Eton, the last vicar, on Sun.

18 Jan. last; patrons, abbess and convent of Polesworth. Ind.: official of Coventry. Bracebridge (*Bracebrugg'*), 20 Feb. 1316.

ANNO [MCCC]XVI.

675 Institution of Walter de Coventr', chaplain, to Weston under Wetherley vicarage near Wappenbury (*Weston juxta Wappenbur'*), vacant by the death of Thomas de Sutham on Mon.[1] 26 Apr.; patrons, prior and convent of Arbury (*Erdbur'*). Ind.: archd. of Coventry. Bishops Itchington, 28 May 1316.

[1 Interlined.]

676 Grant *in commendam* to M. Ellis de St. Albans,[1] priest, rector of Wethersfield (*Wetherisfeld*), London dioc., [2]who has only a single benefice,[2] of Stockton (*Stokton*) church for half a year. Offord Cluny (*Offord*), 17 July 1316.

[1 *BRUO*, iii.1623 notes he was rector of Withersfield, Suffolk.
[2-2] Interlined.]

677 Institution of Roger de Boyvill', chaplain, to Wootton (*Wotton*) vicarage, vacant by the death of Thomas de Coleshull, the last vicar, on Fri. 27 Aug.; patrons, prior and convent of Kenilworth. Ind.: archd. of Coventry. London,[1] 12 Sept. 1316.

[1 Interlined.]

678 Institution of Thomas Betoun of Snitterfield (*Sniterefeld*), chaplain, to Avon Dassett (*Avenederset*) church, vacant by the death of John de Lappeworth, the last rector, on 14 Aug.; patron, Walter de Cantilupo. Ind.: archd. of Coventry. London, 20 Oct. 1316.

679 Institution of John de Persore, chaplain, to Newnham (*Nonham*) vicarage; patrons, prior and convent of Kenilworth. Ind.: archd. of Coventry. 12 Oct. 1316.

680 Institution of M. William de Stonleye to Kenilworth vicarage, vacant by the resignation of Roger de Boyvill' on Fri. 10 Sept.; patrons, prior and convent of Kenilworth. Ind.: archd. of Coventry. Coldham, 14 Feb. 1317.

[Fo. 40v] ANNUS DOMINI :MILLESIMUS :CCC:XVII[us]:

681 Licence to William de Shulton, rector of Baginton, to study for two years from Michaelmas last under the terms of the constitution *Cum ex eo*. 8 Apr. 1317.

682 Grant *in commendam* to Adam de Lymbergh, priest, of Berkswell church. Ind.: archd. of Coventry. London, 18 Apr. 1317.

683 Institution of John de Hovygham, chaplain, to Marton (*Merton*) vicarage; patrons, prioress and convent of Nuneaton. Ind.: archd. of Coventry. London, 16 May 1317.

684   Institution of John Wylimot, chaplain, to Monks Kirby vicarage; patrons, prior and convent of Monks Kirby. Ind.: archd. of Coventry. 22 May 1317.

685   Commission to M. Nicholas de Guthmundele, rector of St. Martin's, Trimley (*Tremele*), Norwich dioc. He is to examine the business of the presentation of Peter de Hertle, clerk, to Stockton church. If Peter is found suitable, and the other circumstances of the business are clear to him, he or another person shall admit, institute, and induct him in the same, with power of coercion. London, ¹19 May 1317¹.
   Note of P[eter]'s institution to Stockton church by the said M. Nicholas; patrons, prior and convent of Hertford (*Herteford*). Ind.: archd. of Coventry.
   [¹⁻¹ Interlined later.
   The rest of the folio is blank.]

[Fo. 41] STAFFORD'.
   [Underlined.]

REGISTRUM ARCHIDIACONATUS STAFFORD' A FESTO SANCTE TRINITATIS ANNO DOMINI
.MILLESIMO .CCC^mo. SEPTIMO ET CONSECRACIONIS W[ALTERI]. DE LANGETON COV-
ENTR' ET LYCH' EPISCOPI UNDECIMO.

686   Note that the inquiry held concerning the vacancy of Colton church, and the character and status of William de Nostrefeld, presented to the same, has said itself to have no knowledge of the orders of the presented, whether he is free and of legitimate birth, or beneficed elsewhere. The same presentee has shown letters testimonial of his orders before M. G[eoffrey] de Blaston and John de Chagele, clerks, which testify that he has been ordained priest.¹ The same presentee has proved before them by trustworthy witnesses, who agreed in their depositions in all things, that he was certainly born of a lawful marriage, and the said witnesses were examined at London in the bishop's house on 3 June 1307².
   [¹ His name does not appear in the ordination lists.
   ² *Septimo* interlined over an erasure.]

687   Note that on 3 June 1307 the same presentee was instituted to Colton church; patron, Lady Hawise le Mareschall. [The church] was vacant by the resignation by letter [quoted] of Thomas de Bradewell, the last rector, sealed with his seal and, because this was unknown to many people, the seal of the official of Norwich (dated Norwich, Fri. 10 Feb. 1307).
   [Margin] He paid the fee.

688   PRO PROVISIONE PRECENTORIS. Letters patent to the dean and chapter of Lichfield. Raymond [de Got], cardinal deacon of the most holy Roman church, has accepted the precentorship of Lichfield church, with the prebend [of Bishops Itchington] annexed to it,¹ which is vacant by the death of M. Thomas de Adberbury, the former precentor, by reason of a provision made to him in the bishop's church of Lichfield by Pope Clement V. He has occupied it by proctor within a month of the vacancy occurring, as is more fully contained in a public instrument made thereon and shown to the bishop. Having ratified and accepted the said acceptance, the bishop has admitted him to the precentorship by proxy. Mandate to induct the proctor in Raymond's name, having presented sufficient mandate for this, to the precentorship with all its rights [etc.], assigning the stall [etc.]. London, 5 July 1307.

[¹ *Fasti*, x.7.]

689 [Fo. 41v] COLLACIO THESAURIATO ECCLESIE LICH'. Letters patent to Thomas de Nevill'. Considering his probity, and the labours and duties he has provided and proposes to provide in future for the bishop's church at Lichfield, the bishop considers him honest and honourable. He collates to him the treasurership of Lichfield church, vacant by the death of M. Alan le Bretoun, the former treasurer, with all its members [etc.], and invests him in the same by his ring, declaring that by this collation he does not intend to derogate the right of Pope Clement V, or the collation made by the same, which can lawfully remain. London, 12 Nov. 1306.

[See **274**.]

690 Mandate to the dean and chapter of Lichfield to induct Nevill' or his proctor, declaring [as in **689**]. London, 12 Nov. 1306.

691 Institution of John de Tok', priest, to Grindon (*Grendon*) church; patron, Alan de Audeleye, as the inquiry has said. Ind.: official of Stafford. Ripon (*Rypon*), 31 July 1307.
[Margin] He paid the fee.

REGISTRUM POST EGRESSUM EPISCOPI A CARCERE ANNO DOMINI [M]CCC^{mo}.VIII. [9 NOV. 1308].
[Underlined.]

692 Licence, in common form, to M. John le Brabazon,¹ priest, rector of Wolstanton, to study for three years from 29 Dec. 1308. London, same date.

[¹ *BRUO*, ii.1117; *CPL*, ii.119, 139, 169, 337, 158, 161.]

693 CONFIRMACIO PRIORIS DE STONE. Letters patent to the prior and convent of Kenilworth. The priory of Stone has recently been deprived of a pastor by the death of Br. Thomas de Mulewych, the late prior. The subprior and convent sought and obtained a licence to elect a prior from them, the patrons. [fo. 42] They have elected unanimously their subprior, Br. John de Attelberge, prior, and have presented the election to the bishop by their letters and suitable proctors. Having examined the election, the bishop has found notable and substantial defects in its form. He has annulled it. Having compassion for their innocence, lest the priory should suffer damage or loss in spiritualities and temporalities by reason of a long vacancy, the bishop has provided the same Br. John de Attelberge prior as an act of special grace, having found him suitable in learning and other respects, understanding him to be circumspect and diligent in the administration of the temporalities of the priory. They are to deliver any seized temporalities belonging to Stone Priory which are in their hands on account of the vacancy to Br. John as prior and pastor, without trouble or delay. London, 23 Feb. 1309.

694   Letters patent to the archdeacon of Stafford. The election recently made by the canons of Stone Priory of their subprior, Br. John de Attelberge, as prior of the same has been presented to the bishop. Having examined it with his council, he has found it defective. He has therefore annulled it and provided John prior [as in **693**]. Mandate to install the said Br. John prior, and to cause him to have possession of all spiritualities and temporalities pertaining to the said priory by the obedientaries of the same. London, 23 Feb. 1309.

695   Letters patent to the convent of Stone Priory. Their election of Br. John de Attelberge, their subprior, as their prior, presented to the bishop, has been examined by him and his council. He has found it defective. He has therefore annulled it and provided the same John prior. Mandate to admit John as their prior, and obey him in all things. [London, 23 Feb. 1309.]
    [The rest of the recto is blank.]

696   [Fo. 42v] Institution of William de Wolvardele, subdeacon, to Quatt church, vacant by the resignation of Richard de Brustollia, the last rector, on Thurs. 28 Nov. last; patrons, prior and convent of Great Malvern. Ind.: archd. Greenford near London (*Greneford juxta London*), 20 Mar. 1309.
[Margin] He paid $\frac{1}{2}$ mark.

697   Letters dimissory to Ellis de Mere, subdeacon, for the order of deacon, in common form, with the addition of this clause: provided that he will have shown sufficient title to his ordainer. London, 30 Apr. 1309.

698   Letters dimissory, in common form, to Robert de Inguarby, subdeacon,[1] rector of Kingsley (*Kingesleye*), for the orders of deacon and priest. London, 1 May 1309.
    [1 Interlined.]

699   Letters dimissory to John de Tybinton, deacon, for the order of priest, in common form, with the addition of this clause [as in **697**]. London, 7 May 1309.

700   Letters patent to M. Andrew de Janna, rector of Forton. He has obtained a prebend in Wolverhampton (*Wolverhamton*) church, in which the bishop understands the charges of residence and expenses are sometimes incumbent on him. He is granted licence to be absent from Forton church for one year from the date of these letters, meanwhile receiving wholly its fruits and, if he personally resides in it, to farm the church to another suitable person, provided that the church is not defrauded of duties [etc.]. London, 9 May 1309.

REGISTRUM ARCHIDIACONI CESTR' VICARII EPISCOPI.
    [**701**, **702** only.]

701   Institution of Br. Thomas de Hales,[1] canon of Halesowen (*Hales'*) Abbey, priest, to Walsall (*Waleshale*) vicarage, vacant by the death of Br. Geoffrey, the last vicar, on Wed. 30 Apr.; patrons, abbot and convent of Halesowen. Ind.: archd. Bowden (*Boudon*), 10 June 1309.
    [1 Thomas Campion in **771**.]

702 Letters patent of R[obert] de Redeswell, archdeacon of Chester, vicar-general. With the bishop's authority he has collated to M. Philip de Turville the prebend and canonry of Curborough,[1] vacant by the resignation of M. John Popard. Davenham, 4 July 1309.

Mandate to the dean and chapter of Lichfield [fo.43] to induct [letter quoted]. Dated as above.

[¹ *Fasti*, x.27.]

703 Institution of William le Bordeleys, priest, to Hanbury (*Hambury*) church, vacant by the resignation of William de Billenia, the last rector; patron, Thomas, earl of Lancaster. Ind.: archd. Ranton, 29 Oct. 1309.

[Margin] Nothing for the fee.

704 Institution of Thomas de Weston, acolyte, to Weston under Lizard (*Weston subtus Brewod*) church, vacant by the resignation of John de Stretton, the last rector, on Sun. 31 Aug.; patron; John de Weston subtus Brewod. Ind.: archd. of Stafford. Ranton, 13 Nov. 1309.

[Margin] He paid the fee.

705 To the dean and chapter [of Lichfield]. Wishing reverently to obey a papal mandate directed to him, the bishop has admitted Bruno de Pedio, proctor of Tydo de Waresio, to the prebend of Whittington and Berkswich (*Berkeswyz*),[1] according to the terms, force, and effect of the mandate, saving the right of all. Mandate to do all that is [required] of them in this matter. Ranton, 23 Nov. 1309.

[¹ *Fasti*, x.67.]

706 Institution of Thomas de Boterwyk, priest, to Worfield (*Worfeld*) church, vacant by the resignation of John de Benstede, the last rector; patron, King E[dward II].[1] Ind.: archd. Tamworth, 14 Mar. 1310.

²Licence to travel overseas from 21 June 1310 to Easter next following.²

[¹ *CPR 1307–13*, 212.
²⁻² Interlined later, duplicating **710**; Boterwyk went to Gascony with John of Brittany, earl of Richmond, in the king's service, see *CPR 1307–13*, 325.]

707 Note that in the presence of the bishop in his chamber at Lichfield probate of Richard Dun of Tamworth's will and the administration of his goods was granted to Margery Dun, his wife, William Symon, and John de Bollehull, his executors. 23 Apr. 1310.

708* [Fo. 43v] Letters patent to John called Wille of Uttoxeter, acolyte. The bishop has received his petition that whereas he secretly received the order of acolyte in innocence some time ago, being ignorant of canonical sanctions, the bishop should compassionately consider granting him dispensation to serve in the order and rise to higher orders. Having imposed salutary penance, the bishop grants dispensation that he might serve lawfully in the same order so secretly received, and rise to higher orders, provided that he will not have been prohibited under threat of excommunication by the bishop, any archdeacon, or other of his ministers, or that other canon law will not obstruct him; provided that he will faithfully complete the penance imposed on him by the bishop, and not transgress in a like manner whenever he rises to higher orders. Lichfield, 1 Apr. 1310.

709 Commission to the official of Stafford. He is to keep the sequestration recently placed on the ecclesiastical goods belonging to Swynnerton church by the bishop for just and legal reasons, act and ordain concerning the same at his discretion, with power of coercion, during pleasure. Duties in the church meanwhile shall not be neglected [etc.], and he shall render an account of his administration. Lichfield, 1 May 1310.

710 Licence to Thomas de Boterwyk, rector of Worfield, to travel overseas until Easter next. Lichfield, 21 June 1310.
    [See **706**, n. 2.]

711 Letters patent to William Meverel, priest, vicar of Colwich (*Colewych*) church. Being favourably inclined to his prayers, and at the supplication of Br. Roland Joorum, O.P., the bishop grants him licence to be in the service of Father T[homas Jorz],[1] cardinal priest of St. Sabina (*Sabine*), until the Nativity of St. John the Baptist next. Meanwhile he will not be troubled regarding his non-residence by the bishop or his ministers, provided that his vicarage is not defrauded of duties and the cure of souls neglected. London, 26 Sept. 1310.
    [[1] *BRUO*, ii.1023.]

712 Institution of Stephen de Hungerford, deacon, to Uttoxeter (*Ottokeshare*) vicarage, vacant by the death of William de Longedon, the last vicar, on 20 July last; patron, John de Hungerford, rector of Uttoxeter (*Huttokeshare*). Ind.: archd. 20 Oct. 1310.
[Margin] He paid the fee.

713 [Fo. 44] Institution of Hugh de Babynton, priest, to the deanery of Tamworth collegiate church, vacant by the resignation of Walter de Bedewynde, the last dean, on 1 Oct. 1310; patron, Sir Alexander de Frevill', kt. Ind.: archd. Lichfield, 15 Nov. 1310.
[Margin] He paid the fee.

714 Note that custody of the sequestration on Sandon (*Sondon*) vicarage has been committed to John Borard, priest, during pleasure. Ind. him or his proctor: archd. Lichfield, 23 Jan. 1311.

715 Licence to Thomas de Weston, subdeacon, rector of Weston under Lizard, to study for one year under the terms of the constitution of Pope Boniface VIII. He is to distribute 40s. among the poor of his parish before Easter next. M. Richard de Norhampt[on][1] will perform this. [Lichfield] 23 Jan. 1311.
    [[1] The sequestrator-general.]

716 Institution of Thomas, son of Adam de Brymton, kt., acolyte, to Water Eaton church, vacant by the resignation of Hugh de Hottot, the last rector, on 27 Nov. [1310]; patrons, abbess and nuns of Polesworth. Touching the holy gospels in the bishop's presence Thomas swore to pay an annual pension of 20 marks [£13 6s. 8d.] to the said religious. Ind.: archd. [Lichfield] 26 Jan. 1311.

¹Licence to study for one year under the terms of the constitution of [Pope] Boniface, and to farm his church for one year. Chesterfield . . .² 1311.¹

[Margin] He owes the fee.

   [¹⁻¹ Interlined later.
   ² Abraded.]

717   Licence to Robert de Esenyngton that he might have an oratory in his house at Essington (*Esenyngton*), and cause divine service to be celebrated there for one year, provided that no prejudice will be caused to the mother church of the place by this. Lichfield, 2 Feb. 1311.

718   Collation to M. William de Bosco,¹ rector of Harrow (*Harewe*), London dioc., of the chancellorship of Lichfield church, with the prebend [of Alrewas] annexed to the same, vacant by the death of M. Luke de Ely, the last chancellor.² Ind.: dean and chapter [of Lichfield], assigning the stall [etc.]. Lichfield, 8 Dec. 1310.

   [Duplicated, see **720**.
   ¹ *BRUO*, i.239.
   ² Emend *Fasti*, x.9, which gives the date of William's collation as 26 Nov. 1310.]

719*   Commission to M. Geoffrey de Blaston, the bishop's commissary-general. He is to admit probate of the wills of the deceased of the diocese whose goods do not exceed £30; to grant to the executors of the deceased free administration of these goods; to audit the executors' accounts; to grant and make letters of acquittance, and to do all [fo. 44v] that is required, with power of coercion. Lichfield, 3 Feb. 1311.

   Note of similar commission to M. Richard de Norh[amp]t[on].¹ Commission to each dean of the archdeaconries of Coventry, Stafford, Derby, and Shrewsbury that they might admit probate of the wills of the deceased in their jurisdictions under 100s. and grant to the executors free administration of their goods. Note of similar grant to Robert de Donechirch, vicar of Lichfield, up to 40s., with an additional clause enabling him to audit the accounts of the executors for these goods.

   [¹ The sequestrator-general.]

720   [Fo. 44] ¹Grant *in commendam* to M. William de Bosco, rector of Harrow, of the chancellorship of Lichfield church with the prebend [of Alrewas] annexed to the same. ²8 Dec. 1310.² 13 Apr. 1311, York.¹

   [¹⁻¹ Added at the foot of fo. 44, cutting in two **719***.
   ²⁻² Interlined; the entry gives both dates, but **718** records William was collated to the chancellorship on 8 Dec. 1310.]

[Fo. 44v] INCIPIT ANNUS DOMINI M^{us}.CCC^{mus} XI^{us}.

721 Collation to John de Berewyco,[1] priest, of Sandon vicarage, which has devolved to the bishop by lapse of time by authority of the Lateran Council. Ind.: John de Cotes, the bishop's clerk. York, 24 Apr. 1311.[2]
[Margin] Nothing for the fee.
    [[1] *DNB*, ii.335.
    [2] Interlined over *predicto* deleted.]

722 Institution of Br. John de Melewych, canon of Ranton, to Seighford (*Cesteford*) vicarage, vacant by the resignation of John de Brugg', the last vicar, on Thurs. 4 Mar. 1311. Ind.: archd. of Stafford. York, 24 May 1311.
[Margin] Nothing [for the fee].

723 Grant *in commendam* to Richard de la Chambre, priest, of Bradley church, who has a only single benefice with cure of souls; patrons, Sir Thomas de Pype, kt., and Margaret, his wife. Ind.: archd. York, 13 June 1311.

724 Institution of Henry le Notte of Solihull, acolyte, to the prebend of Wigginton and Comberford (*Wygynton et Cumberford*) in Tamworth collegiate church, vacant by the death of Ralph de Hengham, the last prebendary, on Wed. 19 May last; patron, Sir Ralph le Botiller, kt. Ind.: archd., assigning the stall [etc. York] 18 June 1311.
[Margin] He owes the fee.
    [See Hughes, 'Clergy list', 8–9, 16.]

725 Institution of Br. John de Leicestr', canon of Kenilworth, as prior of the cell of Calwich (*Calewych*); patrons, prior and convent of Kenilworth. Ind.: archd. This institution was approved with no inquiry [having been made], because other [institutions] have usually been made thus. York, 30 June 1311.

726* Commission to the prior of Repton and M. Adam Byrom, the official of Stafford. The bishop is outside his diocese for pressing reasons.[1] They are to collate by exchange to John de Kynardesleye, rector of Tatenhill, whichever prebend in Lichfield church becomes vacant within 15 days from the receipt of these letters,[2] accept resignations, grant letters of inquiry to a suitable person to be presented to Tatenhill church, and to institute and induct [him], and do all that is required, with power of coercion. The bishop does not intend to derogate in any way the papal provisions pending in Lichfield church. York, 5 July 1311.
    [[1] Langton was held prisoner at York by this date, see the introduction p. xxxiv.
    [2] There is no record in the register of John being instituted to a prebend, but he occurs as prebendary of Eccleshall on 3 Dec. 1319. He resigned this about 14 Apr. 1322 when granted the prebend of Flixton. He received Tatenhill church *in commendam* on 1 Jan. 1312. On 10 Apr. 1319 it was noted that he had been the last incumbent there, but it was vacant on 16 Jan. 1319, see *Fasti*, x.34, 37, 46; *MRA*, nos. 571, 575, 577; **735, 1261**; Hughes, 'Clergy list', 10, 18.]

727 [Fo. 45] Licence to M. Jordan de Canvill', priest, rector of Clifton Campville (*Clifton Canvill'*), to study for two years at university in England or overseas from Michaelmas next, provided that the church [etc.]. London, 15 Sept. 1311.

728 Commission to the archdeacon of Chester. The business of the election of Br. Roger de Aston, recently celebrated in Gresley (*Greseleye*) Priory, should proceed. He is to examine, confirm, or annul the election, and if there are any objections to the person elected to hear them and determine if they are just. If he invalidates the election as defective, and not because of the person's failings, he is to appoint Br. Roger prior of the house, and do all that is required, with power of coercion. York . . .¹ [1311].

Note of similar commission to the dean of Lichfield. Same date.

[¹ Blank space.]

729 Institution of John de Caldecote, priest, to Elford (*Elleford*) church, vacant by the death of John de Pollesworth,¹ the last rector, on Tues. 7 Sept.; patron, Sir John de Ardena, kt. Ind.: archd. of Stafford. London, 25 Sept. 1311.

[Margin] He paid the fee.

[¹ Instituted during the vacancy of the see before 21 Sept. 1296 by Archbishop Winchelsey, see *Reg. Winchelsey*, ii.912.]

730 [Duplication of **723**.]

731 Institution of Richard de la Chambre, priest, to Bradley church, vacant by the death of Ralph de Heyngham, the last rector, on 19 May last; patrons, Sir Thomas de Pype, kt., and Margaret, his wife. Ind.: archd. London, 19 Nov. 1311.

[Margin] Nothing for the fee.

[The rest of the recto is blank.]

732 [Fo. 45v] Institution of Henry de Lich', priest, to the prebend of Bonehill (*Bollenhull*) in Tamworth collegiate church, vacant by the death M. Robert de Pycheford, the last prebendary, on Wed. 27 Oct. last; patron, Sir Alexander de Frevill', kt. Ind.: archd. London, 22 Nov. 1311.

[Margin] He paid the fee.

ANNUS CONSECRACIONIS .W[ALTERI]. COVENTR' ET LICH' EPISCOPI .XVI^{us}.

733 Licence to Thomas de Boterwyk, rector of Worfield, to study for one year. 7 Dec. 1311.

734 Collation to Richard Abel, son of Sir John Abel, kt., of the prebend of Bishopshull (*Byshopeshull*) in Lichfield church,¹ with all its members [etc.]. Ind. him or his proctor: dean and chapter of Lichfield, assigning the stall [etc.]. Lichfield, 29 Dec. 1311.

[¹ *Fasti*, x.21.]

735   Grant *in commendam* to John de Kynardeseye, priest, of Tatenhill church, for the benefit of that church. Ind.: archd. Lichfield, 1 Jan. 1312.

736   Institution of James de Dalby Paynel, priest, to Alton (*Alveton*) vicarage, vacant by the death on 28 Dec. of Henry de Boyfeld, who last held the same; patrons, abbot and convent of Croxden (*Crokesden'*). Ind.: archd. York, 21 Feb. 1312.
[Margin] He paid the fee.

ANNUS DOMINI MILLESIMUS .CCC^{mus}. DUODECIMUS INCIPIT.

737   Institution of William de Tene, priest, to Swynnerton church; patron, Sir Roger de Swynnerton, kt. Ind.: archd. Brington (*Bruynton*), 30 Mar. 1312.
[Margin] He owes the fee.

738   Note that Br. Richard de Keten, canon of Kenilworth, has been admitted to the keepership or rule of the cell of Calwich, and instituted prior of the same, without inquiry; patrons, prior and convent of Kenilworth. Ind.: archd. Same day and place.

739   Note that the bishop has collated to Robert de Clipston, clerk, the prebend ¹of Stotfold¹ in Lichfield church which was John de Berewyk's, declaring that by this his collation he does not intend to derogate the right of Pope Clement V, or the collation made by him. Ind. him or his proctor: dean and chapter of Lichfield. Pont de Sorgue (*Pontem Sorbi*) [France], 19 Sept. 1312.
   [¹⁻¹ Interlined. *Fasti*, x.55.]

[Fo. 46] ANNUS DOMINI MILLESIMUS .CCC^{mus}. XII^{us}.

ANNUS .W[ALTERI]. EPISCOPI .XVII.

740   Note of like collation to Henry de Bluntesdon, priest, of the vacant prebend of Gaia Major (*Gaye Majoris*) in Lichfield church.¹ Ind. him or his proctor: dean and chapter of Lichfield. Pont de Sorgue (*Pontem Sorby*), 17 Jan. 1313.
   [¹ *Fasti*, x.40.]

ANNO DOMINI M^{o}.CCC^{mo}.XIII° INCIPIENTE.

741   Collation to Robert de Clipston, clerk, of the prebend of Handsacre (*Handesacr'*) in Lichfield church,¹ vacant by the death of William de Blyburgh,² the last prebendary. The bishop invested the same by his ring, declaring [as in **739**]. Ind.: dean and chapter of Lichfield. Avignon (*Avinion*), 3 Mar. 1313.
   [¹ *Fasti*, x.43.
   ² *CPR 1292–1301*, 181.]

742 Note of like collation to M. Ralph de Leicestr', D.C.L, of the vacant prebend of Stotfold in Lichfield church.[1] Ind.: dean [and chapter of Lichfield]. Hackington without Canterbury (*Hakinton extra Cantuar'*), 10 July 1313.

[[1] *Fasti*, x.55.]

743 The Benedictine priory of Farewell being vacant by the death of Annabel, the last prioress, on Thurs. 2 Aug. 1313, the nuns have sought a licence to elect a suitable prioress from the bishop. They have elected Iseult de Pype[1] prioress, who came in person to the bishop humbly seeking him to admit her as prioress. Being outside his diocese at that time, hindered by various business, the bishop has commissioned . . .[2] the chancellor of Lichfield church[3] [letter quoted] to examine Iseult de Pype in all matters, and to confirm the election if she is found suitable and worthy, as the right or custom of that monastery has been respected till now. Northampton, 20 Aug. 1313.

[[1] *VCH Staffordshire*, ii.225.
[2] A drawn line measuring 3.5cm.
[3] M. William de Bosco, see **718, 720**.]

744 Licence, in common form, to M. John le Brabanzon, priest, rector of Wolstanton, to study for one year. London, 4 Oct. 1313.

745 Note of similar licence for Thomas de Boterwyk, rector of Worfield. London, 23 Oct. 1313.

746 Collation to M. Robert de Patrica,[1] clerk, of the prebend of Pipa Parva (*Parva Pype*) in Lichfield church,[2] vacant by the resignation of M. Philip de Barton,[3] archdeacon of Surrey (*Surreye*), the last prebendary. Ind.: dean and chapter of Lichfield. London, 26 Oct. 1313.

[[1] *BRUO*, iii.1434–5.
[2] *Fasti*, x.49–50.
[3] *BRUO*, i.122.]

747 [Fo. 46v] Institution of Robert de Waddeworth, priest, to the vacant vicarage of Sandon; patrons, abbot and convent of Combermere. Ind. him or his proctor: archd. London, 26 Dec. 1313.
[Margin] He paid the fee.

748 Collation to Robert de Clypston, clerk, of the prebend in Gnosall collegiate church which was William de Seukesworth's, vacant by William's death. Ind. him or his proctor: rector of Haughton (*Halghton*)[1] . . ., assigning the stall [etc.]. London, 7 Feb. 1314.

[[1] Over an erasure. Followed by a drawn line measuring 3.5cm.]

749 Institution of Thurstan, son of William de Hiland, acolyte, in the person of William de Wyrkesworth, his proctor, to Hanbury (*Hambur'*) church, vacant by the death of William Bordeleys, the last rector, on 6 Jan. last; patron, Thomas, earl of Lancaster and Leicester, steward of England. Ind. him or his proctor: archd. London, 8 Feb. 1314.
[Margin] Nothing for the fee.

INCIPIT ANNUS DOMINI M^{us}.CCC^{mus}. QUARTUSDECIMUS.

750 Note that custody of the sequestrated portion which was Roland [de Viquiria's][1] in Wroxeter church has been committed to John, son of Roger de Cheyny, acolyte, during pleasure. The bishop wishes John to render a faithful account of the fruits and revenues of that portion. Mandate to M. Richard de Norhampt[on], the bishop's sequestrator-general, to deliver custody. Bishops Itchington, 5 June 1314.

    [[1] See **335, 972, 991.**]

751 Licence to Thomas, rector of Weston under Lizard, deacon,[1] to study from the time of his institution to 2 Mar. next under the terms of the constitution. Lichfield, 15 June 1314.

    [Thomas de Weston was instituted rector on 13 Nov. 1309, but he received a licence to study for one year on 23 Jan. 1311, see **704, 715.**
    [1] Interlined.]

752 Institution of William de Hodinet, priest, to Lapley (*Lappelegh*) vicarage; patron, Br. John, prior of Lapley. Ind.: archd. of Stafford. Great Haywood (*Hewode*), 14 June 1314.
[Margin] He paid the fee.

753 Institution of William de Alvereston, priest, to Kingswinford (*Swyneford Regis*) church; patron, Sir John de Somery, kt. Ind.: archd. Lichfield, 18 June 1314.
[Margin] Nothing for the fee.

754* [Fo. 47] Letters patent to Sir William de Bereford, kt., the king's justice.[1] His fervent devotion for religion is unavoidably impeded because he is sometimes apprehensive to ride to his parish church of Sutton Coldfield. He is granted licence to have an oratory at his manor of Langley in the said parish [and] to cause divine service to be celebrated [there] at his pleasure, provided that the rights and income of the parish church shall not be diminished. London, 9 July 1314.

    [[1] Chief Justice of Common Pleas 1309–26, see Foss, *Judges*, 55, 234–7; *DNB*, ii.324–5.]

755 Institution of Walter Hubert, priest, to Sedgley (*Seggeslegh*) vicarage; patrons, prior and convent of Dudley (*Duddelegh*). Ind.: archd. London, 15 July 1314.
[Margin] He owes the fee. He paid.

756 Note that M. James de Yspania[1] resigned his prebend of Wolvey in Lichfield church[2] to the bishop in the presence of M. Gilbert de Bruera, clerk, M. Nicholas de Gudmondele and Richard de Norton, notaries public. Immediately afterwards the bishop collated the prebend to M. Gilbert de Bruera and invested him by his ring. Ind. Gilbert or his proctor: dean and chapter of Lichfield, assigning the stall [etc.]. London, the bishop's manse, 27 Oct. 1314.

[¹ *BRUO*, iii.1736–8.
² *Fasti*, x.68.]

757* Commission to M. Philip de Turvill', canon of Lichfield, appointing him official to hear all *ex officio* or instance causes belonging to the bishop's jurisdiction; also to correct and punish the offences of subjects, with power of coercion. London, 22 Nov. 1313.

758 [Fo. 47v] Collation to Robert de Harewedon, clerk, of the prebend of Darnford in Lichfield church,¹ vacant by the resignation of William de Brikhull, the last prebendary. Ind. him or his proctor: dean and chapter of Lichfield. Lichfield, 24 Mar. 1315.
[Margin] The letters remain in the possession of [the bishop].

[¹ *Fasti*, x.32.]

759 Collation to William de Brikhull, clerk, of the prebend of Gaia Major,¹ vacant by the death of Henry de Blontesdon called le Aumoigner [almoner]. Ind. him or his proctor: dean and chapter of Lichfield. Same day and year.
[Margin] The letters remain in the possession of the official.

[¹ *Fasti*, x.40.]

760 Collation to Philip de Turvill' of the vacant prebend of Colwich in Lichfield church.¹ Ind.: dean and chapter of Lichfield. Brewood, 27 Mar. 1315.
[Margin] The letters remain in the possession of the same [official], but secretly (*set latenter*).

[¹ *Fasti*, x.24–5.]

761 Licence, in common form, to Thomas de Boterwyk, rector of Worfield, to study for one year. Lichfield, 23 Dec. 1314.

762 Grant *in commendam* to William de Astebury, priest, of the vacant vicarage of Alstonfield (*Alstanesfeld*); patrons, abbot and convent of Combermere. 6 June 1315.

763 Institution of John Iwyn of Tean (*Tene*), priest, to Leek (*Lek'*) vicarage, vacant by the death of Thomas de Aula, the last vicar, on Sun. 15 June last; patrons, abbot and convent of Dieulacres. Ind.: archd. Lichfield, 3 July 1315.

764 Institution of William Cornet, priest, to Sandon vicarage, vacant by the resignation of John de la Avurum; patrons, abbot and convent of Combermere. Ind.: archd. of Stafford. 31 July 1315.
[Margin] He paid the fee.

765 [A cancelled copy of **896**.]

766 Collation to Robert de Harwedon of the prebend Flixton in Lichfield church which was M. Roger de Martivall's.[1] Ind. him or his proctor: dean and chapter of Lichfield. Weston near Stanford (*Weston juxta Stanford*), 29 Sept. 1315.

[1 Vacant by his promotion to the bishopric of Salisbury. Consecrated 28 Sept. 1315, see *Fasti*, iii.1; *ibid.* x.36.]

767 Faculty to M. Philip de Turvill' to admit and institute William de Astebur', chaplain, to Alstonfield (*Austanesfeld*) vicarage. Vale Royal, 28 Oct. 1315.

768 [Fo. 48] Collation to Robert de Clipston, canon of Lichfield, of Penn (*Penne*) church, which is vacant and belonging to the bishop's collation by episcopal right. Afterwards, a certain Henry de Bischebur', alleging that he was patron of that church, presented to the same . . .[1] Coleshill (*Coleshull*), 23 Oct. 1315.

[1 Unfinished, followed by six blank lines.]

769 Institution of Philip de Mardewell, chaplain, to the vacant vicarage of Milwich (*Melewych*), vacant by the resignation of Richard Nonynton on Sun. 26 Oct.;[1] patrons, prior and convent of Stone. He swore [to reside]. Ind. him or his proctor: archd. of Stafford. Eccleshall, 7 Nov. 1315.

[1 A fragment of a sequestrator-general's account roll, LJRO MS. D30 M7r, confirms that the vicarage became vacant on 26 Oct. 1315, but it records a vacancy of fifteen days. The bishop received 8d. from this sequestration.]

770 Dispensation for R[ichard Waleys], rector of Walton upon Trent, priest, to remain in the schools for one year from 1 Nov. last. Eccleshall, 10 Nov. 1315.

[Walton upon Trent (Derb.) is on the present day county border with Staffordshire; previous entries (**272**, **563**) have been registered under Derby archdeaconry, but see **1272**, also in Stafford archdeaconry.]

771 Institution of Br. Henry de Derham, monk of Halesowen, to Walsall (*Walshal*) vicarage by virtue of the privilege which the abbot and convent of the same place have obtained in this regard, and before an inquiry has been held concerning the vacancy; patrons, the said religious. The vicarage was vacant by the resignation of Br. Thomas Campion, the last vicar. Ind.: archd. of Stafford. Eccleshall, 22 Dec. 1315.

[See Hughes, 'Clergy list', 6, 14–15.]

772 Institution of John de Kemesey, priest, to Alton vicarage, vacant because James Paynel, the last vicar, was instituted to Whitwell (*Wytewell*) church;[1] patrons, abbot and convent of Croxden. He swore to reside. Ind.: archd. of Stafford. Sandwell, 7 Mar. 1316.

[1 On 2 Feb. 1316, see **1078**. However, a fragment of a sequestrator-general's account roll, LJRO MS. D30 M7r, records that Alton vicarage became vacant on Fri. after the feast of St. Mary (?6 Feb. 1316) and remained so until Mon. before the feast of St. Gregory (8 Mar. 1316), and that the bishop received nothing from this vacancy as the income was needed to pay a chaplain; see also Hughes, 'Episcopate', i.182.]

773 Note that M. Philip de Turvill' has been appointed coadjutor to the rector of Lullington (*Lullynton*) who has impaired eyesight. Packington, 27 Mar. 1316.

774 Institution of Robert de Holedene, the earl of Lancaster's clerk, in the person of M. Ralph de Houghton, his proctor, to Rolleston church, vacant by the death of Robert de Staundon, the last rector, on Thurs. 11 Mar. last; patron, the said earl. Ind.: archd. of Stafford. Arlesey (*Alricheseye*), 20 May 1316.

775 Institution of Thomas de Freford to Elford church, vacant by the death of John de Caldecote, the last rector, on Sat. 7 Aug. last; patrons this turn, William de Freford, John de Codynton, and Thomas le Spenser, keepers of Elford manor. Ind.: archd. of Stafford. London, 25 Aug. 1316.

776 Licence to the same Thomas to study for one year under the terms of the constitution *Cum ex eo*. Same day.

[Fo. 48v] ANNUS DOMINI M^{us}.CCC^{mus}.XVI^{us}.
  [In a later hand.]

777 Note that [the election of] Br. John ¹de Burton,¹ abbot of Burton upon Trent, was confirmed, and he swore obedience on 1 July 1316 in Dronfield (*Dronefeld*) church. He was blessed and made his profession on 5 Aug. at Sheepwash (*Schepewasch*) near Lincoln.
  [¹⁻¹ Interlined.]

778 Note that at the king's request the bishop has collated to Thomas de [Eyton]¹ the treasurership of Lichfield [cathedral], vacant by the resignation of J[ohn] de Sandal on 6 Aug. 1316, as is clear in a public instrument made thereon. Ind.: dean and chapter of Lichfield [etc.]. Lincoln, 7 Aug. 1316.
  [¹ MS. two dots; *Fasti*, x.11.]

779 Note that Richard de Lustrishull has had letters of induction for the dean and canons of St. John's collegiate church, Chester, ¹to induct and receive¹ him into the prebend which was John de Hothum's, which was agreed as a result of the archbishop of Canterbury's collation by authority of the grace issued to him by the apostolic see. Same day.
  [Duplicated, see **908** in a (correct) Chester archdeaconry section, except for ¹⁻¹ which reads 'to admit and induct'.]

780 Institution of Richard le Poyvour, chaplain, to Cheswardine (*Chesewardyn*') vicarage, vacant by the death of John de Dunston, the last vicar, on Sat. 7 Aug. last; patrons, abbot and convent of Haughmond. Ind.: archd. of Stafford. London, 6 Oct. 1316.

781 Note that Robert de Harewedon has had letters of induction for the dean and chapter of Lichfield to induct and receive him into the prebend of Darnford, as is customary. 20 Oct. 1316.
  [See **758**.]

782   Collation to Harvey de Staunton, clerk, of the vacant prebend of Flixton in Lichfield church.[1] Ind.: dean and chapter of Lichfield. 20 Oct. 1316.
   [[1] *Fasti*, x.36.]

783   Institution of Ralph de Novo Burgo to Sandon vicarage, vacant by the death of William Cornet, the last vicar, on Sun. 10 Oct.; patrons, abbot and convent of Combermere. Ind.: archd. of Stafford. 28 Nov. 1316.

784   Institution of Isumbert de Longavilla to Worfield church, vacant by the death of Thomas de Boterwyk on Tues. 26 Oct.; patron King Edward.[1] Ind.: archd. of Stafford. London, 24 Jan. 1317.
   [[1] *CPR 1313–17*, 575.
   The rest of the folio is blank.]

[Fo. 49] FEOFFAMENTA FACTA PER EPISCOPUM IN EPISCOPATU DE VASTIS ET ESCAETIS ET ALIA FORINSECA.
   [Underlined.]

785   [Copy of the] charter of Walter, bishop of Coventry and Lichfield, to Henry in le Mor of Lichfield and Beatrix, his daughter, granting 16 acres of land from his waste land in Cannock (*le Cank'*) which lies in length from that place called 'Leefhull' at 'le Nunnesco' between the road which leads from the town of Cannock (*Canckebury*) towards Lichfield at both ends. To have and to hold the said 16 acres of land with its appurtenances to Henry and Beatrix, his daughter, and to Beatrix's lawful heirs, and their heirs, from the bishop and his successors freely, quietly, well, and in peace forever, rendering thereafter 8s. each year to the bishop and his successors at the usual four terms[1] at his manor of Longdon (*Longedon*) for all secular service exacted and claimed. The bishop and his successors will warrant [it] forever. In witness whereof the bishop's seal is affixed. Witnesses: Thomas, lord of Pipe (*Pype*), John de Hesmerebrock, John de la Burne, Nicholas de Ambriton, clerk, John de Pype in Lichfield, Richard Cardoun of the same, William le Taverner, and others. Selby (*Soleby*), 1 Aug. 1307.
   [[1] Michaelmas, Hilary, Easter, Trinity.]

786   [Copy of the charter, etc.] to Henry in le Mor of Lichfield, his lawful heirs, and their heirs, granting 10 acres of land with its appurtenances from the bishop's waste land in Cannock (*le Canck'*) which lies in length from the road called Ridware Way (*Rydewar' Wey*) at 'le Nunnebrigge' beside M. Luke de Ely's land as divided by the metes and bounds. To have and to hold [etc.] forever, rendering 5s. each year to the bishop and his successors at the usual four terms at his manor of Longdon (*Langedon*) for all service [etc.]. Warranty clause. Sealing clause. Witnesses: Thomas de Pype, John de Esmerebrock, John de la Bourne, Nicholas de Ambriton, clerk, John de Pype in Lichfield, Richard Cardoun of the same, William le Taverner, and others. Selby, 4 Aug. 1307.

787 [Copy of the charter, etc.] to Hugh de la Dale, mason, and Agnes, his wife, granting the part of a tenement with its appurtenances in the town of Lichfield which was John de le Hul's; it lies between Vincent, son of John de le Hul's tenement on the one part and Hawise, widow of John de le Hul's tenement on the other part; it extends in length from the road to the bishop's pool; it is 12ft. in breadth at the head at both ends; [also] the reversion of the dower of the said tenement, which Hawise holds, containing 6ft. in breadth, as it has fallen to the bishop by escheat by the release of Henry, son of John de le Hul. To have and to hold [etc.] forever (with reversion to Robert, Hugh's brother, and his lawful heirs forever), rendering 6d. each year to the bishop and his successors at the usual terms in the town of Lichfield for all service [etc.]. Warranty clause. Sealing clause. Witnesses: William de Frefford, Thomas, lord of Pipe in Lichfield, Nicholas de Ambriton, clerk, William Westwy, William de Hampton, Richard de[1] atte Walle, and others. Lichfield, 4 Aug. 1307.[2]

[1] *Sic*
[2] *Sic.* This charter and **786** are both dated Fri. after the feast of St. Peter ad vincula, **786** at Selby (Yorkshire), **787** at Lichfield.]

788* [Fo. 49v] Letters patent to Richard de Beaumont, rector of Whitlingham, Norwich dioc. The bishop has received letters of Pope Clement V [quoted] allowing him to grant dispensation to six of his clerks lawfully to hold two benefices, each with cure of souls, notwithstanding the constitution of the General Council[1] and any others published to the contrary (dated St. Cyr-au-mont-d'or, 22 Feb. 1306). Including him [one of] the six clerks, the bishop grants him dispensation lawfully to receive another benefice with similar cure of souls if one is offered to him, provided that such benefices are not defrauded of duties. London, 22 June 1307.

[1] Council of Lyon, 1274, canon 18, see 'Decretalium D. Gregorii Papae IX Compilatio', i.16, 3, *Corpus Juris Canonici* (as in **8**).]

789* Letters patent. The bishop has appointed M. R. de P.[1] and M. S. de S.[2] his proctors to contract a loan at the Curia to expedite his business there, for a sum they shall determine according to the nature and demand of the business and the bishop's resources; to bind the bishop, his church and successors, goods, and the moveable and immovable goods of his church, both present and future, ecclesiastical and secular, to the creditors of the loan; to take an oath for the money to be paid to the creditors under any terms and penalties lawfully required by the contract or by the custom of the Curia; to submit the bishop to the jurisdiction of any papal chaplain whom the creditors shall choose, who may condemn him and his proctors concerning the money, or part of it, and impose a sentence of excommunication if the money is not paid within the term to be determined by the same auditor. The bishop renounces for two days the constitution published by the General Council and other constitutions, qualifications, and exceptions by which he could be protected against the creditors and which might prejudice the loan, and promises to approve whatever shall be done, procured, or promised by the proctors. n.d. [?1309.]

[Langton was cited to the Curia in February 1309 and was granted papal licence in

July 1309 to contract a loan of 1000 marks (£666 13s. 4d.) to meet his expenses there, see *CPL*, ii.49, 57, 58; Hughes, 'Episcopate', i.239.
¹ Possibly M. Robert de Patrica, see **746**.
² Possibly M. Simon de Shirleye, see the introduction p. xxix.]

790 Letter to R[obert], archbishop of Canterbury, primate of all England, the agent appointed by the apostolic see to execute the grace issued by the same to Isabella, queen of England, concerning provisions to be made at her nomination.¹ The bishop agrees to grant a canonry and prebend in his church of Lichfield to a suitable person [fo. 50] to be nominated by the queen according to the tenor of the papal letters. n.d.
[Margin] ²Agreement of the bishop and archbishop to provide a prebend at the queen's nomination.²
[¹ Dated 23 July 1308, see *CPL*, ii.45.
²⁻² In a later hand.]

791 Letters patent. The bishop has granted to M. Geoffrey de Eydon,¹ his advocate at the Court of the Arches, London, an annual pension of 40s. (20s. at Easter and 20s. at Michaelmas) for as long as he will be his advocate [there] and he is willing to present his defence counsel and aid for the bishop's business to be expedited in the same court. n.d.
Note of similar letters to M. John de Bloye² and M. Andrew de Brugg'³ for 40s.
[¹ Dean of the Arches, see Churchill, *Canterbury administration*, i.432, note; ii.239.
² *BRUO*, i.205–6; Churchill, *ibid.*, ii.237.
³ Churchill, *ibid.*, ii.242.]

792 [Copy of the] charter [etc.] to John Mauclerk of Leicester granting 60 acres of the bishop's waste land which lies in Cannock beside 'Lefful'', measured by perches of 24½ ft. according to the metes and bounds. To have and to hold for the term of his life [etc.] (with reversion to William Mauclerk of Leicester for the term of his life. Reversion to William, son of William de Shulton, and his lawful heirs. Reversion to Henry, William's brother, and his lawful heirs. Reversion to Agnes Mauclerk, John Mauclerk's sister, and her lawful heirs), rendering 30s. each year to the bishop and his successors at the usual four terms at his manor of Longdon for all service [etc.]. Warranty clause. Sealing clause. Witnesses: John de Hotot, William de Freford, John de Asmerbrok', Henry de la More, William le Taverner of Lichfield, and others. London, 3 May 1309.

793 [Copy of the] charter [etc.] to ¹Roger de Aston,¹ Sibyl, his wife, and their lawful heirs granting a messuage and a moiety of a virgate of land with adjacent meadow and all other appurtenances in the town of Longdon. To have and to hold [etc.] forever, rendering 6s. 4d. each year to the bishop at the usual terms at his manor for all [service]. Warranty clause. [fo. 50v] Sealing clause. Witnesses: Henry Mauveisyn, kt., William de Sandiacre, kt., William de Freford, William de 'Tymmor', John de la Bourne, Reginald de Rous, Ralph de Rous, Ralph Proutfot, and others. London, 5 May 1309.²
[¹⁻¹ Underlined.
² Underlined.]

794 [Copy of the] charter [etc.] to ¹William de Freford,¹ Sibyl, his wife, and their lawful heirs granting 12½ acres of land with all its appurtenances from the bishop's waste land in Lichfield and Fisherwick (*Fisscherwyk*), measured by perches of 24½ ft., which he had by escheat after the death of Robert, chaplain of Whittington (*Whitinton*). To have and to hold [etc.] (with reversion to Richard, William's brother, and his lawful heirs forever), rendering 6s. 3d. each year to the bishop and his successors in equal parts at the usual four terms at his manor of Longdon. Warranty clause. Sealing clause. Witnesses: Sir Robert de Bures, kt., Sir William Trumwyne, kt.,² Sir Henry Mauveysyn, kt., Thomas de Pipa, Roger de Aston, William de 'Thomenhorn', Henry de Alrewas, William de 'Tymmor', and others. London, 5 May 1309.

[¹⁻¹ Underlined.
² Keeper of the peace for Stafford, 1307–8, see *CPR 1307–13*, 23, 31, 53.]

795 [Copy of the] charter [etc.] to ¹William de Freford¹ and his lawful heirs granting 12½ acres of land, measured by perches of 24½ ft., with its appurtenances from the bishop's waste land in Lichfield and Fisherwick (*Fissherwyk*); 8 acres lie on 'le Halsemor', 2 acres lie at Longbridge (*Longebrugg'*) and 2½ acres lie on 'le Rakemor', which he had by escheat after the death of Robert, chaplain of Whittington. To have and to hold [etc.] forever, rendering 6s. 3d. each year to the bishop and his successors in equal parts at the usual four terms at his manor of Longdon for all service [etc.]. Warranty clause. Sealing clause. Witnesses: Sir Robert de Bures, kt., Sir William Trumwyne, kt., Sir Henry Mauveysyn, kt., Thomas de Pipa, Roger de Aston, William de 'Thomenhorn', Henry de Alrewas, William de 'Timmor', and others. London, 5 May 1309.

[¹⁻¹ Underlined.]

796 [Copy of the] charter [etc.] to ¹William Mauclerk¹ of Leicester granting 60 acres from the bishop's waste land in Cannock lying beside 'Lefful'', measured by perches of 24½ ft., according to the metes and bounds. To have and to hold for the term of his life [etc.] (with reversion to [fo. 51] John Mauclerk of Leicester for the term of his life. Reversion to William, son of William de Schulton, and his lawful heirs. Reversion to Henry, the same William's son, and his lawful heirs. Reversion to Agnes Mauclerk, William Mauclerk's sister, and her lawful heirs), rendering 30s. each year to the bishop and his successors at the usual four terms at his manor of Longdon for all service [etc.]. Warranty clause. Sealing clause. Witnesses: John de Hotot, William de Freford, John de Ashmerbrok', Henry de la More, William le Taverner of Lichfield, and others. London, 3 May 1309.

[¹⁻¹ Underlined.]

797* Letters patent to William de Draco,¹ clerk. The bishop has received letters of Pope Clement V [quoted] allowing him to grant dispensation to four secular clerks to receive holy orders and a single benefice, with or without cure of souls, despite being under age, provided that [they are] aged 15, notwithstanding any constitution published to the contrary (dated St. Cyr-au-mont-d'or, 22 Feb. 1306). Since he is of noble birth and assiduous in the study of letters, which is not diminished by his youth, and out of respect for Sir William de Dacre, kt.,² his father, including him [one of] the four clerks, the bishop grants him dispensation lawfully to receive and retain a single benefice, with or without cure of souls, if one is offered to him.[3] London, 12 May 1309.

[[1] Recte *Dacre* (see his father below). Probably ordained acolyte 20 Sept. 1309, see *Reg. Halton*, i.330 (Daker). Ordained subdeacon 14 Mar. 1310, see **1303**.

[2] A retainer of Thomas, earl of Lancaster, see J.R. Maddicott, *Thomas of Lancaster, 1307–1322. A study in the reign of Edward II* (Oxford, 1970), 50.

[3] Instituted rector of Prescot 13 May 1309, see **832, 840, 860**.]

798 Note of similar dispensation for John de Bereford. London, same date.

799 Letters patent to M. Robert de Reddeswelle, archdeacon of Chester, and John de Shoteswelle, clerk. They are commissioned to inquire into, correct, and punish the excesses of the bishop's flock, both clerical and lay, in the parish of Shustoke (*Schustok'*) of the bishop's jurisdiction, whether *ex officio* or at the suit of parties, with power of coercion. London, 22 Feb. 1310.

800 [Fo. 51v] Note that the bishop is bound by his letter to the dean and chapter of Lichfield for £40 to be paid on the Nativity of St. John the Baptist next. London, 7 May 1310.

801* A bond. The bishop is obliged and bound to Ralph de Hengham and his executors for £210 which he received on loan from the same, to be paid to him or his attorney, as follows: 105 marks [£70 (each)] on the quindene of Easter next, the quindene [of the Nativity] of St. John the Baptist, and the quindene of Michaelmas, pledging all his moveable and immovable goods. London, 7 Oct. 1310.

802 [Copy of the] charter [etc.] to John de Heth, Isabella, his wife, and their heirs, granting 15 acres of the bishop's waste land with its appurtenances in the district of Prees, lying under 'le Lee', of which William de Thorpwatervill' previously held 8 acres of the bishop. To have and to hold [etc.] forever, rendering 7s. 6d. each year to the bishop and his successors at the usual terms at his manor of Prees. Reversion to the bishop and his successors if they die without heir. Warranty clause. Sealing clause. Witnesses: Richard, lord of Sandford, Reginald de Sharnes, William, son of Sir Ralph de Sandford, Sir William Herward, Richard de Wottenhull, William Gamel, William de Colton, and others. Eccleshall, 24 Mar. 1311.

803* Letters patent granting M. Geoffrey de Blaston, canon of Lichfield, the hall within the bishop's close at Lichfield which was M. Walter de Clipston's, the bishop's nephew, together with an upper room and a cellar, recently built anew, [another] upper room and cellar, a kitchen and a bakery, provided that M. Geoffrey will have the rooms repaired at his expense within four or five years at the most, otherwise the grant will be void. York, 24 Aug. 1311.

[The rest of the folio is blank.]

804 [Fo. 52. Copy of the] charter [etc.] to John de Carleton granting 12 acres of royal land (*terre regalis*) from the bishop's waste land in Brewood, lying beneath his high wood in a place called 'le Slouhull' and 'le Slougreve'. To have and to hold [etc.] in hereditary fee (with reversion to Joan, [John's] sister, and her lawful heirs), rendering thereafter 6s. each year to the bishop and his successors at the four established terms at his manor of Brewood, for all [service]. Warranty clause. Sealing clause. Witnesses: Sir John Giffard of Chillington (*Chilinton*), kt., John, lord of Weston, Thomas de la Hyde, Thomas de Engleton, Robert de 'Civesteshay', Robert de Bremhale, Jordan le Cotiller of Brewood, and others. Lichfield, 29 Dec. 1315.

805* Letters patent absolving and acquitting Roger de Schulton, rector of Heanor, from all obligation to account and reckon for any bailiwick or office in which he has rendered service to the bishop, his successors and executors, declaring Roger, his heirs, successors and executors free and released from all legal action, impeachment, or claim whereby they might be charged in future. Lichfield, 1 Apr. 1317.

806* Letter to M. Simon [de Radeswelle], rector of West Kirby. He has not been resident in his church since 1310, as the cure of souls requires. The bishop considers the reasons he has given for his non-residence just and lawful. Neither he nor his ministers will proceed against him, or cause him any trouble. Lichfield, 3 Apr. 1317.

> [He received a licence to study for seven years on 4 June 1300 when rector of Whitnash, resigning that benefice for West Kirby on or before 4 Mar. 1302, see **104, 124, 180.**
> The rest of the recto is blank.]

807 [Fo. 52v. Copy of the] charter [etc.] to William, son of Philip de[1] Terven and Alice, his wife, their heirs and assigns, granting 1½ bovates of land with adjoining messuage, cottage and a plot of pasture with appurtenances in Tarvin and Oscroft (*Owescroft*), from which lands and tenements the bishop has been accustomed to receive 18s. rent each year; the bishop's clerk, Adam de Kelsale, however, has held the 1½ bovates, messuage, cottage, and plot of pasture of the bishop for the term of one year in exchange for half a water mill with its appurtenances in Tarvin, as William's charter made to the bishop thereon witnesses. To have and to hold [etc.] as wholly to William and Alice as Adam held those lands and tenements of the bishop and his successors freely, quietly, lawfully, peacably, wholly, and by inheritance forever; with husbold and haybold, quittance of common pannage and easements pertaining to the town of Tarvin, rendering thereafter a rose flower each year to the bishop and his successors at the bishop's manor of Tarvin on the Nativity of St. John the Baptist for all secular service, accustomed and claimed. Warranty clause. Sealing clause. Witnesses: Sir Hugh de Audelee, then justice of Chester, Sirs John de Orreby, Ralph de Vernon senior, Hamon de Mascy, Roger de Chedele, Ralph de Vernon junior, Hugh de Dutton, William de Boydel, kts., Richard de Fouleshirst, then sheriff of Chester, Richard le Brun of Stapleford, Roger de Clutton, Thomas de Hokenhille, and many others. Tarvin, 29 Jan. 1316.

> [1 Interlined.]

808 [Copy of the] charter [etc.] to William, son of Richard Abonethewey of Bishopstone (*Bysopeston'*), and his heirs granting 4½ acres of the bishop's royal land in 'Colweleye' lying between Bishopstone field on the one part and John Ridel's land on the other part, including the ditch and hedge. To have and to hold [etc.] forever (with reversion to John, son of Matilda, daughter of John atte Bruggende, and his heirs. Reversion to Robert, William's son, and his heirs. Reversion to John, Robert's brother, and his heirs), rendering 2s. 3d. each year to the bishop and his successors at the usual terms at his manor of Great Haywood. Warranty clause against all living men. Sealing clause. Witnesses: John de Colwych, Richard de Wolseleye, Henry de Heywode, Robert Aucel, Thomas, son of Felicia de Wolseleye, Richard de Toft, Hugh de Longedon, clerk, and others. Lichfield, 6 Mar. 1316.

809* [Fo. 53] To the abbot and convent of St. Werburgh, Chester. The bishop held a visitation at their monastery on 1 Dec. 1315. He found correction and reform were needed. He decrees as follows:

The house is gravely burdened with debt; useless or unnecessary offices must be removed; the abbot shall robe only six clerks, five esquires or yeomen; he shall be content with his robes in the monastery; robes shall not be given outside, unless necessary.

Neither the abbot, monks, nor seculars shall keep hounds or dogs at the expense of the house.

The abbot shall accept the counsel of the oldest and senior brethren on important and difficult business, not only of one or two.

Corrodies and pensions shall not be sold or granted except in necessity, and then only by common determination and of each of his chapter and the bishop.

The abbot shall not entertain except on solemn feasts, on the arrival of great men, or for another clear reason; nor shall he spend as much on wine and spices as he is accustomed; he shall be content with 10 tuns of wine each year. He shall treat his brethren equally when dining in his room or elsewhere; he shall not believe private denunciations against his brethren. He shall summon his brethren to dine in his room on meat and fish days without exception.

He shall diligently see that the rents and homage of the house are collected and recovered in full.

He shall correct transgressing brethren with due charity and clemency.

The obedientiaries shall be appointed in chapter according to ancient custom.

The abbot shall return the money he has taken from the fabric-fund; henceforth he shall not take a loan from the fabric-fund or alms.

The monks shall be recalled from the manors to the convent; [the manors] will be cultivated by other keepers. In accordance with an old agreement, the abbot shall give £4 10s. for provisions for the monks at Hilbre Island and Saighton.

The prior and his successors shall remain in the convent according to the rule. He shall not hunt beasts in the forests. He shall not use a bow and arrows against the rule, but shall observe religion.

The prior and monks shall dress according to the rule.

The prior shall eat in the refectory, keeping both meat and fish days.

Silence shall be observed.

The brethren shall not eat and drink outside the refectory or other place when they eat; the leftovers shall be turned into alms.

Legal books bought by the abbot with money from the house, or their value, shall be returned to the monastery.

After collation the brethren shall not feast and drink in secret, but shall go to compline.

Br. Matthew de Pentyn, Br. Geoffrey de Bosdoun and Br. John de Gilbesmeire, whose insolence and malice has disturbed the peace and quiet of the brethren, shall be sent to other houses; they shall not be recalled until the bishop ordains: Pentyn to Coventry, Bosdon to Shrewsbury, Gilbesmere to Hilbre Island. Br. Robert de Markynton shall be recalled to the house and remain in the convent.

Because those in the Lord's service have renounced forinsec service [in] another's craft, Br. Robert Mareschall, who several times has meddled in surgery, or any monk, shall not involve themselves in works of that art except in charity to relieve a sick pauper by a little unction; action or consultation regarding any wound shall not be allowed.

All are to obey the bishop's decree which is to be read frequently in chapter before all the brethren, lest any should excuse himself about its observance through ignorance, on pain of excommunication. Astbury, 14 Dec. 1315.

810 [Fo. 53v] To the prior and convent of Wombridge (*Wombrugg'*). In his visitation of their monastery a short time ago the bishop found correction and reform were needed. For their benefit and the application of religion he has provided remedies which he sends by this decree.

The prior shall be more watchful and vigilant concerning the priory's estate, particularly the temporalities.

Liveries shall not be sold without the agreement of the chapter and the bishop.

Br. Thomas de Broughton shall not meddle at all in lay courts, or in any business touching the monastery.[1] He is to be recalled to the monastery and remain there according to the rule.

All the canons shall receive their clothing from a chamberlain appointed by the convent according to their needs and the resources of the house.

Silence shall be observed at the due hours.

Women shall not enter the choir and close as frequently and indiscriminately as they have been accustomed.

Canons who wish to celebrate mass should be allowed to do so, provided that they are not lawfully barred.

The sick shall be provided with more food than the healthy, as their condition requires and the resources of the church allow.

All in the monastery are to observe and keep firmly the foregoing, and their rule, under pain of excommunication, and other penalties. n.d.

[¹ Despite this injunction Br. Thomas was still holding the courts of Roger Corbet in 1324, see *VCH Shropshire*, ii.82.]

811 To the prior and convent of St. Mary's church, Repton (*Repingdon*). In his visitation of their church on 10 June 1316 the bishop found correction and reform fitting, concerning which he has ordained this decree.

The prior shall change his chaplain each year, according to the terms of the constitution.

Annual accounts of the manors and obedientiaries shall be rendered at once before the prior and convent, or the senior members of the convent.

Br. John de Coventr' shall be removed from the office of cellarer. He shall devote himself to choir and cloister and, as he is old, he shall speak to the Lord rather than to women. He shall say a Psalter each week in the cloister for a year. He is forbidden to speak to women, except his sister, or one related to him by marriage.

Br. Ralph de Schepeye shall remain in the choir and cloister all the next year; he shall not leave the monastery except with a mature person and with the prior's licence. He shall say a Psalter each week. He shall abstain from meat and fish on holy days, and from speaking with women, except with a sister, or one related by marriage in the presence of another senior brother. He shall remain in the convent for the whole year.

Liveries shall not be sold or granted, except with the bishop's licence.

One of the brethren shall be put in charge of the infirmary. The sick shall be provided with more food and drink than the healthy, and they shall wear simple clothes.

All are to obey this decree [as in **809***]. Darley, 17 June 1316.

812 To the prior and canons of Gresley. The bishop held a visitation of their church on 9 June 1316. He found certain things in need of correction, concerning which he has ordained this decree.

Liveries and pensions shall not be granted or sold without the bishop's licence.

Women shall not stay within the boundaries of the house; if some have lived there till now, they must be removed.

This must be observed fully by the prior and brethren as soon as possible. n.d.

813 [Fo. 54] IN ROTULO .XXVII°. REGIS .E[DWARDI]. FILII REGIS .H[ENRICI]. IN SALOP' [1298–9]. The sheriff [of Shropshire] has rendered the account of 10d. from John de Broghoton acknowledged because he did not come on Thurs. 3 Sept. and Mon. 7 Sept. before A[dam] de Crok[edayk] and William Inge, having been appointed justices in several counties for the year 27 [Edward I (1299)], as is recorded on the roll of fines and amercements.[1] And 20d. from Richard Gamel of Brandon because he is not prosecuted by Roger, son of Giles and Richard, his brother, by surety of the same, as is recorded there; 9d. from Margery, daughter of Thomas de Chetuln' for a false claim; 20d. from John de Brewode and Margery, his wife, for the same; $\frac{1}{2}$ mark from Geoffrey de Greseleye acknowledged because he did not come; 20d. from William de Stavelegh' acknowledged for the same; 20d. from Hugh de Chalvedon acknowledged for the same there; 9d. from Robert Gerveys for the same; 20d. from William de Hochehull of Lichfield for a false claim; 20d. from Robert de Croxhal' and Richard, son of William the carterer of the same because they have not produced someone; 20d. from Thomas de Handwyk and Robert de Hulton for the same; 20d. from Hugh de Barr' and Thomas le Rus of Longdon for the same; and 20d. from William de Claydon for a false claim. Total: 24s. 2d. In the treasury: nothing.

. And 24s. 2d. to Walter de Langeton, bishop of Coventry and Lichfield, by liberty of the king's charter dated 18 Apr. 27 Edward I [1299], enrolled on the Easter memoranda [roll] 28 [Edward I (1300)],[2] granting for himself and his heirs to the same Bishop Walter, the king's treasurer, for his laudable service to the king and his realm before and after he assumed the pastoral office, that he and his successors shall have on all their episcopal lands the return of all king's writs, pleas of withernaam, the chattels of felons and fugitives, and the fines and amercements of all their men and tenants to be levied by the said bishop and his successors, their bailiffs and officials, for the use of the same bishops, without being hindered or prevented by the king, or by any of his heirs, sheriffs, bailiffs, or officials. By his writ dated 22 Apr. 27 [Edward I (1299)] the king has commanded the treasurer and barons to observe firmly each clause of that charter, and for it to be observed and upheld by all of the king's justices, sheriffs and officials in the king's realm; and for the sheriffs henceforth to have due allowance in their accounts rendered in the Exchequer for the pleas of withernaam, chattels of felons and fugitives, and the amercements of all the men and tenants of the bishopric which they have previously been answerable for, and the sheriffs themselves to be discharged thereof, according to the grant made to the bishop. It is quit.

[[1] PRO Pipe rolls (E 372), no. 144, m. 7.
[2] *Sic.* The regnal year has been altered on the pipe roll from 28 to 27. It is enrolled on memoranda roll Michaelmas 1298 – Trinity 1299 (26–27 Edward I), see PRO K.R. Memoranda rolls (E 159), no. 72, m. 29d; *CChR 1257–1300*, 476. Edward I made only twelve such grants, and decreed in 1306 that henceforth they would be restricted to members of his family, see Hughes, 'Register', 7.]

814 IN ROTULO .VIII°. .E[DWARDI]. FILII REGIS .E[DWARDI]. IN ITEM. STAFFORD [1314–15]. Account rendered by R[oger Cheygny][1], sheriff: 40s. from Robert de Tuppere from a fine for trespass; 40d. from John de Walle from a fine for the same; 40d. from John le Carpenter for the same; $\frac{1}{2}$ mark from Robert Chaumpeneys for the same; 40d. from William de la More for the same; 40d. from Robert de Brerdon junior for the same; $\frac{1}{2}$ mark from Hugh, son of Robert Note for the same; 20s. from Richard de Brumle, tanner, for the same; 20s. from John Buraunt for the same; 40d. from William Harding for the same; 40d. from Simon, son of Robert de Herteshorn for the same; 1 mark from William de Norton and Elizabeth, his wife, from a fine for a licence granted for a tenement in Norton; 1 mark from Thomas le White and Felicia, his wife, from [the same] for a tenement in Huntington (*Huntesdon*); [fo. 54v] 1 mark from Henry de Hughtesdon and Juliana, his wife, from a fine for [the same] for a tenement in Huntington (*Hughtesdon*); 1 mark from John de Hughtesdon, chaplain, from a fine for [the same] for a tenement in Huntington; 1 mark from Thomas, son of Reginald le Bedel from a fine because he is not prosecuted by surety of Reginald le Bedel;[2] 6d. from Robert le Eyr of Podmore (*Podemor'*) because he did not come;[3] 6d. from William, son of Felicia, because he did not come; 6d. from William le Taverner for the same; 6d. from John de Hondesacr' for the same; 3d. from Adam de Whethal' for the same; 3d. from John de Whethales because he has not produced someone; 6d. from John de Coton and Ranulph de Bromle for the same; 6d. from Roger, son of Agnes and Adam Togod for the same; 6d. from John Robyns and Geoffrey Jurdan for the same; 6d. from Adam de Hondesacr' for the same; 6d. from Robert le Eyr of Podmore because he did not come.

On the roll of amercements before the barons from the execution of writs at Hilary term 4 [Edward II (1311)]: 6d. from William le Taverner of Lichfield for the same; 6d. [from][4] Roger le Mareschal for the same; 6d. from John de Coton and Ranulph de Bromle because they have not produced someone; 6d. [from][5] Agnes Wyaunt and Ranulph Lele for the same; 6d. from William the miller and John le Irmongere for the same; 4d. from John de Pipa of Lichfield because he did not come;[6] 6d. from William le Taverner of Lichfield for the same; 4d. from John de Hondesacr' for the same; 4d. from William de Donastthorp and William Fox because they have not produced someone; 4d. from William Scarp and Henry le Walesshe for the same; 4d. from William de Norton and Richard, son of Simon for the same; 6d. from Richard Cardun' because he did not come; 6d. from John de Pipe for the same; 6d. from William le Taverner for the same; 6d. from Thomas le Cotiler and Adam de Wilmend because they have not produced someone; 6d. from Ralph le Seler and Thomas le Porter for the same; 6d. from John le Seler and William le Spicer for the same; 6d. from Richard Cardun' because he did not come; 6d. from Reginald de Charnes for the same; 6d. from Stephen le Cotiler and Thomas le Cotiler because they have not produced someone; 6d. from Richard de Prees and Adam le Serjaunt for the same; 6d. from Reginald de Charnes because he did not come; 6d. from John de Pipe of Lichfield for the same; 6d. from Alan Charnes and Alan Fryet because they have not produced someone; 6d. from William de Donasthorp and John le Seler for the same; 6d. from William Trumwyn because he did not come;[7] 6d. from William, son of William Trumwyn for the same; 6d. from William Trumwyne, son and heir of William Trumwyne for the same; 6d. from Thomas de Dokeseye and Adam Trumwyne because they have not produced someone; 6d. from Adam Trumwyne and John de Canok for the same; 6d. [from][8] Adam Trumwyn and Richard le Keu for the same; 20s. [from][9] Nicholas de Moreby from a fine for a licence granted for the manor of Weeford (*Weford*);[10] 1 mark [from][11] Robert le Eyr of Podmore and Cecilia, his wife, from a fine for a licence granted for a tenement in Podmore;[12] $\frac{1}{2}$ mark from Henry de Lich' from a fine for a licence granted.[13] Total: £11 19s. 8d. In the treasury: nothing.

To Walter de Langeton, bishop of Coventry and Lichfield, of whom the said men are tenants: £11 19s. 8d. by liberty of King Edward I's charter granted to the same Walter on roll [27[14] Edward I] for Shropshire, granting [as in **813**]. By his writ dated 8 [Edward II] the king has commanded the treasurer and barons to allow all and each of the foregoing to the same bishop to have, use, and enjoy as he ought to have them according to the tenor of the said charter, and to allow it to the same bishop at the Exchequer. It is quit.

[[1] *List of sheriffs*, PRO Lists and Indexes, 9, 117; PRO Pipe rolls (E 372), no. 160, m. 16d.

[2] The pipe roll here reads: *In rotulo de finibus et amerciamentis coram rege de termino Pasche anno quinti*

[3] The pipe roll here reads: *In rotulo amerciamentorum coram baronibus ad placita de termino Sancti Michaelis anno .iiij*^{to}.

[4] MS. *pro*

⁵ MS. *pro*

⁶ The pipe roll here reads: *In rotulo de amerciamentis coram baronibus de executionibus brevium de termino Sancte Trinitatis anno .iiij^to.*

⁷ The pipe roll here reads: *In rotulo de amerciamentis coram baronibus de executionibus brevium anno .iiij^to.*

⁸ MS. *pro*

⁹ MS. *pro*

¹⁰ The pipe roll here reads: *In rotulo de finibus et exitibus de banco anno .viij°.*

¹¹ MS. *pro*

¹² The pipe roll here reads: *In rotulo de finibus et exitibus de banco de termino Pasche anno secundo*

¹³ The pipe roll here reads: *In rotulo de finibus et exitibus de banco de termino Sancti Michaelis anno quinto,* followed by a 10cm. blank space.

¹⁴ MS. 17.]

815* [Fo. 55] Letters patent. Religious and circumspect men subject to the bishop's jurisdiction who have rendered endless services and labours to religion for the Lord and men should receive suitable support from the bishop's provision. Br. W[illiam] de Alsop, abbot of Darley, has beseeched that, since he is weak with old age and long service, and he is afraid that in time he shall be less able to govern his house, the bishop might provide for him, whereupon the bishop ordains with the agreement of all [the abbot's] brethren.

If he retires, or is removed from office because of infirmity, he shall have a room in Darley monastery for his lifetime, that is the upper-room which was Sir Roger de Draycote's, with a chapel, a wardrobe with a fire, and an allowance of candles.

He shall also have Shirley church, with the houses of the rectory, and all other things pertaining to it, on condition that he recognizes and supports the ordinary charges pertaining to the church and rectory.

He shall have two conventual loaves and two gallons of better ale each day from the cellar of Darley, and on each feast-day a complete dish with cheese and butter from the kitchen, as the abbot is served in the refectory.

The abbot shall assign him a fellow-canon to serve him as chaplain, who shall have a conventual loaf and a gallon of better ale from the cellar each day with his customary food from the kitchen, as one of the canons is served in the refectory.

He shall have for his ease a servant or chamberlain to serve him, who shall have a small white loaf and a black loaf from the cellar each day, with a gallon of better ale from the kitchen at those times when the abbot's servant is served.

All the said bread and ale shall be dispensed in his room, or taken to him outside the monastery, or wherever he pleases. He shall take nothing from the kitchen as long as he is outside the monastery with his ministers. If he wishes to have some of his fellow brethren from the convent with him at table in his room the bishop grants that the same brethren shall have their accustomed victuals there from both the cellar and the kitchen, just as they have in the refectory.

William shall also have a black loaf and two servants' loaves each day for cutting or slicing at his table, whether he is in or outside the monastery, at Shirley church, or at the bishop's other manors, should he wish to go [there].

When both going and returning he shall have a suitable companion or escort, with horses and grooms from the abbot's stable, as his status requires.

By this ordinance or provision the bishop does not intend to grant or approve the retirement or renunciation which Br. William might make from any spiritual dignity or office. Duckmanton, 29 June 1316.

816 [Fo. 55v] Letters patent to Br. Roger de Crek' and the other monks of Sandwell. The unanimous and amicable election of Br. John de Duckebroc',[1] monk of of St. Milburga's church, Much Wenlock (*Wenlok'*), as prior of their house, which is vacant by the death of Br. Thomas, the last prior, has been presented to the bishop by an instrument under their seal. The bishop has examined the business of the election and has found substantial and notable defects both in its form and circumstances. He has annulled it. Lest their house should suffer loss in any way in spiritualities and temporalities because of a long vacancy the bishop has provided the said Br. John prior as an act of special grace, having examined him concerning his religion, and understanding him to be circumspect and assiduous in the management of temporalities. [Br. John] should make profession according to the rule of the Cluniac order, but cannot comply without his abbot's licence for his election, or the bishop's provision. Br. Henry, abbot of the Cluniac order,[2] has given his deputies a licence from the prior of St. Mary's church, Thetford (*Theford*), Norwich dioc., of the Cluniac order, to be given to the said Br. John showing his agreement to his election or nomination as prior. Br. John has rendered the vow of obedience, whereby he was fully bound to the said abbot and the Cluniac order. The bishop therefore ordains and commands Br. Roger and his house to admit Br. John as their prior, submitting to him in all things. London, . . .[3] Oct. 1316.

[1 Resigned by 1323, see *VCH Staffordshire*, iii.219.
2 Henry de Bonvillers, prior of Much Wenlock, 1285–1320, see *VCH Shropshire*, ii.46.
3 Blank space.]

817 Letters patent of King Edward [II][1]. Theodosius de Camilla, the late dean,[2] and the chapter of Wolverhampton (*Wolvernehampton*) had impleaded Roger [Meuland], then bishop of Coventry and Lichfield, in the court of King Edward [I] concerning the advowson of Penn (*Penne*) church, near Wolverhampton. The same bishop had called to warrant Ralph de Bysshebury against the dean and chapter, who had warranted the same to him. He lost that advowson by default which he made in the same court. It was found subsequently that there had been collusion between Ralph and the dean and chapter but judgment remains to be given and the matter is pending. In consideration of the good service of his clerk, William de Wylyngeston, who was collated and instituted to [Penn] church by the dean and chapter after the collusion, and wishing to make special grace to him, [the king] has accepted William's title in the church; even if judgment be rendered in future on this matter William shall not be removed from that church by [the king] or [his] heirs on this account. Windsor, 14 Jan. 1321. By writ under the privy seal.

[1 *CPR 1317–21*, 553.
2 Dean 1269–1295, see *VCH Staffordshire*, iii.330, 323–4.]

[Fo. 56] .CESTR'. REGISTRUM ARCHIDIACONATUS CESTR' A FESTO SANCTE TRINITATIS
ANNO GRACIE .M°.CCC^mo. SEPTIMO ET CONSECRACIONIS .W[ALTERI]. DE LANGETON
EPISCOPI COVENTR' .XI°.

818 Letters patent to William [de Swetenham],[1] rector of Swettenham
(*Swetinham*), subdeacon. Since he has a mind to study, so that he will bear
seasonable fruit in God's church, and at the request of Arnold, cardinal priest of
St. Marcellus, the bishop grants that he may study at university for one year,
meanwhile receiving wholly the fruits of his church. He shall not be bound to
receive further orders by authority of the new constitution of Pope Boniface VIII
published on this matter,[2] provided that the church meanwhile is not defrauded
[etc.], and he will employ a suitable vicar to whom appropriate support shall be
provided from the fruits and revenues of the church. At the end of his period of
study, and from the place where he has studied, he shall swear complete fealty to
the bishop. Theydon Mount, 24 June 1307.

[1] See **895**.
[2] *Cum ex eo*, see **45**, n. 4.]

819 Letters patent to M. William de Blechele, subdeacon, rector of Waverton,
granting dispensation to study at university for one to two years. Wallingford
(*Walingford*), 27 Aug. 1307.

[Langton had been arrested by this date, see the introduction pp. xxxiv–v.]

[1]QUERERE REGISTRUM .. ARCHIDICACONI CESTR'.[1]

[See the vicar-general's register **489–551** for business between 27 Aug. 1307 and
9 Nov. 1308; also **1027**.

[1–1] Added later.]

REGISTRUM POST EGRESSUM EPISCOPI A CARCERE .V. IDUS NOVEMBRIS
M°.CCC^mo.VIII°. [9 NOV. 1308].

[Underlined.]

820 Letters patent to M. John Marcell, clerk, who has been laudably
commended to the bishop for his probity. Wishing to honour him with an
ecclesiastical benefice because of this, the bishop collates to him the prebend
which was William de Eston's, his clerk, in St. John's church, Chester, vacant by
William's resignation, with all its rights [etc.]. Ind.: dean and chapter. London,
6 Dec. 1308.

821 [Fo. 56v] Letters patent to Nicholas de Blaston, deacon, perpetual[1] vicar of
Tarvin church. Being favourably inclined to his prayers, the bishop grants him
faculty to receive lawfully the order of priest by any Catholic bishop of the realm
of England, notwithstanding that he is beneficed in Coventry and Lichfield
dioc., provided that there is no other canonical impediment. Theydon Mount,
6 Feb. 1309.

[1] Interlined.]

822 Note that on 5 Mar. 1309 Henry de Bugges, monk, was informed that the following monks had obtained letters dimissory. Letters patent to Brothers Alexander de Asthull, John de Foxwist, Henry de Werburgton, William de Binington, subdeacons, and John de Wenlok, Jordan de Mamcestr', and Walter de Penwne, deacons, monks of St. Werburgh's monastery, Chester. Being favourably inclined to their prayers, the bishop grants licence that Alexander, John de Foxwist, Henry, and William may receive the order of deacon, and John de Wenlok, Jordan, and Walter [may receive] the order of priest by any Catholic bishop of the realm of England, or of the principality of Wales, notwithstanding that they received the monastic habit in Coventry and Lichfield dioc., provided that [as in **821**]. London, 5 Mar. 1309.

823 Licence, in common form, to Henry de Walton, chaplain, rector of Tattenhall (*Tatenhale*), to study for one year. London, 6 Mar. 1309.

824 Licence to M. William de Blechesle, subdeacon, rector of Waverton, to study for one year according to the terms of the constitution of Pope Boniface VIII. London, 5 Mar. 1309.

825 Institution of Adam de Ashton, priest, to Huyton vicarage, vacant by the death of Thurstan de Wygan, the last vicar, on 6 Jan.; patrons, prior and convent of Burscough (*Burscow*). Ind.: archd. of Chester. Greenford, 12 Mar. 1309.

826 Letter to William de Tatham and Roger de Shelton. Having great trust in the steadfastness of their faith, the bishop grants them joint custody of his sequestration on the vacant church of Prescot (*Prescote*), during pleasure. They shall answer to him for its fruits and revenues. Mandate to the archdeacon to deliver custody. Greenford, near London, 18 Mar. 1309.

[Fo. 57] INCIPIT ANNUS DOMINI MILLESIMUS .CCC^us. NONUS.

827 Licence to William de Lench, perpetual vicar of Blackburn (*Blakeborne*) church, to go on pilgrimage for one year. London, 30 Apr. 1309.

828 Institution of Henry de Lich', priest, to Ormskirk (*Ormeschirch*) vicarage, vacant by the resignation of Robert de Farneworth, the last vicar; patrons, prior and convent of Burscough. Ind.: archd. of Chester. London, 1 May 1309. [Margin] He paid ½ mark.

829 Licence to William de Prayers, acolyte, rector of Childs Ercall (*Erkalwe*),[1] to study for one year from Michaelmas next under the terms of the constitution of Pope Boniface VIII. Letters dimissory for all holy orders. London, 1 May 1309.

[1 In Shrewsbury archdeaconry.]

830   Letters patent to Richard de Chadesden', priest. Trusting in his laudable probity, and the industrious and fervent zeal which he expects to have from him for God's service and the cure of souls, the bishop collates him to the vacant vicarage of Whalley, with all its rights and appurtenances, which has devolved to him this turn by lapse of time by authority of the Lateran Council.[1] Ind.: archd. of Chester. London, 3 May 1309.

[1 Third Lateran Council, 1179, see **22**, note.]

831   Letters patent to Nicholas de Briddebrok, priest. The bishop admits him to St. Mary's chantry in St. John's collegiate church, Chester, to which he has been presented by Sir John de Orreby, kt., the patron. Ind.: dean and chapter of St. John's church, Chester. London, 14 May 1309.

832   Institution of William de Dacre, clerk, to Prescot church, vacant by the death of Eustach de Cottesbech, the last rector; patrons, William de Dacre and Joan, his wife. Ind.: archd. of Chester. Letters dimissory for all minor and subdeacon's orders. London, 13 May 1309.
[Margin] ½ mark for the fee.

833   [Fo. 57v] Letters dimissory to John, son of Reginald de Tervyn, deacon of Coventry and Lichfield dioc., for the order of priest, in common form, with the addition of this clause [as in **697**]. London, 14 May 1309.

[Followed by two blank lines.]

834   Letters patent of R[obert] de Redeswell, archdeacon of Chester, vicar-general, to Nicholas, son of Richard de Frodesham, subdeacon. He may lawfully be promoted to the orders of deacon and priest by any bishop of the province of Canterbury, notwithstanding that he originates from Coventry and Lichfield dioc., provided that there is no other canonical impediment, and that he will show sufficient title to his ordainer. Davenham, 4 July 1309.

835   To the archdeacon of Chester. The bishop has committed custody of his sequestration placed on the fruits of Childwall church to Adam, son of Hugh de Preston, clerk, during pleasure. Mandate to deliver custody of the sequestration to Adam, or his proctor. Ranton, 9 Nov. 1309.

836   Institution of Adam, son of Hugh de Prestone, clerk, to Childwall church, vacant by the resignation of John de Drokenesford,[1] the last rector, on 6 Oct. last; patron, Sir Robert de Holand, kt. Ranton, same day.

[1 Consecrated bishop of Bath and Wells 9 Nov. 1309, see *Fasti*, viii.1.]

837   Licence to Thomas Trossel, rector of Warmingham, to study for one year from Christmas next. Ranton, 22 Nov. 1309.

838   Licence to M. William de Blechele, rector of Waverton, to study for one year from 2 Mar. next according to the terms of the constitution of Pope Boniface VIII. London, 20 Feb. 1310.

INCIPIT ANNUS DOMINI M^{us}.CCC^{mus}.X^{us}.

839* Note of the profession of Br. Ellis de Workesle, abbot of Whalley, to the bishop, his successors, and [his church] of St. Chad, Coventry and Lichfield [dioc.], in accordance with the rule of St. Benedict. Lichfield cathedral, 12 Apr. 1310.

840* Letter of acquittance. The bishop has received £12 from William de Dacre, rector of Prescot, for the arrears of the tenth imposed on the English clergy by Pope Boniface VIII a short time ago,[1] which £12 is now for the king's use by virtue of the king's writ directed to the bishop. The rector is acquitted of the £12. Great Haywood, 29 Apr. 1310.

Note that the £12 was paid to M. Richard de Norhampton[2] at Lichfield on 1 May 1310 [3]by J[ohn] de Langeton[3] to be paid into the king's Exchequer for the [bishop].

[[1] The tenths were imposed as three separate taxes: 1 Nov. 1305 for two years, 1 Nov. 1307 for one year, 1 Nov. 1309 for three years. Langton was commissioned a collector but, according to Lunt, he remained a silent partner, leaving the collection to the bishops of Lincoln and London, see Lunt, *Financial relations*, 382–95; Hughes, 'Episcopate', i.237–8.
[2] The sequestrator-general.
[3–3] Interlined.]

841* [Fo. 58] Letters patent witnessing that on 8 May 1304 at Westminster the bishop sold, granted and demised all the fruits and revenues of Barthomley church pertaining to him for the same year by grant of Pope Boniface VIII concerning the first fruits and revenues of vacant benefices in his diocese to Robert de Chishull, the rector, for £20, at the request of William de Blibrug', clerk; from which he has assigned £10 to the same William to build his room within the bishop's close at Lichfield, and the remaining £10 has been paid fully to the bishop. Because Robert claims not to have had the letter concerning the sale, grant, and demise till now, the bishop has caused his letters patent to be made. Lichfield, 24 Apr. 1310.

842 Note that the bishop has committed custody of his sequestration on Radcliffe (*Radeclyve*) church to Richard de Radeclyve, clerk, who has been presented to the same, provided that he renders a faithful account. Reservation to revoke the sequestration, during pleasure. Lichfield, 8 May 1310.

843 Institution of Richard de Radeclive, acolyte, to Radcliffe church, vacant by the death of John de Hulton, the last rector, on Sat. 11 Apr. last; patron, William de Radeclive. Ind.: archd. Licence to study at university for one year from Michaelmas next. Coventry, 14 June 1310.

844 Licence to William Pentyn, priest, rector of Handley, to study for one year from Michaelmas next and to farm his church, provided that the church is served by a suitable vicar who will answer to the bishop and his ministers for episcopal dues. Lichfield, 21 July 1310.

845 Institution of Ranulph called Torald, deacon, to Bowdon (*Boudon*) vicarage, vacant by the death of Richard de Aldescroft, the last vicar, on 15 Aug. last; patrons, prior and convent of Birkenhead. Ind.: archd. London, 16 Oct. 1305.
[Margin] He paid the fee.

846 Licence to Robert de Clyderhou, rector of Wigan, to study for one year from Easter next. [London] 1 Nov. 1310.

847 Licence to Thomas Trussel, subdeacon,[1] rector of Warmingham, to study for three years from Christmas next in England or overseas, according to the terms of the constitution of Pope Boniface VIII. London, same day.
  [1 Interlined.]

848 Licence to Richard [de Radeclive],[1] rector of Radcliffe, acolyte, to study for two years under the terms of the constitution [etc.]. Lichfield, 16 Dec. 1310.
  [1 See **843**.]

849 [Fo. 58v] Institution of Robert de Dotton, acolyte, to Eccleston church; patron, Sir Hugh de Venables, kt. Ind.: archd. He was given a curate before this time, [1 because of his youth,1] by the archd. of Chester, then vicar-general, as is evident in his register.[2] Lichfield, 16 Dec. 1310.
  [1-1 Interlined.
   2 See **494**, also **883***.]

850 Note that William le Gede, priest, was admitted to the chapel of Upholland near Wigan (*Holande juxta Wygan*), with this additional clause: saving forever the mother church from loss in all things; patron, Sir Robert de Holande, kt. Ind.: archd. 30 Dec. 1310.

851 Institution of William de Lancastr', priest, to Croston church, vacant by the death of M. Walter de Clypston, the last rector, on 21 Dec. last; patrons, the religious men of Lancaster. Ind.: archd. Lichfield, 2 Feb. 1311.
[Margin] Nothing for the fee.

852 Licence to M. William de Blecchesle, rector of Waverton, to study for one year from 2 Mar. next under the terms of the constitution [etc.]. Lichfield, 2 Feb. 1311.

853* Commission to M. Geoffrey de Moeles, rector of Coddington, to exercise the office of penitentiary in the archdeaconry of Chester. Similar commission to Br. John de Notyngham, monk of St. Werburgh, Chester. Lichfield, 14 Jan. 1311.

854 Licence, in common form, to William de Bromyord, rector of Plemstall, to study for one year. 12 Feb. 1311.

855 Letters patent to William de Wyco and Adam de Dyseworth, canons of Norton Priory. The bishop has heard the vehement and clamorous report of the canons of the priory, and other faithful men, that the prior, Br. Gilbert, wastes and squanders [the priory's] goods. Unless remedy is applied quickly, the priory will suffer irreparable damage and the opprobrium of desolation. The bishop bears the care and responsibility of the whole of his diocese. Trusting in their faith, integrity, purity of conscience, and industry for the Lord, he appoints them coadjutors to the prior. The prior will do nothing pertaining to the administration without their counsel until the bishop thinks fit to make other provision by virtue of the facts found at visitation.[1] All kind of alienation is meanwhile prohibited. Lichfield, 12 Sept. 1310.

[[1] See **859**.]

856 [Fo. 59] Institution of M. Ralph de Tunstal, acolyte, to Eccleston church, vacant by the resignation of M. William de Lancastr', the last rector, on 2 Feb.; patrons, prior and monks of St. Mary, Lancaster. Ind.: archd. Letters dimissory for all holy orders. Eccleshall, 6 Mar. 1311.
[Margin] He paid the fee.

857 Institution of Henry de Leycester, acolyte, to Childwall church, vacant by the resignation of Adam de Preston, the last rector, on 31 Jan. 1311; patron, William le Gode, dean of St. Thomas the Martyr's chapel, Upholland. Ind.: archd. Eccleshall, 18 Mar. 1311.
[Margin] Nothing for the fee.

INCIPIT ANNUS DOMINI M^us.CCC^us.XI^us.

858 Institution of Richard de Swyneflet, priest, to Whalley vicarage, vacant by the resignation of Richard de Chadden', the last vicar, on 7 Mar.; presented by M. Geoffrey de Blaston, canon of Lichfield, by the authority given him by the abbot and convent of Whalley, of the Cistercian order, the patrons. Ind.: archd. Commission to absolve his parishioners in all cases for one year only, except those specially reserved to the bishop. Eccleshall, 27 Mar. 1311.
[Margin] Nothing for the fee.

859 Commission to William de Brichull, canon of Lichfield, and M. Richard de Norh[amp]t[on], the sequestrator-general, with power of coercion. Wishing to provide for the benefit of the religious house of Norton, the bishop has recently appointed coadjutors to the prior.[1] They are to go in person to the house and inquire diligently concerning the state of the house, both in chief and in part, and what they find needing correction they will correct with justice. Beauchief (*Beauchef*), 4 Apr. 1311.

[[1] See **855**.]

860 Letters patent to William de Daker, subdeacon, rector of Prescot. The bishop discerns he has the aptitude and disposition for study. He grants him licence to study at university for three years from the time the rule of his church was committed to him[1] under the terms of the new constitution. York, 23 Apr. 1311.

[[1] 13 May 1309, see **832**.]

861 [Fo. 59v] Licence to Richard de Swyneflet, vicar of Whalley, to travel to the Roman Curia on the business of his vicarage for one year, on condition that the vicarage shall not be defrauded of duties, etc. York, 5 June 1311.

862 Institution of Ralph de Sondbache, priest, to the deanery of St. Thomas the Martyr's chapel, Upholland, vacant by the death of William le Gode, the last dean, on Sun. 9 May last; patron, Sir Robert de Holande, kt. Ind.: archd. York, 20 June 1311.
[Margin] He owes the fee.

863 M. Thomas de Cherleton,[1] clerk, who has been presented Walton church by the abbot and convent of Shrewsbury, the patrons, as they claim, has had a letter of inquiry in common form. Mandate to the dean of Lichfield that, if the same inquiry finds all to be clear for the presenting and the presented, he should deliver possession of the church to him with the bishop's authority. Note of his institution. York, 4 June 1311.

   [1 *BRUO*, i.392–3.]

864 Collation to M. Roger de Haselarton,[1] clerk, of the prebend in St. John's collegiate church, Chester, vacant by the death of Ralph de Heynham. Ind.: dean of that church, assigning the stall [etc.]. York, about the beginning of August.[2]

   [1 *BRUC*, 301–2.
   2 *Circiter principium mensis Augusti*]

865 Institution of Guy de Neuton, subdeacon, to St. Peter's church, Chester, vacant by the death of Robert de Maklesfeld, the last rector, on Wed. 23 June last; patrons, abbot and convent of St. Werburgh, Chester. Ind.: archd. London, 15 Sept. 1311.
[Margin] He owes the fee.

866 Collation to John de Hothum, clerk, of the prebend in St. John's collegiate church, Chester, which was M. Ellis de Napton's, the former archdeacon of Derby. Mandate to the dean of that church to induct him and assign the stall [etc.]; and to sequestrate all the fruits and revenues pertaining to the said archdeaconry by right of the prebend, to inquire concerning the defects to be repaired in the prebendal manse, and quickly provide an estimate for this. London, 11 Sept. 1311.

867 Institution of John de Falhes, priest, to the vicarage of St. Oswald's altar in St. Werburgh's coventual church, Chester; patrons, the religious of the same place. Ind.: archd. London, 22 Nov. 1311.
[Margin] He owes the fee.

[Fo. 60] ANNUS CONSECRACIONIS DOMINI W[ALTERI] COVENTR' ET LICH' EPISCOPI
SEXTUSDECIMUS INCIPIT .IX. KAL. JANUARII [24 DEC. 1311].

868   Institution of Richard de Donynton, priest, to Ormskirk vicarage, vacant
by the death of Henry de Melling', the last vicar, on Mon. 25 Oct. last; patrons,
prior and convent of Burscough. He swore [etc.]. Ind.: archd. London, 6 Dec.
1311.
[Margin] He owes the fee. Nothing [for the fee].

869   Licence to Thomas de Cherleton, subdeacon,[1] rector of Walton, to study
for one year under the terms of the constitution of [Pope] Boniface. 31 Jan. 1312.
    [1 Interlined.]

870   Institution of Robert, son of William de Donecastre, acolyte, to Grappenhall (*Gropenhale*) church, vacant by the resignation of William[1] de Rodyerd,
the last rector, on 19 Oct. last; patrons, prior and convent of Norton. Ind.:
archd. Lichfield, 10 Feb. 1312.
[Margin] He owes the fee.
    [1 Interlined.]

ANNUS DOMINI MILLESIMUS .CCC^mus. DUODECIMUS INCIPIT. [1]QUERAS IN REGISTRO DE
TEMPORE MAGISTRI RADULFI DE LEICESTR' VICARII EPISCOPI.[1]
    [1–1 Added by another hand, see **552–601**.]

ITEM DE ANNO DOMINI MILLESIMO .CCC^mo.XIII^mo. ET CONSECRACIONIS DOMINI
WALTERI COVENTR' ET LICH' EPISCOPI .XVII^mo.

871   Institution of M. Geoffrey de Moeles, priest, to Handley (*Hanlegh'*)
church, vacant by the death of William Pentyn, the last rector, on Tues.
10 Apr. last; patrons, abbot and convent of St. Werburgh, Chester. Ind.:
archd. 2 Dec. 1313.
[Margin] He paid the fee.

872   Licence to M. Thomas de Cherleton, rector of Walton, to study for two
years under the terms of the constitution of Pope Boniface VIII, and to farm his
church. 6 Oct. 1313.

873   Note that custody of the sequestration placed on the fruits and revenues of
Hordley (*Hordelegh'*) church [1]or chapel[1] has been committed to Robert de
Marchumlee, acolyte, during pleasure; patrons, abbot and convent of Shrews-
bury. London, 7 Oct. 1313.
    [1–1 Interlined. The benefice was said to be a chapel in **577, 933**.]

874   Collation to Robert de Clypston, clerk, of the prebend in St. John's
collegiate church, Chester, which was M. William de Henovere's.[1] Ind.: dean of
the same church. London, 30 Oct. 1313.
    [1 *BRUO*, ii.909.]

[Fo. 60v] ANNUS DOMINI .M^{us}.CCC^{mus}.XII^{us}. ET CONSECRACIONIS DOMINI .W[ALTERI]. EPISCOPI .XVIII^{us}.

875 Note that custody of the sequestration on the vacant chapel of Brereton[1] has been committed to Ralph de Brereton, clerk, during pleasure. London, 24 Dec. 1313.

[Instituted 3 Mar. 1314, see **882**.
[1] The second *re* are interlined.]

876 Institution of M. John Deverdon, priest, to Manchester (*Mamcestre*) church; patron, Sir John la Ware, kt. Ind. him or his proctor: archd. London, 24 Jan. 1314.
[Margin] Nothing [for the fee].

877 Commission to M. Geoffrey de Blaston, archdeacon of Derby, and M. Philip de Turvill', the bishop's official. The bishop is hindered by various and difficult business. He is unable to expedite the election of Br. John de Colton, canon regular of Trentham, as prior of the vacant priory of Norton. They are to examine both the election and its form, and the person elected, confirm or annul the election, commit the temporalities and spiritualities, receive canonical obedience from the same, if he is confirmed, and induct him in possession, doing all that is required, with power of coercion. Kirkstead (*Kirkested*), 15 Jan. 1314.

878 Institution of Guy de Neuton, subdeacon, to Coddington church; patrons, abbot and convent of St. Werburgh, Chester. The church became vacant on Sat. 21 Oct. last because M. Geoffrey de Moeles, the last rector, was then admitted to another benefice with similar cure of souls.[1] Ind.: archd. of Chester.
London, 31 Jan. 1314.
[Margin] He paid the fee.
[[1] *Sic.* Instituted rector of Handley 2 Dec. 1313, see **871**.]

879 Institution of Roger de Chyn, priest, to St. Peter's church, Chester, vacant by the resignation of Guy de Neuton, the last rector, on Fri. 21 Sept. last; patrons, abbot and convent of St. Werburgh, Chester. Ind.: archd. of Chester. London, 6 Feb. 1314.
[Margin] He owes the fee.

880 Commission to M. Philip de Turvill', the bishop's official. From the report of trustworthy men the bishop understands that the perpetual vicar of Wynbunbury (*Wybonbury*) parish[1] church labours with such severe illness and physical infirmities that he requires the care of another person. The bishop wishes to provide suitable relief for him and his vicarage. He is to go in person to the vicarage and summon the neighbouring clerks and laity before him to inquire into the state of the same. If the inquiry and physical inspection find the vicar inadequate for the rule of his vicarage, he is to assign another suitable and circumspect man, of whom he has full trust, as his coadjutor. Eccleshall, 5 Mar. 1314.

[See **891**.

¹ Interlined.]

881 [Fo. 61] Note that William Hereward, Hugh de Fossebrok, William de Sallowe, Hugh le Spenser of Norwich, William de Wyco, and John de Donstaple, priests, were instituted to prebends in St. Thomas the Martyr's collegiate church, Upholland, with no inquiry having been made; patron, Sir Robert de Holand. Ind.: dean of the same church, assigning the stall[s, etc.]. Eccleshall, 6 Mar. 1314.

[See **583, note.**]

882 Institution of Ralph de Brerton, acolyte, to Brereton chapel; patron, Sir William de Brereton, kt.¹ Ind.: archd. Lichfield, 3 Mar. 1314.

[¹ Interlined.]

883* Letters patent. As each constraint of the law ought to excuse a lawful impediment, it is fitting for the pastoral office to hear the lawful excuses of the flock and to apply a suitable remedy. [Robert]¹ de Dotton, acolyte, was recently instituted to Eccleston church,² after which he caused himself to be promoted lawfully to the orders of subdeacon and deacon at the next decreed terms,³ wishing to be ordained priest within a year after receiving the order of deacon, in accordance with canon law. He was suffering from a very severe illness so that he was unable to assume the priestly order without grave physical danger. He remains a deacon, unable to rise to higher orders, whereupon he has beseeched the bishop to pronounce compassionately. The bishop has examined the impediment by the testimony of faithful men [without] exception. He excuses the rector as having been hindered by just and reasonable cause. He should be ordained priest at the next holy orders to be celebrated.⁴ London, 8 Dec. [1313].

[¹ MS. *Thomas*
² See **849**.
³ Ordained subdeacon 19 Dec. 1310, deacon 6 Mar. 1311, see **1306, 1307**.
⁴ No record of Robert being ordained priest has been found.]

884 Licence, in common form, to Thomas Trussel, subdeacon, rector of Warmingham, to study for one year. 29 Dec. 1313.

INCIPIT ANNUS DOMINI Mᵘˢ.CCCᵐᵘˢ.XIIIIᵘˢ.

885 Institution of Robert de Clipston, in the person of M. Richard de Abindon,¹ his proctor, to St. Mary's church, near Chester castle; patrons, abbot and convent of St. Werburgh, Chester. ²Licence to study for seven years under the terms of the constitution of Pope Boniface VIII.² London, 29 Apr. 1314.

[¹ *BRUO*, i.4–5.
²⁻² Interlined later.]

886 Licence, in common form, to M. Ralph de Tunstal, priest, rector of Eccleston, to study for one year. London, 11 July 1314.

887 [Fo. 61v] Institution of M. Robert de Wakefeld, acolyte, to Heswall church, vacant by the resignation of William de Folbourn, the last rector, on Mon. 22 July last; patron, Ralph, son of David de Haselwell. Ind.: archd. of Chester. York, 11 Sept. 1314.

888 Licence to Guy de Neuton, deacon, rector of Coddington, to study for two years under the terms of the constitution of [Pope] Boniface. York, 12 Sept. 1314.

889 Institution of John de Esseby la Souche, priest, to Plemstall parish church, vacant by the resignation of William de Bromyerd, the last rector, made to the bishop at Barnwell (*Bernewell*) . . .[1] Ind.: archd. Wybunbury (*Wybonburi*), 11 Dec. 1314.
[[1] A 2cm. blank space.]

890 Institution of Robert de Preston, priest, to North Meols church, vacant by the resignation of Nicholas de Herty, the last rector, on 2 Oct.; patrons, abbot and convent of Evesham. Ind.: archd. Eccleshall, 20 Dec. 1314.
[Margin] He paid the fee.

ANNUS CONSECRACIONIS DOMINI W[ALTERI] .XIX[us].

891 Letter to Thomas [de Prestecote], priest, perpetual vicar of Acton.[1] The vicar of Wybunbury (*Wybbenbur'*) is very old, and is impeded and hampered by physical infirmity. He is unable to exercise adequately the cure of his vicarage in person. [Thomas's] character, knowledge, and experience of affairs in many ways recommend him for the office of coadjutor to the vicar and his vicarage. The bishop appoints him coadjutor so that both the vicar and his vicarage will be taken care of by his administration. Eccleshall, 29 Dec. 1314.
[[1] See **171**. Appointed coadjutor following an inquiry, see **880**.]

892 Institution of M. Richard de Vernoun, priest, to Davenham church, vacant by the death of M. Robert de Reddeswell, archdeacon of Chester, the last rector; patron, Sir Ralph de Vernoun, senior, kt. Ind. him or his proctor: Adam de Keleshale. Grove, 17 Jan. 1315.
[Margin] Nothing for the fee.
[See **1200**, and note.]

893 Note that custody of the sequestration on Swettenham church has been committed to Laurence de Knuttesford, priest, until 3 May, having been presented to the church. Ind.: M. Richard de Vernoun, keeper of the archdeaconry of Chester. Coldham, 17 Feb. 1315.

894 [Fo. 62] Licence to M. Robert de Wakefeld, subdeacon,[1] rector of Heswall, to study for one year. Lichfield, 17 Mar. 1315.
[[1] Interlined.]

895 Institution of Laurence de Knuttesford, priest, to Swettenham church, vacant by the resignation of William de Swetenham, the last rector; patron, Richard, lord[1] of Swettenham. Ind.: archd. Lichfield, 18 Mar. 1315.
[Margin] He owes the fee.
  [[1] Interlined over *de* deleted.]

896 Note that custody of the sequestration on Barthomley (*Bertomlee*) church has been committed to William de Praers, clerk,[1] during pleasure. The bishop wishes that William should not be troubled concerning the account to be rendered.[2] 16 Aug. 1315.
  [A copy of **765**, which was cancelled.
  [1] Instituted 25 Oct. 1315, see **898**.
  [2] The bishop received nothing from this sequestration, see LJRO MS. D30 M7d; Hughes, 'Episcopate', i.181.]

897 Note that custody of the sequestration on Hawarden (*Hawardin*) church was committed to William de Melton,[1] priest, during pleasure, at Eccleshall on 24 May 1315. William later advised the bishop that the letter issued to him concerning the custody had been taken from his proctor. William obtained a new letter at Coldham on 21 Aug. Archd. of Chester to deliver custody to W[illiam], or his proctor. William is not bound to render an account.[2]
  [[1] Consecrated archbishop of York, 25 Sept. 1317, see *HBC*, 282.
  [2] The bishop received nothing from this sequestration also, see LJRO MS. D30 M7d; Hughes, 'Episcopate', i.181.]

898 Institution of William de Praers, acolyte, to Barthomley (*Bertumlee*) church, vacant by the death of Robert de Chishull, the last rector, on 14 June last; patron, Richard called le Praers, lord of Barthomley (*Bertumlegh*). Ind.: archd. of Chester. Stone, 25 Oct. 1315.

899 Note that the same William has had dispensation concerning holy orders and to study for one year. Eccleshall, 2 Nov. 1315.

900 Note of similar dispensation for Ralph [de Brerton][1], rector of Brereton chapel. Cheadle (*Chedle*), 17 Nov. 1315.
  [[1] See **882**.]

901* Institution of Thomas de Cressacr' of York dioc. to Mottram in Long-dendale church; patron, Thomas de Burg'. Ind.: archd. of Chester. The church is vacant by the resignation of M. Jordan de Maclesfeld,[1] who last held the same, against whom proceedings to deprive were begun by the bishop in his visitation of the archdeaconry of Chester the same year,[2] but he, anticipating the sentence, freely resigned that benefice. Bracebridge near Lincoln. 4 Feb. 1316.
  [[1] See **174**, and note.
  [2] Probably about 17 Nov. 1315 when the bishop was nearby at Cheadle, see **900**, and the itinerary, Appendix D in Volume II.]

902 The same day the said Thomas had dispensation to attend the schools for one year and concerning holy orders, provided that he shall be ordained subdeacon in that year according to the terms of the constitution of [Pope] Boniface.

[No record of Thomas having received the subdiaconate has been found. The register of William Greenfield notes only that he had letters dimissory for minor orders on 19 Mar. 1315, see *The Register of William Greenfield, lord archbishop of York, 1306–1315*, ed. W. Brown, A Hamilton Thompson (Surtees Society, 145, 149, 151–3, 1931–40), v, no. 2785, note.]

ANNO DOMINI M^{o}.CCC.XVI.

903 Dispensation for M. Robert de Wakefeld, rector of Heswall, concerning holy orders and to remain in the schools for one year. 2 May 1316.

904 Grant *in commendam* to Richard de Osgodby, priest, a kinsman of Sir Adam de Osgodby, of the vacant[1] church of Hawarden (*Hawarthyn*). Ind.: archd. of Chester. 6 May 1316.

[1 Interlined.]

905 [Fo. 62v] Institution of Robert de Notingham to Bebington church; patrons, abbot and convent of Chester. Ind.: official of Chester or the dean of Wirral (*Wyrhal*). Tutbury (*Tutebur'*), 7 July 1316.

906 Institution of Adam de Wetenhal to Woodchurch church, vacant by the death of John de Tewe, the last rector; patron, Richard de Praers. Ind.: archd. of Chester. 16 June 1316.

907 Institution of John called Travers to Prestwich (*Prestwych*) church, vacant by the death of M. William de Markelawe, the last rector, on Wed. 5 May last; patron, Adam de Preswych. Ind.: archd. of Chester. Sheepwash near Lincoln, 7 Aug. 1316.

908 [Duplicate copy of **779**.]

909 Institution of M. Roger de Soterleye to Stoke on the Wirral (*Stok' in Wyrhal*) church, vacant by the death of Robert de Hulmo, the last rector, on Fri. 20 Aug. last; patron, Edmund de Soterleye. Ind.: archd. of Chester. [1]Dispensation for the same [to study] from 8 Oct. under the terms of the constitution of [Pope] Boniface.[1] Hackington (*Hakyngton*) near Canterbury, 4 Oct. 1316.

[1-1 Added later near the spine.]

910 Institution of Andrew de Aston, chaplain, to St. Mary's chantry in St. John's church, Chester, vacant by the death of Nicholas de Brodbrok' on 7 Sept. last; patron, Sir John de Orreby, kt. Ind.: dean of St. John's, Chester, or his commissary. 12 Oct. 1316.

911 Note that the election of Lady Emma de Vernoun as prioress of the nuns of Chester was examined and confirmed in Eccleshall prebendal church on

29 Nov. [1316]. She swore obedience to the bishop. Mandate to the nuns to obey her. Ind.: archd. of Chester.

912 Institution of Adam del Clif, priest, to Eastham (*Estham*) vicarage, vacant by the death of Simon de Aston on Fri. 26 Nov. last; patrons, abbot and convent of St. Werburgh, Chester. Ind.: archd. of Chester. Sawley (*Sallowe*), 12 Dec. 1316.

913 Institution of Adam, son of Robert de Mascy, to the moiety of Lymm (*Lymme*) church vacant by the death of Peter de Lymme, the former rector, on Fri. 5 Nov. last; patron, Thomas, son of Thomas de Leg'. Ind.: archd. of Chester. London, 22 Jan. 1317.

914 Licence to the same Adam to study for one year, on condition that he will be promoted at least to the order of subdeacon within that time according to the terms of the constitution *Cum ex eo*. Same day.
    [He is not listed in the ordination lists for Coventry and Lichfield diocese.]

915 [Fo. 63] Dispensation for William de Praers, deacon, rector of Barthomley, to enter the schools for one year; he shall not be compelled to further orders meanwhile[1]. [London] 22 Jan. 1317.
    [[1] Interlined.]

916 Institution of William de Wyco to Runcorn (*Runcovere*) vicarage; patrons, prior and convent of Norton. Ind.: archd. of Chester. 21 Mar. 1317.

917 Institution of Richard del Grene, chaplain, to Taxal (*Takishal*) church; patron, Edmund de Dounys. Ind.: archd. of Chester. 30 Mar. 1317.

ANNO DOMINI MILLESIMO .CCC^{mo}. SEPTIMODECIMO.

918 Licence to M. Robert de Wakfeld, rector of Heswall, to study for one year under the terms of the constitution of Pope Boniface VIII. Brington (*Bryngton*), 9 Apr. 1317.

919 Institution of Gilbert de Ringstude to the chapel of the Rood, Tarporley (*la Rode de Torperle*); patron, Sir John de Grey. Ind.: archd. Eccleshall, 30 May 1317.

920 [Copy of the] charter of Prior Andrew and the convent of Norton to Hugh, son of Hugh de Dotton and his heirs granting all the dead wood from Brewood wood to give and to sell, saving forever to the house and brethren all necessities for building and burning by view of their forester, without hindrance of the forester, and without the destruction of the wood.
    They remit all their rights of common in 'Hulteleth' wood, except that for 60 pigs and 60 cattle.
    They will provide a chaplain to celebrate mass forever at Poolsey (*Pullishey*), and a lamp burning at mass and at the office for the souls of his father and mother, their ancestors, and heirs.

They grant an adequate right of way for all necessities, provided that no damage occurs to corn and hay.

They remit the 5 marks (£3 6s. 8d.) which they were claiming from his father's will, and which he was obliged to pay to them.

Sealing clause. Witnesses: J[ohn] de Lacy, earl of Lincoln, Sir Roger de Cestr', Henry de Longchamp, Geoffrey, son of Adam de Dotton, Geoffrey de Clifton, Gilbert de Lymme, Graham de Lostok, Hubert, parson of Donington (*Doninton*), William, lord of Desborough (*Derisbur'*), Ranulph Starki, William the clerk, and many others. [?1236.]

[For the date see J.P. Greene, *Norton Priory* (Cambridge, 1989), 9, 10; G. Ormerod, *The history of the county palatine and city of Chester*, 2nd. edn., ed. T. Helsby, 2 vols., (London, 1882), i, pt. ii.643. An Andrew occurs as prior 1224–31 and 1238, see *The heads of religious houses in England and Wales 940–1216*, ed. D. Knowles, C.N.L. Brooke (Cambridge, 1972), 178. John de Lacy was recognized as earl of Lincoln 1232 and died 1240, see *HBC*, 470; *DNB*, xi.380.]

921 Acta of the visitation of the archdeaconry of Chester by the bishop's commissaries Adam Burum and Nicholas de Gunthumdelee concerning the aforesaid charter. The prior and convent of Norton of the Augustinian order have resisted the findings of the visitation. At the provision of Sir Hugh de Dutton, kt., the defendants were called. Br. John de Colton, the prior, who had sufficient mandate on behalf of his convent, came before the commissaries on the said day. Sir Hugh was also present, asserting that the religious were obliged to provide a chaplain to celebrate mass forever in Poolsey chapel, with a lamp burning at mass and the office at the due and accustomed hours. They had withdrawn the chaplain and lamp. The prior acknowledged himself and his convent to be bound to provide the foregoing. Sir Hugh produced the above-written charter [fo. 63v]. The commissaries have condemned the religious to provide the chaplain and lamp in accordance with their acknowledgement, as is evident by the commissaries' certificate. St. John's prebendal church, Chester, 15 Feb. 1316.

[The rest of the folio is blank.]

[Fo. 64] SALOP'. REGISTRUM ARCHIDIACONATUS SALOP' A FESTO SANCTE TRINITATIS ANNO GRACIE .M°.CCC^{mo}. SEPTIMO ET CONSECRACIONIS W[ALTERI] [1]DE LANGETON[1] EPISCOPI COVENTR' .XI.

[[1–1] Interlined.]

922 Note that custody of the bishop's sequestration on Ness church has been committed to Philip de Harleye, acolyte, until Michaelmas next, having been presented to the church by the abbot and convent of Shrewsbury.[1] Note of the letter to the archdeacon of Shrewsbury [quoted]. Ind. him or his proctor, with all its rights [etc.]. London, 18 June 1307. Letters dimissory for all minor and subdeacon's orders.

Note that the church became vacant on[2] Thurs. 6 Apr. last by the death of Hugh de Ballecot, the last rector.

[[1] Instituted 27 Nov. 1307, see **504**.
[2] Interlined.
Followed by a line drawn across the folio.]

REGISTRUM POST EGRESSUM EPISCOPI A CARCERE V. IDUS NOVEMBRIS [9 NOV. 1308].

923 Letter to Thomas Crok', clerk. He has been commended to the bishop for his probity. He proposes to honour his pious and meritorious person with an ecclesiastical benefice. He collates to him that prebend in St. Chad's church, Shrewsbury, which was John de Kirkeby's, and which is vacant by his death, with all its rights, [etc.]. Ind.: dean and chapter. London, 12 Dec. 1308.

924 Letters patent to Philip de Harle, subdeacon,[1] rector of Ness (*Nesse le Strange*). Since he has the mind to study, so that he will bear full fruit in God's church, the bishop grants him the desired licence to study at university for one year, receiving wholly the fruits and revenues of his church, provided that the church is not defrauded of duties [etc.]. London, 2 Feb. 1309.
   [1 Interlined.]

925 Note that Philip de Halis, subdeacon, has obtained letters dimissory for the orders of deacon [1]and priest[1] to the title of a 50s. annual pension from William de Morton, rector of Holme-next-the-Sea (*de Hulmo juxta Mare*), Norwich dioc. London, 3 Mar. 1309.
   [1-1 Interlined.]

926 [Fo. 64v] Licence, in common form, to John de Burton, rector of West Felton, to study for two years. London, 5 Mar. 1309.

927 Note that Brothers William de Burg' and Thomas de Acton, monks and professed of St. Peter's monastery, Shrewsbury, have had letters dimissory for the order of priest. London, 7 May 1309.

928 Note that M. Ralph de la Bolde, rector of Edgmond (*Egmundon*), and Robert de Atterlegh, rector of Tong (*Tonge*), have had licences in common form to study for two years from Assumption next. London, 9 May 1309.

INCIPIT ANNUS DOMINI M[us].CCC[mus]. NONUS.

929 Letters patent to Peter de Fomython, rector of Ightfield (*Hythefeld*). Because he wishes to attend to the business of his church, the bishop grants him licence that he may be absent until 1 Mar. next, putting the fruits to his use meanwhile, provided that the church is not defrauded [etc.]. Ranton, 16 Nov. 1309.

930 Licence to Roland [de Viquiria],[1] portioner of Wroxeter (*Wrokcestre*), to study at university for one year. [Ranton] 3 Dec. 1309.
   [1 See **335**.]

931 Licence to Simon de Cotenham, rector of Berrington (*Byriton*), to be absent for one year; and the same for Hugh de Byriton, and to farm [the benefice]. Ranton, 17 Dec. 1309.

932 Note that custody of the sequestration on Wem (*Wenne*) church has been committed to the proctor of M. John de St. Amand,[1] clerk, having been presented to the same church, during pleasure. Ranton, 18 Dec. 1309.

[1 *BRUO*, iii.1623–4.]

933 Licence to Richard de Deryngton, rector of Hordley (*Hordyleg'*) chapel, to study at university for one year. Ranton, 6 Jan. 1310.

934 Licence to Thomas Colle of Shrewsbury to have an oratory at his manor of Uckington (*Oxindon*) and to cause divine service lawfully to be celebrated there, on condition that no prejudice will be caused to his mother church, during pleasure. Ranton, 8 Jan. 1310.

935* [Fo. 65] Note that on 12 Jan. 1310 at Ranton the bishop absolved Sir Richard de Leghton, kt., from a sentence of excommunication imposed for his many contumacies before the bishop's commissary[-general] in the consistory court at Lichfield. He is enjoined to go to Rome before Michaelmas and offer 12 pounds of wax candles in St. Peter's church, and make a similar oblation in St. Paul's church, on pain of 40 marks [£26 13s. 4d.].

936 Institution of M. John de Bruneshope, subdeacon, to Upton Magna (*Opton*) church, vacant by the death of John le Ensaunt on 11 June last; patrons, abbot and convent of Shrewsbury. Ind.: archd. Ranton, 27 Jan. 1310.

937 Licence to Philip de Harle, subdeacon, rector of Ness, to study for one year under the terms of the constitution of Pope Boniface VIII. Ranton, 3 Feb. 1310.

938 Licence to Thomas de Charnes, priest, rector of a moiety of Condover, to study at university for one year. Ranton, 3 Feb. 1310.

939 Letters patent to Philip de Warle, clerk. On account of his probity the bishop is persuaded to honour him with an ecclesiastical benefice. He collates to him that prebend which Ingelard de Warle, his brother, held in St. Chad's church, Shrewsbury, which is vacant by his resignation, with all its rights [etc.]. London, 19 Feb. 1310.

940 Collation to Owen de Montgomery, priest, of the deanery of St. Chad's church, Shrewsbury, vacant by the resignation of Robert called Peet of Worcester, the last dean. Ind.: archd. London, 28 Feb. 1319.

941 Institution of Walter, son of John de Perton, acolyte,[1] to Stirchley (*Stirchleye*) church, vacant by the resignation of Roger de Esthop, the last rector, on Tues. 13 Jan. last; patrons, prior and convent of Much Wenlock. Ind. him or his proctor: archd. Lichfield, 17 Mar. 1310.

[1 Interlined.]

942 Licence, in common form, to M. John de Knouvill', rector of Whitchurch (*Whytchurch*), to study for one year from Easter next. Lichfield, 19 Mar. 1310.

[Fo. 65v] INCIPIT ANNUS DOMINI MILLESIMUS .CCC^{mus}.X^{us}.

943 Institution of Hammond de la More, acolyte, to the vacant chapel of Isombridge (*Esnebrigg'*), which has devolved to the bishop's collation by lapse of time by authority of the General Council.[1] Ind.: archd. Lichfield, 3 June 1310.
    [[1] See **22**, note.]

944 Institution of Thomas de Cheynneye, acolyte, to West Felton church, vacant by the death of John de Byriton, the last rector, on Mon. 4 May last; patron, Hugh, son of Philip de Felton. Ind.: archd. 25 July 1310.

945* Letter to Emma Sprenghose. She has aspired to the solitary life of an anchorite from childhood. Wishing to know the truth concerning her life, manner of living, and suitability, the bishop has caused an inquiry [to be made] by suitable men who have known her. He has learned that she is suitable for this solitary life. He admits her as an anchorite in the houses of the churchyard of St. George's chapel, Shrewsbury, in order to serve God. Ind.: archd. of Shrewsbury, or the dean of St. Chad's church, Shrewsbury, or his proctor. Eccleshall, 17 Jan. 1311.

946 Licence, in common form, to M. John de Knevill', rector of Whitchurch, to study for one year from 2 Mar. next. He is to cause 40s. to be distributed to the poor[1] before Whitsun. 23 Jan. 1311.
    [[1] Interlined.]

947 Note that Peter de Ware, priest, has been collated and instituted to Prees vicarage, vacant by the resignation of John de Pritewell, the last vicar, in an exchange of benefices lawfully and legitimately made between Peter[1] and J[ohn] of St. Dunstan's church, near the Tower of London, and the said vicarage. Ind. him or his proctor: William de Thorp, priest. Eccleshall, 24 Mar. 1311.
[Margin] Nothing for the fee.
    [[1] Interlined.]

948 Licence to Walter, son of John de Perton, subdeacon, rector of Stirchley (*Stirchesleye*), to study for one year under the terms of the constitution of Pope Boniface VIII. Same place.

949 [Fo. 65A][1] Letter to the abbot and convent of Haughmond (*Hagmun'*). The bishop recently[2] visited their monastery on Tues.[3] 10 June 1315. He found certain things assailed and observed [4]by them[4] . . . of the decrees and provisions of St.[5] Peter.
    The diocesan's agreement is required . . . concerning the corrody or allowance granted by them to Roger de Crabs' for his lifetime. Moreover, because[6] . . . the clothes and shoes of the canons have been accustomed to be

assigned[7] to each brother [from] [8]a certain sum of money[9] till now,[8] wishing to provide for the benefit of their monastery, and as property was being removed by them, . . . they shall not sell or commend[10] any[11] allowance or corrody henceforth without the bishop's express agreement, or that of his successors, nor . . . shall they presume to assign any [12]clothes to the brethren.[12] Henceforth, they shall have a chamberlain who shall provide and supply clothes and shoes and other such things[13] . . . to each brother[14] according to the custom of their religion. But in consideration of their grace, the bishop shall not impose a penalty for the said excesses. n.d.

[[1] This folio is a piece of parchment measuring approximately 20.4cm. by 9.5cm. A vertical tear in the centre of the piece, some 2cm. from its foot, measures approximately 4cm.; it has been stitched. Both sides are working records, and have many deletions and interlineations, and some of the text is illegible.
[2] Deleted and underdotted.
[3] Interlined over *lune* deleted.
[4-4] Interlined.
[5] MS. *sanctorum*
[6] Interlined, followed by two deleted and illegible words.
[7] Over an illegible erasure.
[8-8] Interlined.
[9] MS. *pecunie summam* followed by *pecuniam* deleted.
[10] Interlined.
[11] Followed by *absque* deleted.
[12-12] Interlined.
[13] Followed by *juxta more religionis vestre* interlined and deleted.
[14] See **950, 984**; *VCH Shropshire*, ii.66; Hughes, 'Episcopate', i.289.
The rest of the recto is blank.]

950 [Fo. 65Av] Letter to the abbot and convent of Haughmond. In his visitation of their monastery on Tues.[1] 10 June 1315 the bishop granted the retirement of Br. Gilbert de Caumpedene, the abbot. He committed the ordinance of the provision to be made for Br. Gilbert's maintenance to M. John Popard, his clerk, who has put it in writing, which ordinance or provision is as follows:

Br. Gilbert shall have that room which he had before, sustenance in food and drink from the commons as for two canons in[2] the refectory, also a canon serving him as[3] a canon in the refectory, and two servants serving him with bread and ale from [4]the cellar[4] as[5] two of the abbot's servants, on condition that the leftovers are given for alms.

[6]The abbot and convent shall have their church of Cheswardine (*Chestwarthyn*),[7] which they are disputing, notwithstanding the said ordinance, etc.[6]

Br. Gilbert shall receive 10 marks [£6 13s. 4d.] each year from the common purse of the house (5 marks [£3 6s. 8d.] at Michaelmas, 5 marks at Annunciation) for his clothes[8] and other necessities, and those of his ministers.[9]

Br. G[ilbert] shall attend divine service in the choir of the monastery, especially at mass and at the principal canonical hours, as often as his faculties or infirmities allow.

[10]Br. Gilbert shall obey the abbot instituted to the monastery in all things.[10]

This ordinance shall be observed firmly on both sides, and they shall affix their common seal to this document. n.d.

[¹ Interlined over *lune* interlined and deleted.
² Interlined over *de* deleted.
³ Interlined.
⁴⁻⁴ Interlined.
⁵ Interlined.
⁶⁻⁶ Interlined.
⁷ For the confirmation of this church, see **984**, and note.
⁸ Followed by *ipsum* deleted.
⁹ Interlined.
¹⁰⁻¹⁰ Interlined.
The rest of the folio is blank.]

[Fo.66] INCIPIT ANNUS DOMINI .MILLESIMUS .CCC^mus. UNDECIMUS.

951   Institution of Richard de Polyleye, subdeacon, to Donnington (*Dunyton*) church, vacant by the death of Richard de Albriston, the last rector, on Tues. 4 May; patrons, abbot and convent of Shrewsbury. Ind.: archd. York, 5 June 1311.
[Margin] He paid the fee.

952   Institution of Thomas de Brocton, priest, to Buildwas (*Parva Buldewas*) church, vacant by the death of Richard de Morton, the last rector, on 5 Aug.; patrons, abbot and convent of Buildwas. He is to pay an annual pension of 5s. to the mother church of Wroxeter. Ind.: archd. London, 10 Sept. 1311.

953   Licence, in common form, to M. Ralph de la Bold, rector of Edgmond, to study for one year.¹ London, 11 Nov. 1311.
[¹ *Annum* interlined.]

954   Institution of Robert de Longeley, clerk, to Ruckley (*Rocley*) chapel, vacant by the death of Ivon, the last rector, on Sun. 31 Oct.; patron, Richard Burnel, lord of Langley (*Longeley*). Ind.: archd. London, 23 Nov. 1311.
[Margin] Nothing for the fee because he is poor.

955   Note that custody of the sequestration placed on the fruits and revenues of Pitchford (*Picheford*) church has been committed to John Giffard, clerk, during pleasure. M. Richard de Norhampton, the sequestrator, to deliver custody. London, 18 Dec. 1311.

956   Institution of Roger, son of Roger de Smythecote, acolyte, to Smethcott (*Smythecote*) church, vacant by the death of Richard, the last rector, on Tues. 7 Dec. last; patron, Sir Edward Burnel. Ind.: archd. Lichfield, 2 Jan. 1312.
[Margin] He owes the fee.

ANNUS CONSECRACIONIS W[ALTERI] EPISCOPI .XVI^us.

957 Institution of M. John de St. Valery, priest, to Pitchford church; patron, the bishop, because the manor of Pitchford, with its appurtenances and the advowson of the church have been enfeoffed to him and his heirs by Sir Ralph de Pycheford, kt. Ind.: archd. York, 26 Feb. 1312.
[Margin] ¹He owes the fee.¹ ²M. John was not instituted, nor swore canonical obedience.²
[¹⁻¹ In the right-hand margin.
²⁻² Added later in the left-hand margin.]

958 Note that custody of the sequestration on Albright Hussey (*Adbriston Heose*) chapel has been committed to Richard de Lilleshull, priest. Archd. and the sequestrator to deliver custody. 28 Dec. 1313.

[Fo. 66v] ANNUS DOMINI MILLESIMUS .CCC^mus. DUODECIMUS INCIPIT.

959 Grant *in commendam* to M. John de Stanton, priest, of Cound church for half a year. Ind.: archd. Brington (*Bruynton*),¹ 30 Mar. 1312.
[¹ Interlined.]

960 Institution of the same M. John de Stanton to Cound church; patron; Lady Matilda called Burnell. He swore [etc.]. The bishop granted that [John's] possession of the church *in commendam* should now be by title of institution. 1 Apr. 1312.
[Margin] He paid nothing.

INCIPIT ANNUS DOMINI MILLESIMUS CCC^mus.XIII^us. CONSECRACIONIS DOMINI EPISCOPI XVII.

961 Licence to M. John de St. Valery, priest, rector of Pitchford (*Pycheford*), to study at any university for one year. London, 26 Oct. 1313.

962 Licence, in common form, to Richard de Polileye, rector of Donnington (*Donynton*), to study at university for one year. 6 Nov. 1313.

963 Mandate to M. Richard de Norhampton, the bishop's sequestrator-general, to deliver custody of the sequestration on Wem (*Wemme*) church to any suitable person, during pleasure, until the bishop comes to his diocese in person. The church is to be served [etc.], and a faithful account rendered. London, 14 Nov. 1313.

964 Institution of John de Leicestr', acolyte, to Harley church, vacant by the resignation of Thomas de Langeton, the last rector, in . . .¹ Oct.; patron, Sir Richard de Harle. Ind.: archd. London, 27 Nov. 1313.
[Margin] He owes the fee.
[¹ 2cm. blank space.]

965 Institution of Amaury (*Almaricus*) le Botiller, acolyte, to Wem church, vacant by the resignation of John de St. Amand, the last rector, on 18 Oct. last; patron, Sir William le Botiller, kt. Ind.: archd. 24 Dec. 1313.
[Margin] He owes the fee.

966 Institution of Walter de Wrokwardyn, priest, to Ightfield (*Ithtefeld*), vacant by the death of Peter le Fuchun, the last rector, on 29 Nov. last; patron, Sir Fulk le Strange, kt. Ind.: archd. 26 Dec. 1313.
[Margin] He paid the fee.

967 [Fo. 67] Licence, in common form, to [M.] Jordan de Caunvill', rector of Clifton Campville, to study for one year. 3 Mar. 1314.

968 Note of like licence for Simon [de Cotenham],[1] rector of Berrington, for two years. 3 Mar. 1314.
[[1] See **931**.]

969 Letters patent to Richard de Lilleshull, priest. The pastoral office is incumbent on the bishop's shoulders. He is obliged to grant suitable support to those of tender age. Thomas de Whitinton, clerk, has been presented to the bishop for the vacant chapel of Albright Hussy (*Adbriston Hoesee*) by John Heose, the patron. Thomas is under age; he cannot be admitted lawfully to the same because of this. Wishing to make special grace to Thomas and to provide beneficially for the said [chapel],[1] the bishop appoints Richard keeper as well as curate until the presentee attains full age, provided that the chapel is served in duties [etc.] and he shall release the fruits and revenues belonging to the chapel for the use of the presentee. London, 30 Jan. 1314.
[[1] MS. *ecclesie*]

970 Note that custody of the sequestration placed on the fruits and revenues of Ruyton church has been committed to John de Stevynton, acolyte, during pleasure. The bishop wishes John to take the fruits entirely for himself, and not render his account. The sequestrator shall deliver custody. Prees, 12 June 1314.

971 Licence to Amaury le Botiller, acolyte, rector of Wem, to study for two years from the date of his institution[1]. Same day, and place.
[[1] 24 Dec. 1313, see **965**.]

972 Commission to M. Philip de Turvill', the bishop's official, to examine and determine the business of the presentation of John de Cheyne to the portion of Wroxeter church which is vacant by the death of Roland [de Viquiria],[1] the late portioner; with power to institute and destitute, and induct, to make and grant letters of institution and induction, or to sequestrate or grant the portion *in commendam*, and to do all that the business requires, with power of coercion. York, 21 Sept. 1314.
[[1] See **335**, **750**, **991**.]

973 Institution of John de Styventon, acolyte, to Ruyton church, vacant by the death of Adam de Picheford, the last rector; patron, Sir John la Ware, kt. He swore canonical obedience.[1] London, 1 Nov. 1314.

[[1] There is no mandate to induct.]

974 Note that custody of the sequestration on Prees vicarage has been committed to Richard de Norton, priest, under these terms: Richard is not bound to render an account of the fruits and revenues. Prees, 7 Dec. 1314.

975 [Fo. 67v] Institution of John le Kent, priest, to Lilleshall vicarage, vacant by the resignation of Simon, the last vicar, on Sun. 22 Sept. last; patrons, abbot and convent of Lilleshall. Ind.: archd. 25 Nov. 1314.

976 Licence to Thomas de Cheynee, rector of West Felton, to study for one year under the terms of the constitution. 7 Dec. 1314.

977 Institution of William de la Rode, acolyte, to Newport (*de Novo Burgo*) church, vacant by the death of Richard de Geidon, the last rector, on 1 Jan. last; patrons, abbot and convent of Shrewsbury. Ind.: archd. London, 7 Feb. 1315. [Margin] He owes the fee.

978 Commission to the dean of St. Chad's church, Shrewsbury. The bishop has admitted Isolda de Hungerford to follow the life of an anchorite, to be enclosed in the houses of St. Romuald's cemetery, Shrewsbury, where other anchorites live. Mandate to enclose her. London, 29 Jan. 1315.

979 Institution of Robert de Preston, acolyte, to Fitz (*Fyttes*) church, vacant by the death of M. Richard de Golden, the last rector, on Mon. 24 Mar. last; patrons, abbot and convent of Haughmond. Ind.: archd. Eccleshall, 23 May 1315.

[Calendared in *The cartulary of Haughmond Abbey*, ed. U. Rees (Shropshire Archaeological Society and University of Wales Press, Cardiff, 1985), no. 325.]

980 Licence to Amaury le Botiler, subdeacon,[1] rector of Wem, to study for one year from Christmas next under the terms of the constitution. 8 June 1315.

[[1] Interlined.]

981 Letters patent to Richard de Norton, priest. Considering his laudable probity, and industrious and fervent zeal for the service of God and the cure of souls, the bishop collates him by ordinary right to Prees vicarage, which is vacant by the death of Peter de Ware, with all its rights [etc.]. Prees, 5 June 1315.

982 Collation to Hugh de Lemmistr' of the prebend in St. Chad's collegiate church, Shrewsbury, which was John de Sutham's. Ind.: archd. of Shrewsbury. Weston near Stanford (*Weston juxta Stanford*), 4 Oct. 1315.

983 Institution of Thomas de Coventr', chaplain, to Newport church, vacant by the resignation of William de la Rode, the last rector, as William was instituted to another church;[1] patrons, abbot and convent of Shrewsbury. Ind.: archd. Everton, 6 Oct. 1315.

[[1] Instituted rector of Ness, 1 May 1315, see **1069**.]

984 [Fo. 68] Letters patent to the prior and convent of Haughmond, confirming the grant of Cheswardine (*Cheswardyn'*) church with its fruits, revenues, and appurtenances, and income from rents of lands in Naginton and Hisland (*Nagynton et Hydeslond*), to provide the canons' clothing. These revenues are to be administered by the chamberlain [of Haughmond]. Lichfield, 2 July 1315.

[Printed in *The cartulary of Haughmond Abbey* (see **979**), no. 452. See also *ibid.*, no. 223; **949, 950**.]

985 Dispensation for M. Robert de Preston, subdeacon,[1] concerning non residence, [2]holy orders,[2] and to study for one year. 3 Mar. 1316.
[Margin] Licence to study for the rector of Fitz (*Fittes*).

[[1] Interlined.
[2–2] Interlined.]

ANNO DOMINI[1] [MCCC].XVI.
[[1] Interlined.]

986 Note that the bishop granted a licence to study for one year under the terms of the constitution *Cum ex eo* to William de la Rode, rector of Ness, beginning on 26 June 1315. William has not received this letter. He later obtained dispensation from the bishop for two years, under the same terms, to be reckoned from the same day, 26 June, and he has received a letter for both the first and the following year.

987 Note that . . .[1] [in] Sept. Gerard, the proctor of M. Stephen de Segrave,[2] came before the bishop and presented a certain process made by an auditor at the Curia, the seal of whom was unknown, depriving M. Richard de Leycester of all his ecclesiastical benefices, and enjoining the bishops in whose dioceses Richard held benefices to provide other persons to them within six days of the process having been presented, under pain of excommunication. Since the same M. Richard had obtained a prebend in St. Chad's church, Shrewsbury, the bishop collated that prebend to M. Thomas de Teffunt . . .[3] [in] September.

[[1] Blank space.
[2] *BRUC*, 516.
[3] Blank space.]

988 Dispensation for M. Robert de Preston, rector of Fitz, concerning non residence, holy orders, and to study in the schools for one year. Haughmond, 25 Nov. 1316.

989 Collation to John de Wyndesovere, rector of Newton (*Newenton*), of the prebend in St. Chad's collegiate church, Shrewsbury, which was M. Hugh de Musele's. Ind.: dean and chapter. London, 5 Feb. 1317.

990 Institution of William Mynch, chaplain, to Acton Pigot (*Acton Pygot*) chapel; patron, Sir John de Handle, kt. Ind.: archd. of Shrewsbury. Coldham, 16 Feb. 1317.

ANNUS [MCCC].XVII^{us}.

991 Institution of John de Cheyne to the portion of Wroxeter church which was Roland [de Viquiria's]; patron, Edmund, earl of Arundel. Ind.: archd. of Shrewsbury. Lichfield, 2 Apr. 1317.
　　[See also **750, 972**.]

[Fo. 68v] ANNUS DOMINI .M^{us}.CCC^{us}.XVII^{us}.

992 Note that Adam Husee, clerk, 17 years of age according to the inquiry, has been instituted to Albright Hussy (*Adbrighton Husee*) chapel, without cure of souls, by dispensation; patron, John Husee. Ind.: archd. of Shrewsbury. Prees, 3 July 1317.

993 Institution of Thomas de Charnes to Middle (*Mydle*) church; patrons, abbot and convent of Shrewsbury. Ind.: archd. of Shrewsbury. Pitchford, 4 July 1317.

994 Licence to William de la Rode, ¹rector of Ness,¹ to study for one year. He shall not be compelled to further orders during that term. Same day.
　　[¹⁻¹ Interlined.]

995 Collation to M. Richard Het of the prebend in St. Chad's collegiate church, Shrewsbury, vacant by the resignation of Robert Eles. Brington, 13 July 1317.

996 Licence to John de Cheyne, portioner of Wroxeter church, to study in the schools for one year, and concerning holy orders, under the terms of the constitution of [Pope] Boniface. 3 Feb. 1318.

997 Institution of John de Cheyne to Cound church, vacant by the resignation of M. John de Staunton, the last rector, on 14 Feb. last; patron, Edmund, earl of Arundel. Ind.: archd. of Shrewsbury. 10 Mar. 1318.

998 Institution of John de Braundon to the portion of Wroxeter church which was John Cheyne's; patron, Edmund, earl of Arundel. Ind.: archd. of Shrewsbury. 10 Mar. 1318.

HIC INCIPIT ANNUS DOMINI MILLESIMUS .CCC^{us}.XVIII^{us}.

999 Institution of John de London to the vacant chapel of Hordley (*Hordeleye*); patrons, abbot and convent of Shrewsbury. Ind.: archd. of Shrewsbury. 17 May 1318.

1000 Institution of Reginald de Chetewynde, acolyte, to Chetwynd (*Chetewinde*) church, vacant by the death of M. John de Uphavene on Tues. 2 May last. Ind.: archd. 27 June 1318.

[Fo. 69] ANNUS DOMINI .M.CCC.XVIII.

1001 Institution of John de Hatton, chaplain, to Upton (*Upton Parva*) chapel [1]with cure of souls,[1] vacant by the resignation of Robert Ridel on 29 June. Ind.: archd. of Shrewsbury. 14 July 1318.

    [[1–1] Interlined.]

1002 Licence to William de la Rode, rector of Ness, to study for one year, and concering holy orders, according to the constitution [1]*Cum ex eo*.[1] 4 July 1318.

    [[1–1] Underlined.]

1003 Collation to William Vacc' of Wales of the prebend in [St. Chad's] collegiate church, Shrewsbury, which was M. Thomas de Teffunte's. 4 Nov. 1318.

1004 Dispensation for John Cheyni, rector of Cound, [to study] for one year under the terms of the constitution [1]*Cum ex eo*[1]. 8 Nov. 1318.

    [[1–1] Underlined.]

1005 Note of similar dispensation for Reginald [de Chetewynde],[1] rector of Chetwynd. 1 Jan. 1319.

    [[1] See **1000**.]

1006 Note of similar dispensation for Robert, rector of Albrighton (*Albrichton*). 1 July 1319.

1007 Note of similar dispensation for [1]M. Richard de Longenohe,[1] rector of Ness. 13 Sept. 1319.

    [[1–1] Interlined.]

1008 Institution of Robert Power, acolyte, in the person of John de Hakchop', his proctor, to Adderley (*Adderdelegh*) church, vacant by the death of M. Richard de Norhampton on 11 June last; patron, the king.[1] Ind.: archd. of Shrewsbury. 15 Sept. 1319.

    [[1] *CPR 1317–21*, 387.]

1009 Dispensation for Roger [de Smythecote],[1] rector of Smethcott, to study for one year. 13 July 1319.

    [[1] See **956**.]

1010 Institution of Stephen de Godwyneston, chaplain, in the person of John de Cotes, clerk, his proctor, to Acton Burnell church, vacant by[1] the institution of John de Torrynge to Tarring (*Torryng*) church, Chichester dioc., on 24 Feb.

1318; patron, Sir John de Handlow, kt. Ind.: archd. of Shrewsbury. 31 Oct. 1319.

[¹ Followed by a line drawn through an erasure of 1.2cm.]

ANNO DOMINI M°.CCC°.XX°.

1011 Dispensation for the rector of Edgmond¹ to study for one year. 7 Apr. 1320.

[¹ John de Scheynton, see **1014**.]

1012 Institution of Thomas de Coventr', chaplain, to Donnington church, vacant by the resignation of M. Richard de Polyleye, the last rector, on Sun. 27 Apr. last; patrons, abbot and convent of Shrewsbury. Ind.: archd. of Shrewsbury. 3 May 1320.

1013 Institution of Thomas de Neuvill' to Newport church, vacant by the resignation of Thomas de Coventr', the last rector, on 3 May; patrons, abbot and convent of Shrewsbury. Ind.: archd. of Shrewsbury. 9 May 1320.

1014 Institution of John de Scheynton to Edgmond church by M. Geoffrey de Blaston, archd. of Derby, the bishop's special commissary; patrons, abbot and convent of Shrewsbury. 14 May 1319. The institution was confirmed by the bishop on 19 June.

[Entry added later at the foot of the folio.]

1015 [Fo. 69v] Institution of Thomas Honold, clerk, to Frodesley chapel, vacant by the resignation of John de Haldenham, ¹proctor of Hugh, the first rector,¹ on Sat. 26 Apr.; patron, John Honold, lord of Frodesley. Ind.: archd. of Shrewsbury. 1 Aug. 1320.

[¹⁻¹ Interlined. Hugh de Aldenham, see **359**.]

1016 Institution of Roger de Scheffeld, acolyte, to Ruyton church, vacant by the resignation of John de Stivynton, the last rector, on 26 July; patron, Sir John la Warr', kt. Ind.: archd. of Shrewsbury. Bishops Itchington (*Ichynton*), 29 Nov. 1320.
[Margin] The church of Ruyton in the deanery of Newport.

1017 Institution of Robert de Budiford, priest, to Hinstock (*Hynestok*) church, vacant by the death of William de Brugge, the last rector, on Thurs. 15 Oct. last; patrons, abbot and convent of Alcester (*Alyncestr'*), Worcester dioc. Ind.: archd. of Shrewsbury. London, 1 Feb. 1321.

1018 Institution of Nicholas de Cheyne, clerk, to Cound church, vacant by the resignation of John de Cheyne, the last rector, on 9 Feb.; patron, Edmund, earl of Arundel. Ind.: archd. of Shrewsbury. Coldham, 10 Feb. 1321.

REQUIRATUR REGISTRUM DE ANNO DOMINI .M^{o}.CCC^{o}.XXI°. IN NOVO QUATERNO.
[The rest of the folio is blank.]

[Fo.70] DERB'. REGISTRUM ARCHIDIACONATUS DERB' A FESTO SANCTE TRINITATIS
ANNO GRACIE .M^{o}.CCC^{mo}. SEPTIMO ET CONSECRACIONIS .W[ALTERI]. DE LANGETON
COVENTR' EPISCOPI .XI^{mo}.

1019   Letters patent to Ralph de Bakeputz, acolyte. He has been presented to
the vacant church of Barton Blount (*Barton*) by [Sir] John Bakepuz, kt., the
patron. The bishop admits and institutes him rector of the same, saving the right
[etc.] of the churches of Coventry and Lichfield in all things. Ind. him or his
proctor: archd. of Derby [quoted]. Letters dimissory for the order of subdeacon.
[Margin] He owes the fee. He paid nothing at institution because he accompanied the bishop to Scotland, and he had nothing. Ongar, Essex (*Aungre in Essex*),
29 May 1307.

1020   Letters patent to John de Hykelinge, priest. He has been presented to
the vacant[1] vicarage of Lowne (*Lound*) by the abbot and convent of Croxton
Kerrial (*Croxton*), the patrons. The bishop admits and institutes him in
accordance with the constitution of the legate published concerning this.[2]
Ind.: archd. of Derby.
[Margin] He owes $\frac{1}{2}$ mark for institution. Loughborough (*Luchtebourgh*), 7 Aug.
1307.
   [1 Interlined.
   2 See **118**, n. 2.
   Followed by a line drawn across the folio.]

REGISTRUM POST EGRESSUM EPISCOPI A CARCERE .V. IDUS NOVEMBRIS ANNO
M^{o}.CCC^{o}.VIII [9 NOV. 1308].
   [Underlined.]

1021   Letters patent to Roger[1] le Wyne, who was instituted rector of
Normanton on 13 Nov. 1307[2] by M. Robert de Reddeswell, archd. of Chester,
vicar-general. Since he has a mind to study, so that he will bear seasonable fruit
in God's church, the vicar-general granted him licence to study for one year
from the time of his institution. Being favourably inclined to his prayers, the
bishop grants him licence to study for another year at university in England,
receiving wholly the fruits of his church meanwhile. He shall be promoted to the
order of subdeacon at least by authority of the newly published constitution of
Pope Boniface VIII[3] [fo. 70v] within a year of the date of his institution. If he
resides in person, he shall appoint a good and adequate vicar in his church to
exercise the cure of souls and to serve it laudably in duties, according to the said
constitution; which vicar shall be supported from the revenues of the church.
Theydon Mount (*Theyden Montfichet*), 7 Feb. 1309.
   [1 Interlined.
   2 See **501**.
   3 *Cum ex eo*]

1022 Letters patent to William de Neville, acolyte. He has been presented to the vacant church of Sudbury by Sir Walter de Montgomery, kt., the patron. The bishop admits and institutes him rector of the same, saving the right [etc.], and the right to present to Somersall (*Somersale*) chapel, which is contested in the king's court. The church is vacant by the death of Robert de Montgomery, the last rector, on Fri. 24 Jan. Ind.: archd. of Derby. Letters dimissory for the order of subdeacon. Licence to study for one year according to the terms of the constitution of Pope Boniface VIII. London, 23 Feb. 1309.
[Margin] $\frac{1}{2}$ mark [for the fee].

1023 Institution of Henry de Marchinton, chaplain, to Cubley (*Cobeleye*) church, vacant by the death of Robert de Montgomery, the last rector, on Fri. 24 Jan. Ind.: archd. of Derby. Licence, in common form, to study for one year. London, 23 Feb. 1309.
[No patron is recorded.]

1024 Licence, in general form, to Reginald de Cusaunce, chaplain, rector of a moiety of Eckington, to study for one year. 21 Feb. 1309.
[He had received a licence to study for five years in England and France by 19 Nov. 1307, when he was granted papal dispensation to hold his moiety and two canonries and prebends in France, see *CPL*, ii.41.]

1025 Letters dimissory for William Talbot, acolyte, of the bishop's dioc., for the orders of subdeacon and deacon, to the title of Br. Robert, the prior, and the convent of Gresley. London, 25 Feb. 1309.

1026 Institution of Robert de Chaundoys, to the vacant moiety of Mugginton church; patron, Sir John de Chaundoys, kt. 20 Dec. 1308.
[There is no mandate to induct.]

1027 [Fo. 71] Letter to M. Robert de Reddeswelle, archd. of Chester, vicar-general. The appointment or provision of a prior for the vacant church of St. Mary, Tutbury (*Tuttebury*), has devolved to the bishop this turn by diocesan right. Trusting fully in his diligence, the bishop commissions him to provide a suitable person as prior from either the priory or elsewhere. London, 17 July 1308.
[Langton was still imprisoned at this date.]

1028 Letter to Br. Robert de Langedon, prior of St. Mary's church, Tutbury. M. R[obert] de Reddeswell, archd. of Chester, the former vicar-general, has appointed him prior and pastor of the said priory with the bishop's authority. Having approved the said provision and appointment, the bishop confirms it. Greenford, 12 Mar. 1309.

1029 Letters dimissory for William de Overa and Henry Overa, acolytes, for all holy orders, in common form, with the addition of this clause: provided that they will have shown sufficient title to their ordainer. London, 30 Apr. 1309.

INCIPIT ANNUS DOMINI .M^{us}.CCC^{us}. NONUS.

1030   Institution of William de Derby, clerk, to Weston upon Trent church, vacant by the death of Henry de Legh', the last rector, on Mon. 18 Aug.; patrons, abbot and convent of St. Werburgh, Chester. Ind.: archd. of Derby. Pentlow (*Pentelowe*), 7 Sept. 1309.

1031   Licence to M. Thomas de Pontesbury, subdeacon, rector of Trusley, to study for one year from Michaelmas next under the terms of the constitution of Pope Boniface VIII. 6 Nov. 1309.

1032   [Fo. 71v] Letters patent to Br. Hamond de Merston, canon of Holy Trinity, Breadsall Park (*de parco Breydeshale*). He has been presented to the cure and rule of the said house by Richard de Corzon of Breadsall. The bishop admits him and appoints him prior, saving the right [etc.]. The priorate is vacant by the death of Br.[1] Hugh de Mackeworth, the last prior. Ind.: archd. of Derby. Ranton, 15 Nov. 1309.
[Margin] Nothing for the fee.
   [1 Interlined.]

1033   Letters patent to Br. Ralph de Grymeston, canon of Darley, of the Augustinian order. He has been commended to the bishop by the purity of his conscience and circumspect industry. He commits to him the office of penitentiary, to be exercised throughout the archdeaconry of Derby only. London, 25 Feb. 1310.

1034   Note that custody of the sequestration [placed] on a moiety of Staveley church has been committed to Robert de Wodehouse, subdeacon, during pleasure, having been presented by Sir Ralph de Fretheuvill', kt., the patron. Ind.: archd. 9 Mar. 1310.

1035   Institution of Herbert Poucher, priest, to the vacant vicarage of Horsley (*Horseleye*); patrons, prior and convent of Lenton, of the Cluniac order. The vicarage is vacant because William le Palmere, the last vicar, was instituted to Cotgrave (*Cotegrave*) church by the archbishop of York on [Fri. 30 May] 1309.[1] Ind.: archd. Tamworth, 15 Mar. 1310.
   [1 MS. *die jovis proxima post festum sancti Bonifacii pape*, that is 12 June 1309, but see *The Register of William Greenfield, lord archbishop of York, 1306–1315* (as in **902**), v.183, where his institution is dated 30 May 1309.]

INCIPIT ANNUS DOMINI .M^{us}.CCC^{mus}.X^{us}.

1036   Licence to Robert [de Bollesovere],[1] vicar of South Wingfield (*Suth Wynfeld*) church, to go on pilgrimage to the Curia until [the Nativity of] St. John the Baptist next. Lichfield, 28 Mar. 1310.
   [1 See **1045**.]

1037   Institution of William David of Tutbury to the moiety of Mugginton (*Mogynton*) church which became vacant on 6 Nov. last; patrons, Sir Robert de

Tok', kt., and Ermintrude, his wife. Ind.: archd. Licence to study for two years. Lichfield, 7 May 1310.
[Margin] He owes the fee.

1038 [Fo. 72] Letters patent to Robert de Ibole, priest. He has been presented to the bishop for Ashbourne (*Eshebourne*) vicarage by Raymond Fabri, proctor of Raymond [de Got], dean of Lincoln,¹ the patron, who has special authority for this. He is admitted and instituted perpetual vicar of the same, saving the right [etc.]. The vicarage became vacant on Tues. 5 May last by the death of Thomas de Welton, the last vicar. Ind.: archd. Lichfield, 16 May 1310.
[Margin] He paid the fee.
    [¹ Dean 1306–10, see *Fasti*, i.3.]

1039 Licence to John [de Becco],¹ priest, rector of Swarkeston, to be absent and to farm his church for one year, provided that the church is not defrauded of duties etc. Lichfield, 23 Aug. 1310.
    [¹ See **419.**]

1040 Licence to Henry de Berleston, portioner of Darley (*Derleye in Pecco*), to be in the service of M. William de Prato, papal clerk, for one year and longer if M. William requires his services, at the request of M. William de Testa, archd. of Aran (*Aranen'*), provided that the church is not defrauded of duties etc. Lichfield, 4 Sept. 1310.
    [Testa, collector-general of papal taxes in England, was collecting annates, the revenue from the first fruits of vacant benefices appropriated to Pope Clement V for three years in 1306. Prato assisted Testa in the province of York, see Lunt, *Financial relations*, 487–90, 621–2.]

1041 Institution of Henry de Derby, acolyte, in the person of his proctor, who has sufficient mandate for this, to Aston upon Trent church, vacant by the resignation of John de Sandale, the last rector, on 7 Oct.; patrons, abbot and convent of St. Werburgh, Chester, saving forever an annual pension of 5 marks [£3 6s. 8d.] due to the said religious. Ind.: archd. 15 Nov. 1310.
[Margin] Nothing [for the fee] because the bishop has remitted [it].

1042 Institution of Br. Robert de Carleton, canon of Welbeck, to Duckmanton (*Dugmanton*) vicarage, vacant by the death of Br. William de Bollesovere, canon of Welbeck, the last vicar, on Mon. 28 Dec. last; patrons, abbot and convent of Welbeck. Ind.: archd. Eccleshall, 17 Jan. 1311.
[Margin] He paid the fee.

1043 [Fo. 72v] Institution of Br. Henry de Norwell, canon of Thurgarton (*Thurgerton*), to Blackwell (*Blacwelle*) vicarage, vacant by the death of Br. Ralph de Thistelton, canon of Thurgarton, the last vicar, on 19 Oct. last; patrons, prior and convent of Thurgarton. Ind.: archd. Eccleshall, 17 Jan. 1311.
[Margin] He paid the fee.

1044   Institution of Br. Hugh de Suwelle, canon of Shelford, to Alvaston vicarage, vacant by the resignation of Br. Godman, the last vicar, on 20 Nov. last; patrons, prior and convent of Shelford. Ind.: archd. 21 Jan. 1311.
[Margin] He paid the fee.

INCIPIT ANNUS DOMINI .M^{us}.CCC^{mus}. UNDECIMUS.

1045   Institution[1] of William de Hambury, priest, to South Wingfield vicarage, vacant by the death of Robert de Bollesovere, the last vicar, on Fri. 22 Jan. last; patrons, abbot and convent of Darley. Ind.: archd., or his official, or the dean of Scarsdale (*Scharvesdale*). 2 Apr. 1311.
[Margin] He paid nothing.
   [1 Interlined.]

1046   Institution of Philip de Cotes, priest, to Shirley vicarage, vacant by the institution of John de Berewyk, the last vicar, to Sandon vicarage on Sat. 24 Apr.;[1] patrons, abbot and convent of Darley, at the bishop's nomination. Ind.: archd. York,[2] 10 June 1311.
[Margin] Nothing for the fee.
   [1 See **721**.
   2 Interlined.]

1047   Institution of Br. Robert de Coventr', canon of Beauchief, to Alfreton vicarage, vacant by the resignation of Br. Ralph de Pecco, the last vicar, on Sun. 8 Aug. last; patrons, abbot and convent of Beauchief. He swore [etc.]. Ind.: M. Richard de Norh[amp]t[on], the sequestrator. Gainsborough (*Geynesborugh*), 31 Aug. 1311.
[Margin] Nothing for the fee.

1048   Institution of William de Woderore, canon of Dunstable (*Donestaple*), to Bradbourne (*Bradeborne*) vicarage, without any inquiry. Ind.: archd. London, 3 Oct. 1311.
[Margin] He paid the fee.

1049   Institution of M. Hugh de Warkenhamby,[1] priest, to Carsington (*Kersington*) church, vacant by the death of William del Bough, the last rector, on 1 Nov. last; patron, M. Roger de Martivall, dean of Lincoln. Ind.: archd. London, 9 Dec. 1311.
[Margin] Nothing for the fee.
   [1 *BRUO*, iii.1992.]

1050   [Fo. 73] Collation to M. Geoffrey de Blaston, clerk, of the archdeaconry of Derby, vacant by the death of M. Ellis de Napton, the former archdeacon.[1] Ind.: M. Richard de Norhampton, the sequestrator. St. Albans, 19 Dec. 1311.
   [1 On 12 July 1311, see **635**.]

ANNUS DOMINI MILLESIMUS .CCC^{mus}. DUODECIMUS INCIPIT ET REQUIRE IN QUATERNO DE TEMPORE MAGISTRI RADULPHI DE LEICESTR'.¹ ITEM INCIPIT ANNUS DOMINI .M^{us}.CCC^{mus}.XIII^{us}.

[¹ See **552–601**.]

1051 Note that Adam de Longeford, clerk, was admitted to Barlborough (*Barleburgh*) church, which became vacant on Mon. 13 Aug. last.; patron, Nicholas de Longeford. Ind.: archd. 5 Sept. 1313.
[Margin] Longeford,¹ Barlborough (*Barlbrugh*')².
[¹ Deleted.
² In a later hand.]

1052 Institution of William de Baliden', deacon, to Crich (*Crugh*) vicarage, vacant by the resignation of John de Walleye, the last vicar, on Fri. 5 Oct. last; patrons, abbot and convent of Darley. He swore [etc.]. London, 20 Oct. 1313.
[Margin] He paid the fee.

1053 Licence, in common form, to Henry de Berleston, priest, portioner of Darley, to study for one year. London, 1 Feb. 1314.

1054 Note of similar licence for M. Henry [Byran],¹ rector of Weston upon Trent. 3 Mar. 1314.
[¹ See **552**.]

1055 Note that custody of the sequestration placed on the fruits and revenues of Stanton (*Staunton*) church has been committed to Thomas de Staunton, acolyte, during pleasure. M. Richard de Norhampton, the sequestrator, to deliver custody to Thomas, or his proctor. Brewood, 9 June 1314.

1056 Note that custody of the sequestration placed on the vacant church of Carsington (*Kersington*) has been committed to John de Kesnes,¹ subdeacon. M. Richard de Norhampton, the sequestrator, to deliver custody. Bishops Itchington, 24 June 1314.
[¹ *BRUC*, 338.]

1057 Institution of John de Keynes, subdeacon, to the vacant church of Carsington; patron, M. Roger de Martivall, dean of Lincoln. Ind.: archd. Licence to study for one year under the terms of the constitution of Pope Boniface VIII. London, 11 July 1314.
[Margin] Nothing for the fee.

1058 [Fo. 73v] Letters patent to M. Geoffrey de Blaston, archdeacon of Derby. The bishop is hindered by various and difficult business and unable to come to his diocese. Gilbert de Mildelton, clerk, has been presented to Whittington (*Whitington*) church. Wishing to spare labours and expenses, he is commissioned to admit and institute Gilbert or his proctor to the church, provided that the inquiry to be made shall decide sufficiently for the presenting and the presentee and nothing shall prevent his institution, doing all things required, with power of coercion. London, 12 July 1314.

1059 Institution of Thomas de Staunton, acolyte, to Stanton church, vacant by the death of M. Geoffrey de Staunton, the last rector, on 31 Mar. last; patron, Sir Robert de Staunton, kt. He swore [etc.]. 29 Sept. 1314.
[Margin] Nothing for the fee.
   [There is no mandate to induct.]

1060 Institution of M. William de Pontesburi,[1] acolyte, to Trusley (*Trusselegh*) church, vacant by the resignation of M. Thomas de Pontesburi, the last rector; patrons, prior and convent of Trentham. Ind.: archd. London, 27 Jan. 1315.
[Margin] He owes the fee.
   [1 *BRUO*, iii.1498.]

1061 Institution of Br. Gilbert de Kyrketon, canon of Welbeck (*Welebek*), of the Premonstratension order, to Etwall vicarage; patrons, abbot and convent of Welbeck, according to the tenor of the privilege of Pope Lucius granted to the said religious.[1] He swore [etc.]. Ind.: archd. Coldham, 23 Feb. 1315.
[Margin] He owes the fee.
   [1 *Sic*, see **248**, and n. 1.]

1062 Institution of William de Wykleswod', acolyte, to Boyleston (*Boileston*) church, vacant by the death of Henry de Coleshull, priest, on Mon. 17 Feb. last; patron, Walter Waldeshef. Ind.: archd. of Derby. Bishops Itchington, 12 Mar. 1315.
[Margin] He owes the fee.

1063 Licence, in common form, to Henry Sauvage, rector of Hartshorne, to study for one year. Same day.

1064 Note that Roger de Shelton, rector of Heanor (*Henovere*), has been appointed curate to William, perpetual vicar of Sawley, because of William's physical infirmities. He is to prepare and render a faithful account of the administration of his goods and vicarage. Roger has authority to substitute another suitable person in his place. 25 Mar. 1315.

1065 [Fo. 74] Letters patent to William, rector of Ilkeston. Having compassion for the physical infirmities with which he labours, the bishop wishes to provide for his well-being and welfare. He is granted faculty to be absent from his church occasionally, according to the needs of his illness, in order to obtain the help of physicians, provided that his church is not defrauded of duties [etc.]. Lichfield, 25 Mar. 1315.

1066 Institution of Ralph de Brantingham, acolyte, to Bonsal (*Bonteshale*) church, vacant by the resignation of M. John de Brantingham, the last rector; patron, M. Roger de Martivall, dean of Lincoln. He swore obedience [etc.]. London, 10 Apr. 1315.
[Margin] He owes [the fee].
   [There is no mandate to induct.]

1067 Institution of John de Campania,[1] acolyte, to Carsington church, vacant by the resignation of John de Keynes, the last rector; patron, M. Roger de Martivall. He swore obedience. Licence to study for one year. Letters dimissory for all holy orders. London, same day.
[Margin] He owes [the fee].
> [There is no mandate to induct.
> [1] *BRUC*, 119.]

1068 Institution of John de Hokenhale, priest, to Pleasley (*Pleseleye*) church, vacant by the death of William de Bruera, the last rector, on 27 Dec. last; patron, Thomas de Shirbrok. Ind.: archd. Greenford, 14 Apr. 1315.
[Margin] He owes the fee.

1069 Institution of William de la Rode, subdeacon, to Ness church,[1] vacant by the resignation of Philip de Harle, the last rector, on Thurs. 6 June 1314; patrons, abbot and convent of Shrewsbury. Ind.: archd. Eccleshall, 1 May 1315.
[Margin] He owes the fee.
> [[1] In Shrewsbury archdeaconry.]

1070 Institution of Br. William de Bollesovere, priest, canon of Welbeck, to Etwall (*Etewell*) vicarage, vacant by the free and spontaneous resignation of Br. Gilbert de Kyrketon, the last vicar, on Sat. 21 June last; patrons, abbot and convent of Welbeck. Ind.: archd. Merevale (*Miram vallem*), 5 July 1315.

1071 [Fo. 74v] Note that M. John de Focerby has been admitted to Kirk Ireton (*Irton*) chapel, vacant by the resignation of M. Harvey de Luda on Wed. 17 Sept.; patron, dean of Lincoln. Ind.: archd. of Derby. London, 9 Oct. 1315.

1072 Licence to the same M. John to study for one year from the time of his institution under the terms of the constitution of Boniface VIII. Same day.

1073 Licence to Gilbert de Middelton, rector of Whittington, to study for three years from the time of his institution.[1] Dispensation concerning holy orders. London, 13 Oct. 1315.
> [[1] After 12 July 1314, see **1058**; *BRUO*, ii.1274–5.]

1074 Dispensation for John [1]de Campania,[1] rector of Carsington, concerning holy orders and to study for three years from the time of his institution.[2] Same day.
> [[1-1] Interlined.
> [2] 10 Apr. 1315, see **1067**.]

1075 Dispensation for M. William de Pontesbur', rector of Trusley, concerning holy orders and to study for one year. London, 13 Oct. 1315.

1076 Institution of Ralph de Ergum, in the person of M. Robert de Bridelington, his proctor, to Matlock church, vacant by the death of M. Walter de

Fodderingeye, the last rector, in . . .¹ September; patron, dean of Lincoln. Ind.:
archd. of Derby. Grove, 16 Oct. 1315.
  [¹ Blank space.]

1077 Institution of Nicholas de Kirkeby, chaplain, to Ault Hucknall (*Hautho-
kenal*) vicarage, vacant by the resignation of J[ohn] de Hokenhal¹ on
Sun. 14 Sept.; patrons, prior and convent of Newstead in Sherwood (*de Novo
loco in Schirewode*). He swore [etc.]. Ind.: archd. of Derby. Wolstanton, 27 Oct.
1315.
  [¹ *Alias* Torkard, see **221**.]

1078 Institution of James Paynel, priest, to the vacant church of Whitwell
(*Whytewell*); patron this turn, Christine de Ry. Ind.: archd. of Derby. Brace-
bridge, 2 Feb. 1316.
  [See **772, 1086**.
  Followed by one word deleted and two blank lines.]

1079 Institution of Herbert Pouger, chaplain, to Horsley vicarage, vacant by
the resignation of his brother, the last vicar.¹ He swore [etc.]. Ind.: archd. of
Derby. Bracebridge, 3 Feb. 1316.
  [The patrons, the prior and convent of Lenton, have not been noted, see **568, 1035**.
  ¹ Henry Pouger, see **568**.]

1080 Institution of M. Robert de Brydelington¹ to Matlock (*Matloc*) church,
vacant by the resignation of Ralph Ergoun; patron, dean of Lincoln. Ind.: archd.
of Derby. Bracebridge, 11 Feb. 1316.
  [¹ *BRUO*, i.265.]

1081 Dispensation for the same to study in the schools for one year and
concerning holy orders under the terms of the constitution. Same day.

1082 [Fo. 75] Institution of William de Brademere to Edlaston (*Edulston*)
church, vacant by the death of John Payn, the last rector; patron, dean of
Lincoln. Ind.: archd. of Derby. 11 Feb. 1316.

1083 Note that on 4 Feb. [1316], in the dean of Lincoln's house, Henry de
Mammesfeld, dean of Lincoln,¹ swore canonical obedience to the bishop, his
successors, officials, and ministers for the churches of Wirksworth, Ashbourne,
Chesterfield, and others appropriated or annexed to his office.
  [¹ Elected before 15 Dec. 1315, and in office until 1328, see *Fasti*, i.3.]

1084 Dispensation for M. John [de Focerby],¹ rector of Kirk Ireton chapel, to
study for six years from Michaelmas next in an established place. He shall not
be compelled to further orders. Bracebridge, 21 Feb. 1316.
  [¹ See **1071**.]

1085   Institution of M. John de Nassington,[1] junior, to Clowne church, vacant by the resignation of John de Leicestr'; patrons, abbot and convent of Worksop (*Wyrcsop*). 5 Mar. 1316.

[There is no mandate to induct.
[1] *BRUO*, ii.1337.]

1086   Note that following the death of John de Prestwyk, the last rector of Whitwell, a law-suit was brought in the king's court concerning the lawful patronage of the church between Christine de Ry on the one part and Robert, son of Adam de Brydeling' on the other part, and also between Christine on the one part and Nicholas de Longested and Walter de Goushull on the other part. Within half a year of the church becoming vacant Christine had recovered her presentation to it from Robert by his default against Nicholas and Walter, because Nicholas and Walter went to the king's court and granted Christine their presentation that turn, saving to the same Nicholas and Walter their other turns to present. n.d.[1]

[[1] Before 2 Feb. 1316, see **1078**.]

1087   Institution of John de Houton to the moiety of Staveley (*Staveleigh*) church vacant by the resignation of John de Wodehous, who last held that portion; patron, Ralph de Frefthevill'. Ind.: archd. of Derby. Sandwell, 7 Mar. 1316.

1088   Institution of Richard de Staunton to Stoney Stanton (*Stonistaunton*) church; patron, Ranulph de Stonistaunston. Ind.: archd. of Derby. Packington, 15 Mar. 1316.

ANNUS [MCCC] SEXTUS DECIMUS.

1089   Institution of John de Bradeleig', chaplain, to Tibshelf (*Tybeschulf*) church, vacant by the resignation of Stephen de Brawode, the last rector; patrons, prioress and convent of Brewood White Ladies. Ind.: archd. of Derby. 28 Mar. 1316.

1090   Institution of Nicholas de Norton, chaplain, to Stretton church, vacant by the resignation of William de Stretton, the last rector, on 12 Apr. last; patron, Isabella, widow of Walter de Stretton. Ind.: archd. of Derby. 12 June 1316.

1091   Institution of Richard de Wycumbe, chaplain, to Hartington vicarage, vacant by the death of Alexander [de Wylghton], the last vicar,[1] on Wed. 7 Apr. last; patrons, abbess and convent of B.V.M. of the house of St. Clare, without the walls of London. Ind.: archd. of Derby. 9 Oct. 1316.

[[1] See **6, 224**.
Followed by two blank lines.]

1092   Dispensation for the same to study for two years from 16 Mar. [1317] under the terms of the constitution *Cum ex eo*.

1093   [Fo. 75v] Institution of John de Hale, clerk, to Fenny Bentley (*Benteleye*) church, vacant by the death of Robert Malet on Fri. 20 Aug. last; patron, dean of St. Mary's church, Lincoln. Ind.: archd. of Derby. 15 Oct. 1316.

1094   Institution of Thomas de Ledenham, rector of St. Mary [Magdalene] on the Hill, Lincoln, to the portion of Darley church vacant by the death of Marmaduke de Hormingwod, the former portioner, on Thurs. 12 Aug. last; patron, dean of Lincoln. Ind.: archd. of Derby. 17 Oct. 1316.

1095   Institution of Robert de Stowa to Edlaston church, which became vacant on 23 Aug. last; patron, dean of Lincoln. Ind.: archd. of Derby. 17 Oct. 1316.

1096   Dispensation for William de Pontesbur', rector of Trusley (*Trusseleig'*), concerning holy orders and to study at university for ¹one year¹ from 14 Oct. last according to the terms of the constitution *Cum ex eo*. 7 Nov. 1316.
    [¹⁻¹ Interlined.]

1097   Institution of Br. William de Bohun, canon of Dunstable, to Bradbourne (*Bradebourn'*) vicarage according to the terms of the bishop's ordinance for its rule; patrons, prior and convent of Dunstable. It is vacant by the recall and resignation of Br. William de Wederor', the last vicar, but his letters of institution are dated 20 Nov. because he ought to have been instituted then, but the bishop was delayed because of . . .¹ Eccleshall, 1 Dec. 1316.
    [¹ Unfinished.]

1098   Institution of M. Alexander de Thurgarton to Upper Langwith (*Languath*) church, vacant by the death of Nicholas de Henovere, the last rector, at Martinmas last; patrons, prior and convent of Thurgarton. Ind.: archd. of Derby. Eccleshall, 5 Dec. 1316.

1099   Institution of Gilbert de Otrington, chaplain, to Elmton (*Elmeton*) vicarage, vacant by the death of Robert de Batheley, the last vicar, on Tues. 19 Oct. last; patrons, prior and convent of Thurgarton. Ind.: archd. of Derby. Eccleshall, 5 Dec. 1316.

1100   Institution of Ralph de Langedon, priest, to Marston vicarage, vacant by the death of Robert de Horseleye, the last vicar, on Sat. 2 Oct. last; patrons, prior and convent of Tutbury. Ind.: archd. of Derby. 9 Dec. 1316.

1101   Institution of Ralph de Bromleye to Stapenhill vicarage, vacant by the death of Thomas [de Pakinton],¹ the last vicar, on Sat. 6 Nov. last; patrons, abbot and convent of Burton upon Trent. Ind.: archd. of Derby. 10 Dec. 1316.
    [¹ See **561**.]

1102   [Fo. 76] Licence to M. Alexander [de Thurgarton]¹, rector of Upper Langwith, to study for one year under the terms of the constitution of Pope Boniface VIII; he shall not be compelled to the orders of deacon and priest during this time. 12 Dec. 1316.
    [¹ See **1098**.]

1103 Institution of Bartholomew de Cotyngham to the vacant church of Beighton (*Beghton*); patron, the king.¹ The church was held in return for the chapel of Eckington, because the king recovered his presentation to that church ²by assize² in his court against John de Stotevill', the patron of Eckington church. Ind.: archd. of Derby. 14 Dec. 1316.

[¹ *CPR 1313–17*, 440.
²⁻² Interlined.]

1104 Institution of William de Wyrkesworth, clerk, to the moiety of Mugginton (*Moginton*) church vacant by the resignation of Richard de Wamberge, the last rector, on 21 Sept.; patron, Thomas, earl of Lancaster and Leicester, steward of England. Ind.: archd. of Derby. Coldham, 7 Jan. 1317.

1105 Institution of Richard de Baugnell to Chesterfield vicarage, vacant by the death of Walter de South Leverton on Tues. 14 Dec.; patron, dean of Lincoln. Ind.: archd. of Derby. 24 Jan. 1317.

1106 Institution of William de Bretford to Blackwell vicarage; patrons, prior and convent of Thurgarton. Ind.: archd. of Derby. London, 2 Feb. 1317.

ANNUS [MCCC]XVIIᵘˢ.

1107 Institution of M. Adam de Hasulbech, in the person of Robert de Hasulbach, his proctor, to Carsington church; patron, dean of Lincoln. Ind.: archd. of Derby. 22 May 1317.

1108 Institution of M. John de Sutton¹ to the vacant moiety of Eckington (*Egynton*) church; patrons, abbot and convent of Dale.² Ind.: archd. of Derby. 25 May 1317.

[¹ *BRUO*, iii.1820.
² *Sic*. The d'Estotevilles apparently held the manor of Eckington and the advowson of the church until at least Nov. 1322, although the right of presentation to the church was constantly contested by the king, see *Calendars of Inquisitions Post Mortem*, v, no. 237; vi, no. 417; ix, no. 49; **252, 558, 559, 1103**.]

1109 [Fo. 76v] Institution of Henry de Halum to Horsley vicarage, vacant by the resignation of Herbert Pouger, the last vicar, on 23 Aug.; patrons, prior and convent of Lenton. Ind.: archd. of Derby. 15 Sept. 1317.

1110 Institution of William de Bautr' to Eyam church, vacant by the death of William de Wine on Sat. 28 May; patron, Sir Thomas de Furnivall, kt. Ind.: archd. of Derby. 25 Sept. 1317.

1111 Institution of Henry de Schobenhal' to the chantry of Stoney Stanton parish church, newly ordained and of the endowment of Ranulph de Stonistaunton. Ind.: archd. of Derby. Ashley (*Assheleye*), 7 Oct. 1317.

1112 Institution of Br. [1]Henry de Notingham[1] to Kirk Hallam (*Kyrkehalum*) vicarage; patrons, abbot and convent of Dale. Ind.: archd. of Derby. 1 Oct. 1317.

[[1-1] Interlined.]

1113 Institution of M. William de Stretton to Stretton church; patron, Isabella de Stretton, widow of [Walter][1] de Stretton. The church became vacant . . .[2] 2 Dec. 1317

[[1] Blank space, see **1090**.
[2] Unfinished.]

1114 Institution of William de Novelton, chaplain, to Clowne church, vacant by the resignation of M. John de Nassington, junior, the last rector; patrons, prior and convent of Worksop. Ind.: archd. of Derby. 16 Nov. 1317.

1115 Institution of Robert May to the vacant church of Mugginton;[1] patron,[2] Thomas, earl of Lancaster and Leicester, steward of England. Ind.: archd. of Derby. 17 Dec. 1317.

[[1] Interlined over *Cloune* deleted.
[2] Interlined.]

1116 Institution of M. Ellis Pouger to the portion of Darley church [1]which M. W. de Birton held;[1] patrons, dean and chapter of Lincoln. The [portion][2] became vacant about 30 Nov. last. Ind.: archd. of Derby. 2 Mar. 1318.

[[1-1] Added down the spine.
[2] MS. *vicaria*]

1117 Note that Henry de Stone, acolyte,[1] has been admitted to the vacant church of Swarkeston; patron, Lady Joan de Wek'. Ind.: archd. of Derby. 3 Mar. 1318.

[[1] Interlined.]

1118 Institution of William Curson, acolyte, to Kedleston (*Ketliston*) church, vacant by the death of Hugh Brabazon on Tues. 13 June last; patron, Richard Curson [1]of Kedleston.[1] Ind.: archd. of Derby. 4 Aug. 1318.[2]

[[1-1] Interlined.
[2] MS. *xviij* interlined over *predicto* deleted.]

1119 [Fo. 77] Dispensation for John de Ayleston, subdeacon, rector of Hathersage (*Haversech'*), concerning further orders and to study at university for one year under the terms of the constitution *Cum ex eo*. 30 Aug. 1318.

[The rest of the folio is blank.]

[Fo. 78] REGISTRUM :W[ALTERI]: COVENTREN' ET LICH' EPISCOPI A FESTO ANNUN-CIACIONIS DOMINICE ANNO DOMINI :MILLESIMO :CCC^mo:XVII^mo: ET CONSECRACIONIS EJUSDEM EPISCOPI :XXI^mo: :ARCHIDIACONATUS COVENTR':

1120 Institution of Roger de Lodbrok', deacon, to the vacant vicarage of Offchurch (*Offechirch*); patrons, prior and convent of Coventry. Ind.: archd. of Coventry. 25 Mar. 1317.

1121 Institution of Peter Mallori to the vacant vicarage of Wolston; patron, prior of Wolston. Ind.: archd. of Coventry. Wolston, 16 Nov. 1317.

1122 Institution of Richard de Someredeby to the vacant church of Berkswell; patron, Edward, king of England, lord of Ireland, and duke of Aquitaine.[1] 29 Nov. 1317.

    [[1] *CPR 1317–21*, 24.]

1123 Dispensation for the same Richard to study in the schools for one year and concerning holy orders under the terms of the constitution of [Pope] Boniface. 2 Feb. 1318.

1124 Institution of Robert Hillari to the vacant church of Sutton Coldfield (*Sutton in Colefeld*); patron, the king.[1] Ind.: archd. of Coventry. 9 Mar. 1318.

    [[1] *CPR 1317–21*, 104.]

1125 Collation to M. John de Everisdon,[1] dean of Wolverhampton (*Wolverne-hampton*), of the prebend of Bubbenhall. Ind.: dean and chapter of Lichfield. London, 3 Mar. 1318.

    [[1] *BRUO*, i.654–5.]

1126 Institution of Thomas de Stodham to the vacant church of Shelden (*Scheldon*); patron, Ralph de Phicut. Ind.: archd. of Coventry. 13 May 1318.

1127 Collation to John de Assheby, clerk, of Baddesley Clinton (*Baddesle Clinton*) church, having devolved to the bishop's collation. Ind.: archd. of Coventry. 28 May 1318.

1128 Institution of Thomas de Blyburgh to Nuneaton (*Nouneton*) vicarage; patron, Br. Peter de Cryketot, proctor-general in England of the abbot and convent of Lire. The vicarage is vacant by the resignation of Geoffrey de Vilers and by his acquisition of Raunds (*Raundes*) church, Lincoln [dioc.], which he then held. [1]Ind.: archd. of Coventry.[1] 7 July 1318.

    [[1–1] Over an erasure.]

1129 [Fo. 78v] Licence to Richard de Someredebi, rector of Berkswell, to study for one year from 3 Feb. next and concerning holy orders according to the constitution [1]*Cum ex eo.*[1] 4 Nov. 1318.

    [[1–1] Underlined.]

1130 Note of similar licence to Robert Hillari, rector of Sutton Coldfield. 13 Jan. 1319.

1131 Institution of John del Heth of Baginton to the perpetual chantry of St. John the Baptist's church, Baginton, vacant by the resignation of the last incumbent on 3 Apr. last; patron, Richard de Herthull, lord of Baginton. London, 27 Apr. 1319.

1132   Institution of Roger de Lodbrok' to Ladbroke church, vacant by the death of William de Daleby, the last rector, on 1 June last; patron, Hugh, son of Sir John de Lodbrok'. Ind.: archd. of Coventry. Lichfield, 10 June 1319.

1133   Institution of Nicholas de Bramham, priest, to Offchurch vicarage; patrons, prior and convent of Coventry. The vicarage became vacant on Sat. [9][1] June because Roger, the last vicar, was instituted to Ladbroke church, and inducted in the same. Ind.: archd. of Coventry. 27 June 1319.

> [[1] MS. *die sabbati proxima post festum Sancti Barnabe* (16 June), but Roger de Lodbrok' was instituted to Ladbroke church on 10 June, see **1132**.]

1134   Institution of Robert de Beverlaco, priest, in the person of William de Ellisworth, his proctor, to Solihull (*Sulihull*) church; patron, J[ohn Hotham], bishop of Ely.[1] The church is vacant by the resignation of Robert de Perham on 16 July by reason of an exchange made with Hadstock (*Hadestok*) church, London dioc. Ind.: archd. of Coventry. 3 Sept. 1319.

> [[1] *HBC*, 244.]

1135   Institution of William de Neusum, priest, to the vicarage of Bishops Itchington church, vacant by the resignation of Warin de Neusum, the last vicar, on 10 Aug. last; patron, Francis de Luco, canon of York,[1] proctor of Peter de Columpna, the precentor of Lichfield.[2] Ind.: Nicholas [de Guldeford],[3] rector of Chesterton (*Cesterton*). 18 Oct. 1319.

> [[1] *Fasti*, vi.64.
> [2] Precentor 1311–39, see *Fasti*, x.7.
> [3] See **93**.]

1136   Dispensation for M. John de Shoteswell[1] to study for one year. 22 Oct. 1319.
[Margin] Licence for the rector of Cubbington.

> [[1] *BRUO*, iii.2215–6.]

1137   Dispensation for M. Richard [de Someredebi],[1] rector of Berkswell, to study for one year from Christmas under the terms of the constitution *Cum ex eo*. 7 Nov. 1319.

> [[1] See **1129**.]

1138   Institution of John de Schulton, priest, to Southam church, vacant by the resignation of John de Croxton, the last rector, on Mon. 19 Mar. 1319; patrons, prior and convent of Coventry. Ind.: archd. of Coventry. Butterley (*Boturle*), 14 Jan. 1320.

1139   [Fo. 79] Institution of John de Chadleshonte, chaplain, to the vicarage of Radford Semele (*Radeford*) church, vacant by the death of Thomas de Kenilworth, the last vicar, on Fri. 28 Mar.; patrons, abbot and convent of Kenilworth (*Kenylworth*). Ind.: archd. 12 Apr. 1320.

1140   Institution of John de la Warde, chaplain, to Newton Regis (*Kyngesneuton*) church; patron, Sir Hugh de Meyngnyl, kt.[1] The church became vacant on

9 Feb. last because Thomas de Poley, the last rector, was instituted to Quinton (*Quenton*) church, Worcester dioc.[2] Ind.: official of Coventry. 8 Apr. 1320.

[[1] Interlined.
[2] *The register of Thomas Cobham, bishop of Worcester, 1317–1327*, ed. E.H. Pearce (Worcestershire Historical Society, 40, 1930), 233.]

1141   Collation to M. John de Stratford, archd. of Lincoln, of the prebend of Bishops Tachbrook[1] [2]in Lichfield church[2] in an exchange with the prebend of Wartling and Hooe (*Writlinggerhoo*) in the king's free chapel of [St. Mary] Hastings (*Hastingges*), Chichester dioc.[3] Ind.: chapter of Lichfield, or their commissary, the deanery being vacant. 4 June 1320.

[[1] *BRUO*, iii.1796–7; *Fasti*, i.6, 48; *Fasti*, x.57.
[2–2] Interlined.
[3] *VCH Sussex*, ix.141.]

1142   Institution of John de Norton, chaplain, to the vacant church of Brinklow in an exchange of benefices with East Lexham (*Estlexham*) church, Norwich dioc., by commission of M. Thomas de Foxton, the official of Norwich. He swore obedience to the bishop on 15 July; [1]patrons, prior and convent of Kenilworth.[1] Ind.: archd. of Coventry, [his] official,[2] or the dean of the same place. n.d.

[[1–1] Interlined later.
[2] Interlined.]

1143   Institution of Henry de Barewe, priest, to the vicarage of Harbury (*Herburbur'*) church, vacant by the death of the last vicar[1] on Sun. 6 July; patrons, prior and convent of Kenilworth. Ind.: archd. 29 July 1320.

[[1] John Libener', see **527**.]

1144   The bishop has received the original papal letters, and others, which mention the exchange made between John,[1] cardinal deacon of St. Theodore,[2] of the canonry and prebend which he held in Reims church, and Richard de Anibaldis of the archdeaconry of Coventry, which he held. The bishop has admitted the said venerable father in the person of Nicholas Ciceronis, his proctor, who has sworn obedience. A copy and comparison of all the documents has been made by Richard de Ulsby, papal notary, with these being present: M. Walter de Askeby, Robert de Patrica, the said notary, William de Ovencle, Robert de Langeton, chaplains, John Laci, clerk, and others. Westhall, 29 Aug. 1320.

[[1] Interlined.
[2] John Gaetani de Urbe, see *Fasti*, x.14.]

1145   Institution of John de Olenesel, deacon, to Hampton in Arden (*Hampton in Ardena*) vicarage, vacant by the death of Simon de Weston, the last vicar, on 11 Apr. last; patrons, prior and convent of Kenilworth (*Kenylleworth*), at the nomination of Sir John Pecche, kt. Ind.: archd. of Coventry. Sawley, 21 Sept. 1320.

1146   Institution of Geoffrey de Nounham, priest, to the vicarage of Coleshill church in an exchange of benefices. Institution of Alan de Bickenhill to the vicarage of Bickenhill (*Bykenhull*) church in an exchange of benefices; patrons, prioress and convent of Markyate. Ind.: archd. of Coventry. London, 26 Oct. 1320.

1147   [Fo. 79v] Licence to Richard de Someredy, subdeacon, rector of Berkswell, to study for one year under the terms of the constitution *Cum ex eo*. 23 Oct. 1320.

1148   Institution of William Sars, acolyte, to Stockton (*Stocton*) church, vacant by the resignation of Peter de Hertle, the last rector, on 6 Nov.; patrons, prior and convent of St. Mary's monastery, Hertford. Ind.: archd. of Coventry. London, 9 Nov. 1320.

1149   Institution of Adam de Kyngesford, priest, to Maxstoke (*Maxstok'*) church, vacant by the death of Peter de Ilmedon, the last rector, on 25 Nov. last; patron, Lady Ida de Clynton, lady of Maxstoke. Ind.: archd. of Coventry. 4 Jan. 1321.

ANNO [MCCC].XXI°.

1150   Institution of John de Kent, acolyte, to Churchover (*Chirchewavere*) church; patron this turn, John de Schireford. The church became vacant on Mon. 11 May last because Richard de Blaby, the last rector, was instituted to Woodford Halse (*Wodeford*) parish church, Lincoln dioc., which has cure of souls. Ind.: archd. of Coventry. Blyth (*Blith*), 23 May 1321.

1151   In the presence of the bishop, Thomas called Legat, priest,[1] who holds the perpetual chantry of William de Capston's chapel at Coventry, and John de Brochurst, priest, vicar of Alspath church, resigned their benefices on account of an exchange to be made. Institution of the said Thomas to Alspath vicarage; patrons, prior and convent of Coventry cathedral. Institution of the said John to the said chantry; patron, prior of the said cathedral. Ind.: archd. of Coventry. Walton on Thames (*Waleton*), [?13][2] June, 1321.

   [1 Interlined.
   2 This letter is dated *xix kal. Julii* in error; *xviij kal. Julii* is 14 June, and the bishop was at Walton on Thames then, see **1240**.]

1152   Institution of William Eborum, chaplain, to Radway (*Radewey*) vicarage, vacant by the death of Thomas de Heyford, the last vicar, on Sun. 5 July last; patrons, abbot and convent of Stoneleigh in Arden (*Stonl' in Ardena*). Ind.: archd. of Coventry. 21 July 1321.

1153   Licence to Richard de Someredeby, subdeacon, rector of Berkswell, to study for one year under the terms of the constitution *Cum ex eo*. 23 Oct. 1321.

1154   Letters patent ordaining the vicarage of Grandborough. The bishop has inspected the following composition or covenant dated 15 July 1297, which was made with the agreement of M. Walter de Thorp, who was then the bishop's official, between the prior and convent of Ranton, who have Grandborough church appropriated to them, and John de Rogeleye, the perpetual vicar of the same.

The vicar's portion will be the entire income pertaining to the altarage, except for the tithes of wool and lambs, and money from the same, and the mortuary payments from the two lords of Grandborough if it is a horse, or arms; [fo. 80] but, if it is another animal, it will pertain to the vicar.

The vicar will retain for himself the houses, buildings, curtilage and croft which he or his predecessors have had previously, and three selions in 'Madewell', a selion in 'Bauedich', four selions next to 'Smalebrok', two roods of meadow below Sawbridge (*Silebrigg'*), four roods of meadow next to 'Schirrindale' towards Hardwick (*Herdewyk*), and a cartload of hay from the same meadow to be taken from the tithe of hay, which the vicar and his predecessors have been accustomed to take. The vicar will take nothing from the tithe of sheaves, or anything else from the tithe of hay, which he and his predecessors have taken previously, but the aforesaid religious will take wholly all the tithes of sheaves and [the remaining] hay. The vicar will receive forever the tithes of the cultivated curtilage, and 6s. 6d. from the men of Caldecote for all the tithes of their meadowland for horses, and headlands in Caldecote.

The vicar will provide a suitable deacon to reside continuously, whom the religious have been accustomed to provide, and the vicar will receive from the religious a quarter of corn and all the tithes of all the mills in the said parish each year at Christmas for the support of a deacon.

The prior and convent will pay the procurations and synodalia of the archdeacon.

Both parties have pledged to observe the foregoing, and their seals, and the seal of M. W[alter] de Thorp, the bishop's official, have been affixed to this memorandum.

The bishop considers the above portion and agreement to be canonical, and that the incumbent charges can be supported adequately from the resources of the church, as the inquiry, made with his authority by the neighbouring rectors, vicars and other faithful men has established. It should be accepted and approved by all future vicars without any challenge or additional claim. With the prior and convent and Geoffrey de Botuldon, the present vicar, being present, the bishop assigns, ordains and provides the above portions of the church to the vicarage of Grandborough and the future vicars thereof forever, wishing them to be content with the same without an additional portion. Lichfield, 16 Apr. 1321.

[The rest of the folio is blank.]

[Fo. 81] REGISTRUM ARCHIDIACONATUS SALOP' A FESTO ANNUNCIACIONIS BEATE MARIE ANNO DOMINI MILLESIMO .CCC^{mo}.VICESIMO PRIMO.

1155 The election of Br. Richard de Melton to the rule of Wombridge Priory, of the Augustinian order, vacant by the death of Br. Philip, the last prior, has been presented to the bishop. He has found it defective, and has annulled it, proclaiming it invalid. Because he has learnt that the same Br. Richard is wise, prudent, of laudable life, begotten of a lawful marriage, watchful of temporalities and spiritualities, and is otherwise greatly to be commended, the bishop has decreed, ordained and appointed him prior by the right devolved to him in this matter, and by special grace. Lichfield, 19 Apr. 1321.

1156   Institution of John de Cheynee, subdeacon, to Cound church, vacant by the resignation of Nicholas de Cheynee, the last rector, on 14 May; patron, Edmund, earl of Arundel. Ind.: archd. of Shrewsbury. London, 15 May 1321.

1157   Licence to Edmund, priest, rector of Buildwas, to study for one year, and to farm his church. London, 21 July 1321.

1158   Licence to John de Cheyney, subdeacon, rector of Cound, to study for one year from Michaelmas next under the terms of the constitution *Cum ex eo*. London, 2 Aug. 1321.

1159   Dispensation for John de Scheynton, rector of Edgmond (*Egemondon*), [to study] for one year under the terms of the constitution *Cum ex eo*. 18 Sept. 1321.

1160   Institution of William de Baggefor', priest, to Kinnerley (*Kynardeseye*) church, vacant by the death of the last rector on Fri. 5 June; patrons, abbot and convent of Shrewsbury. Ind.: archd. of Shrewsbury. 30 Oct. 1321.

1161   Licence to William de Hugeford, clerk, rector of Stockton, to study for one year under the terms of the constitution *Cum ex eo*. William was instituted to Stockton church by M. John de Turvill', canon of Lichfield, on 31 May [the same year] by a commission issued to him in this regard. London, 30 Oct. 1321. Note that William has had letters dimissory for all minor orders and the orders of subdeacon and deacon. 5 Nov. [1321].

[¹⁻¹ Interlined.
The rest of the folio is blank.]

[Fo. 82] REGISTRUM W[ALTERI] COVENTR' ET LICH' EPISCOPI A FESTO ANNUNCIA-
CIONIS BEATE MARIE ANNO DOMINI MILLESIMO :CCC: DECIMO OCTAVO: CONSECRA-
CIONIS VERO EJUSDEM EPISCOPI :VICESIMO SECUNDO: ARCHIDIACONATUS DERBEYE.

1162   Institution of John de Ayleston to Hathersage (*Havereshegg'*) church; patrons, prior and convent of Launde. Ind.: archd. of Derby. 25 Mar. 1318.

1163   Institution of Edmund Touschet to Mackworth (*Macworth*) church; patron, Sir Robert Touschet, kt. Ind.: archd. of Derby. 12 Apr. 1318.

1164   Institution of Richard de Hasilbech' to Fenny Bentley church, vacant by the resignation of M. John de Hal',¹ the last rector; patron, dean of Lincoln. Ind.: archd. of Derby. 23 Apr. 1318.

[¹ *BRUO*, ii.849.]

1165   Dispensation for Edmund Tuchet, rector of Mackworth (*Mackeworth*), [to study] for one year under the terms of the constitution *Cum ex eo*. . . .¹ Nov. 1318.

[¹ Blank space.]

1166   Dispensation for William Bautre, rector of Eyam, concerning holy orders and to study for one year under the terms of the constitution *Cum ex eo*. 12 Feb. 1319.

1167   Grant *in commendam* to M. Ralph de Querndon,[1] priest, of Hathersage church. 10 Mar. 1319.
[2]On 17 May M. Ralph was instituted to the church in the person of Henry Underwod', his proctor; patrons, prior and convent of Launde. The church was vacant by the resignation of John de Ayleston, the last rector, who had acquired Denton church. Ind.: official of Derby, or the vicar of Chesterfield.[2]
   [[1] *BRUO*, iii. p. xxxix.
   [2–2] Added later.]

1168   Institution of Thomas de Stokes, priest, to the vicarage of St. Werburgh's church, Derby, vacant by the death of Walter de London, the last vicar, on Sat. 26 May last; patrons, prioress and convent of Derby. Ind.: archd. of Derby. Great Haywood, 11 June 1319.

1169   Institution of William de Gonaltston, priest, to the ordained and assigned vicarage of Tibshelf (*Tybschulf*) church; patrons, prioress and convent of Brewood White Ladies. Ind.: archd. of Derby. Eccleshall, 9 July 1319.

1170*   [Fo. 82v] Letters patent appropriating Tibshelf church. The prioress and convent of Brewood White Ladies have requested the appropriation of the church of St. Peter and St. Paul, Tibshelf, now vacant, and of their advowson, which they submit to the bishop's regulation and ordination by their letter given at Brewood, 12 Jan. 1319.
   Considering their poverty and the hardships which they frequently suffer, their devotion to God and to the neighbourhood, namely piety and hospitality, and their care of the poor and infirm, in order that they might perform these things better in future, and having made careful inquiry, the bishop appropriates the church of Tibshelf to the nuns, their successors, and their monastery forever with the agreement of his chapters of Coventry and Lichfield, and the agreement and assent of King Edward II by his charter.[1]
   The nuns and their successors shall pay 20s. at Michaelmas at Lichfield each year forever to the vicars of Lichfield church. The bishop reserves to himself and his successors the assessment of the vicarage, to which the prioress and convent shall present a suitable person to him, his successors, and to whomsoever institution and deprivation shall pertain during vacancies of the see, now and whenever the vicarage becomes vacant, and who shall maintain procurations and other ordinary charges forever. Lichfield, 14 Jan. 1319.
   [Calendared also in *MRA*, nos. 325–7.
   [1] *CChR 1300–26*, 391.]

1171   [Fo. 83] Letters patent ordaining the vicarage of Tibshelf. The bishop has considered the intimations of the prioress and convent of Brewood White Ladies who possess Tibshelf church, of which they are the patrons, which he has appropriated and assigned to them forever. He has reserved to himself and his successors the right to ordain or assess the vicarage of the church, institute the vicar presented to him by the nuns, and assign a suitable portion to the vicar from the revenues and goods of the church.

The nuns have presented William de Gonaltston juxta Soutwell to the bishop for the vacant vicarage.[1] An inquiry has been held in the presence of the parties concerning the resources (*statu*), value and revenues of the church, which the bishop ordains and assigns as follows.

Each vicar at the time shall have all the fruits and revenues of the church, excepting only the tithe of sheaves.[2] He shall also have half the land of the church, to be divided equally from both the better and inferior, together with the headlands containing meadow or pasture lying at the head of the selions of the said land, the small church-yard of the church, which is opposite the church and contains half an acre of land, for a manse, and half the hay of the church from both the headlands of the church lands assigned to him and from the tithe of the parishioners of the same town. The nuns shall pay 40s. each year to William and his successors in the vicarage from the fruits of the church in equal parts at Michaelmas and Easter, commencing at Michaelmas next. If they fail to pay the pension at these terms the bishop, his successors, his ministers of Lichfield, and whomsoever custody of the spiritualities of the vacant see of Coventry and Lichfield will pertain, may compel the nuns to do so by ecclesiastical censure and sequestration of the fruits of Tibshelf church. William and his successors in the vicarage will support the procurations and other ordinary charges; the nuns will support all the extraordinary charges. Eccleshall, 9 July 1319.

[Calendared also in *MRA*, no. 506.
[1] Instituted 9 July 1319, see **1169**.
[2] Followed by *et feni* deleted.]

1172 Institution of Henry de Walton, priest, to Aston upon Trent church, vacant by the death of M. Robert de Frodesham, the last rector, on Sat. 1 Dec. last; patrons, abbot and convent of St. Werburgh, Chester. Ind.: archd. of Derby. 11 Dec. 1319.

1173 Institution of Br. William de Aslacton, canon of Welbeck, to Etwall vicarage, vacant by the death of Br. William de Bollesovere, the last vicar, on Sun. 9 Dec. last; patrons, abbot and convent of Welbeck. He swore to reside [etc.]. Ind.: archd. of Derby. 2 Jan. 1320.

1174 [Fo. 83v] Institution of M. William de Longedon, priest, to Doveridge (*Douvebrug'*) vicarage, vacant by the death of Nicholas de Underwode, the last vicar, on Wed. 2 Jan. last; patrons, prior and convent of Tutbury. Ind.: official of the archd. of Derby. Eccleshall, 8 Jan. 1320.

[MCCC] VICESIMO.

1175 Institution of Robert de Scharneford, chaplain, to Lowne (*Lund'*) vicarage, vacant by the death of John de Hyclyng', the last vicar, on Sun. 23 Mar.; patrons, abbot and convent of Croxton Kerrial. Ind.: archd. 12 Apr. 1320.

1176   Institution of Hugh de Dalby, chaplain, to Shirland (*Schyrlaunde*) church, vacant by the resignation of Robert de Deneford, the last rector, on 18 Feb. last; patron, Sir John de Grey, lord of Dyffryn, Clwyd (*Deffrencloyt*). Ind.: archd. of Derby. 26 Apr. 1320.

1177   Institution[1] of Roger Fitzherbert of Parwich (*Peverwych'*), acolyte, to Norbury church, vacant by the death of Roger [Fitzherbert],[2] the last rector, on Fri. 10 Jan.; patron, Sir John Fitzherbert of Norbury, kt. Ind.: archd. of Derby. 23 June 1320.
   [[1] Interlined.
   [2] See **426**.]

1178   Institution of John de Schiringham, clerk, to Heanor church, vacant by the death of Roger de Schulton, the last rector, on 31 Jan. last; patron, Sir Richard de Grey of Codnor (*Codenovere*), kt. Ind.: archd. of Derby. 29 June 1320.

1179   Institution of Br. Robert de Coventr', canon of Beauchief, to Alfreton vicarage, vacant by the death of Br. Ralph, canon of the same house; patrons, abbot and convent of Beauchief (*de Bello Capite*). No inquiry was made because of the confidence the bishop had in the presenters and the presentee, by reason of the presentee's oath. Ind.: archd. of Derby.[1] Westhall, 10 Aug. 1320.
   [[1] Interlined.]

1180   Licence to John [de Schiringham],[1] subdeacon, rector of Heanor, to study until 20 July next under the terms of the constitution *Cum ex eo*. Coldham, 2 Mar. 1320.
   [[1] See **1178**.]

ANNO DOMINI .M°.CCC°.XXI°.

1181   Note that the same John was ordained deacon on 18 Apr. 1321.[1] On 19 Apr. he had licence to study for one year from 20 July next[2] under the terms of the constitution *Cum ex eo*, and letters dimissory for the order of priest.
   [[1] The ordination list for this service is incomplete and John's name is not recorded, see **1329**.
   [2] Interlined.]

1182   Dispensation for William de Bautre, subdeacon, rector of Eyam, to study for one year under the terms of the constitution [1]*Cum ex eo*[1]. 4 Feb. 1321.
   [[1–1] Underlined.]

1183   Institution of John de Melbourn',[1] subdeacon, to Hartshorne church, vacant by the resignation of John de Riston, the last rector, on 29 Dec. last[2]; patron, Sir Hugh de Meignyl, kt. On 25 May Richard de Lucy, who had been presented to the said church by John de Nevill', renounced all his right, if he had any [3]in the same[3] by virtue of the aforesaid presentation, before the bishop, in the presence of M. Walter de Askeby, William de Longedon, John de Hoby,

priests, and John Blaby and John de Lacy, clerks. Ind. John de Melborn':
archd. of Derby. Pontefract (*Pountfrett*), 25 May 1321.

[¹ *BRUC*, 400.
² Interlined.
³⁻³ Interlined.]

1184 Institution of John de Overa, priest, to Glossop vicarage, which became
vacant on Tues. 28 Apr.; patrons, abbot and convent of the Cistercian
monastery of St. Mary, Basingwerk. Ind.: archd. of Derby. London, 3 June
1321.

1185 [Fo. 84]¹ Dispensation for John de Melbourn', subdeacon, rector of
Hartshorne, concerning holy orders and non-residence under the terms of the
constitution *Cum ex eo*. 9 July 1321.

[¹ This folio is a piece of parchment measuring approximately 20.5cm. by 6.5cm.]

1186 Institution of Br.¹ Richard de Roderham, priest, ²canon of Beauchief
(*Beuchef*)², to Alfreton (*Alferton*) vicarage, vacant by the resignation of Br. Robert
de Coventr', the last vicar, on Sun. 12 July last; patrons, abbot and convent of
Beauchief. Ind.: archd. of Derby. Everton, 8 Sept. 1321.

[¹ Interlined.
²⁻² Interlined.
Fo. 84v is blank.]

[Fo. 85] ARCHIDIACONATUS CESTR' DE ANNO DOMINI :MILLESIMO :CCC^mo:XVII^mo:

1187 Collation to Robert de Clipston of the prebend in St. John's collegiate
church,¹ Chester, which was M. W[illiam le] Constabl's.² Ind.: dean and
chapter of the same place. 15 May 1317.

[¹ Interlined.
² See **386**.]

1188 Institution of Gilbert le Waleys, clerk, to Acton church, vacant by the
death of Thomas le Waleys, the last rector, on Thurs. 5 May last; patron,
Richard le Waleys. Ind.: archd. of Chester. Abbots Bromley (*Bromlegh' Abbatis*),
5 June 1317.

1189 Institution of Adam de Wallebouk, chaplain, to Blackburn (*Blakeburn*)
vicarage, vacant by the death of William de Lenche on Fri. 20 May last;
patrons, abbot and convent of Whalley (*Whallegh'*). Ind.: archd. of Chester.
16 June 1317.

1190 Licence to Gilbert le Waleys, rector of Acton, to study for one year from
Michaelmas next. He shall not be compelled to be promoted in the first year
except to the order of subdeacon. 20 June 1317.

1191 Institution of M. John Walewayn,¹ junior, to Hawarden (*Hawardyn*)
church; patron, Sir Robert de Montalt. The church became vacant on Tues.
29 Apr. 1315.² In the meantime several presentations have been made: William

de Melton,[3] William de Osgodeby,[4] and M. John Walewayn, senior. Their presentations for institution were not pursued. Ind. M. John, junior: archd. of Chester. Fulbrook (*Fulbrok*), 12 July 1317.

[[1] *BRUO*, iii.2225.
[2] Interlined.
[3] Granted custody of the sequestration on the church on 24 May 1315, see **897**.
[4] Granted the church *in commendam* on 6 May 1316, see **904**.]

1192 Licence to the same M. John to study for one year. He shall not be obliged to be promoted to holy orders in the said term except to the order of subdeacon. 12 July 1317. Note of similar licence from 23 June 1318.

1193 Institution of Thomas de Boulton, chaplain, to Rochdale (*Rachedal'*) vicarage, vacant by the death of Richard Perbald, the last vicar, on Tues. 13 Sept. last; patrons, abbot and convent of Whalley (*Whall'*). Ind.: archd. of Chester. 25 Oct. 1317.

1194 Institution of Thomas de Leye, acolyte,[1] to Mottram in Longdendale church, vacant by the resignation of Thomas de Cresacr'; patron, Sir Thomas de Burg', kt. Ind.: archd. of Chester. 6 Dec. 1317.

[[1] Interlined.]

1195 [Fo. 85v] Institution of Thomas de Vernoun to the vacant chapel of Haslington (*Haselington*); patron, Sir Ralph de Vernoun, kt. Ind.: archd. of Chester. 6 Dec. 1317.

1196 Institution of William de Bristoll to Aldford (*Aldeford*) church, vacant [1]by the death of[1] [the last rector][2]; patron this turn, Edward, first-born son of the king of England, by reason of the custody of John, son of John de Arden, a minor. Ind.: archd. of Chester. 1 Feb. 1318.

[[1-1] Interlined.
[2] Blank space.]

ANNUS [M].CCC.XVIII[us].

1197 Licence to the rector of Mottram in Longdendale[1] to study for one year and dispensation concerning holy orders under the terms of the constitution *Cum ex eo*. 23 Apr. 1318.

[[1] Thomas de Leye, see **1194**.]

1198 Note of similar licence and dispensation for M. Robert de Wakfeld, rector of Heswall. 9 May 1318.

1199 Institution of John de Hurmeston, priest, to Leigh (*Legh*) church; patron, Sir Robert de Holand, kt. The church became vacant by the same John's resignation, and he was re-instituted as Sir Robert had possession of the presentation. Ind.: archd. of Chester. Eccleshall, 9 July 1318.

1200   Note that Thomas de Vernoun, clerk, has been admitted to Davenham church, vacant by the surrender (*per dimissionem*) of M. Richard de Vernoun by reason of the new constitution published against pluralism;[1] patron, Sir Ralph de Vernoun, senior, kt. Ind.: archd. of Chester. Coldham, 23 Aug. 1318.

> [[1] The constitution *Execrabilis* of Pope John XXII, published 19 Nov. 1317, see *Extravagantes Johannis Papae XXII* in *Corpus Juris Canonici* (as in 8), ii, 3, 2.4 (p. 1259); W.T. Waugh, 'Archbishop Peckham and pluralities', *English Historical Review*, 112 (1913), 625–635.
>
> Adam Orleton's register records that Richard de Vernoun resigned Davenham on 2 Feb. 1318, see *Registrum Ade de Orleton episcopi Herefordensis A.D. MCCCXVII–MCCCXXVII*, ed. A.T. Bannister (CYS, 5, 1908), 59. Vernoun was Orleton's official and vicar-general, see *ibid.*, 31, 43, 67, 76, 92, 106, 180. See also *BRUO*, iii.1946.]

1201   Note that William de Vernoun, clerk, has been admitted to Haslington chapel, without cure of souls, which is vacant because Thomas de Vernoun, who was the chaplain, has been admitted to Davenham church;[1] patron, Sir Ralph de Vernoun, senior, kt. Ind.: archd. of Chester. Coldham, 24 Aug. 1318.

> [[1] See **1200**   above.]

1202   Institution of Richard Longespeye, chaplain, to Warmingham church, vacant by the resignation of Thomas Trussel made to the bishop at Lincoln on 11 Feb. 1318 according to the constraints of the new constitution [*Execrabilis*]. Ind.: archd. Coldham, 3 Sept. 1318.

1203   Dispensation for William de Dacr', rector of Prescot (*Prestcote*), for one year under the terms of the constitution ¹*Cum ex eo*.¹ 8 Nov. 1318.
[Margin] Licence to study for the rector of Prescot.

> [¹⁻¹ Underlined.]

1204   [Fo. 86] Institution of M. Ralph de Tunstall, chaplain, to Croston church, vacant by the death of [William de Lancastr'] the [last] rector[1] on Sat. 4 Nov.; patrons, prior and monks of St. Mary's church, Lancaster. Ind.: archd. 22 Nov. 1318.

> [[1] See **851**.]

1205   Institution of Richard de Radeclif', priest, to Bury (*Buri*) church, vacant by the resignation of Roger de Frekelton, the last rector, in an exchange of benefices; patron, Margery, lady of Bury. Institution of Roger de Frekelton, priest, to Radcliffe (*Radeclif*) church, vacant by the resignation of Richard de Radeclif' in an exchange, as above; patron William de Radeclif'. Ind.: archd. of Chester. Tamworth, 14 Jan. 1319.

1206   Institution of John le Waleys, acolyte, to Acton church, which became vacant on Sat. 18 Nov. 1318; patron, Richard le Waleys. Ind.: archd. 20 Jan. 1319.

¹ANNUS .M^{US}.CCC.XIX.¹ ²ET CONSECRACIONIS DOMINI EPISCOPI ANNO .XXVIII°.²
[¹⁻¹ Underlined.
²⁻² Added later by another contemporary hand.]

1207 Note that because St. Olaf's church, Chester, has been vacant for such a long time its ordination has devolved to the bishop, and he has collated Jordan de Marchale, clerk. Ind.: official of Chester. 5 Apr. ¹1319.¹
[¹⁻¹ Underlined.]

1208 Institution of M. Ralph de Salop' to Walton church, vacant by the resignation of M. Thomas de Cherlton, the last rector, who was instituted to Downton (*Dounton*) church; patrons, abbot and convent of Shrewsbury. Ind.: official of Chester. 22 Apr. 1319.

1209 Licence to M. John Walewayn, junior, subdeacon,¹ rector of Hawarden, to study for one year under the terms of the constitution ²*Cum ex eo*². 23 June 1319.
[¹ Interlined.
²⁻² Underlined.]

1210 Note of similar licence for the rector of Acton (*Acton Bloundel*)¹ from 7 Apr. 1319.
[¹ John le Waleys, see **1206**.]

1211 Institution of M. Adam de Southwyk, in the person of John de Southwyk, rector of Ongar (*Aungre*), his proctor, to Rostherne (*Routhesthorn*) church, vacant [Fo. 86v] by the death of Roger de Venables, the last rector, on Fri. 13 July last; patron, Edward, earl of Chester, first-born son of the king of England. Ind.: archd. of Chester. 8 Sept. 1319.

1212 Institution of Richard de Womberegh, priest, in the person of William de Pakynton, his proctor, to Eccleston church, which became vacant on Mon. 27 Nov. 1318; patrons, prior and monks of St. Mary's church, Lancaster. Ind.: archd. of Chester. 22 Oct. 1319.

1213 Dispensation for Thomas de Vernoun, rector of Davenham, [to study] for one year under the terms of the constitution *Cum ex eo*. 24 Oct. 1319.

1214 Institution of Thomas de Turvill', acolyte, to the moiety of Malpas (*de Malo passu*) church vacant by the death of William Duyn, the last rector, on Wed. 3 Oct. last; patron, Sir John de Sutton, kt. Ind.: archd. of Chester. 7 Nov. 1319.

1215 Licence to the same Thomas to study for one year under the terms of the constitution *Cum ex eo*. Same date.

1216 Institution of John de Stonlee, chaplain, to Harthill (*Herthull*) chapel, vacant by the resignation of Thomas de Potyngton, the last rector, on 18 Nov.

last; patrons, William Ingg and Iseult, his wife, by reason of Iseult's dower. Ind.: archd. of Chester. 8 Nov. 1319.

1217 Collation to John Hustwayt, priest, of the prebend of Flixton (*Flyxton*) in Lichfield church, vacant by the resignation of Harvey de Staunton on 25 Oct. in an exchange with the prebend of Husthwaite (*Hustwayt*) in York church,[1] which John held. Ind.: chapter of Lichfield. 11 Nov. 1319

    [[1] *Fasti*, vi.58; x.36–7.]

1218 Institution of Nicholas de Hareweld, priest, to Tarporley (*Thorperlegh*) church; patron, Sir John de Grey, kt. The church is vacant by the resignation of Robert de Blescheleye, the last rector, on 10 Nov., and by his institution to Great Brickhill (*Magna Brychull*) church [Salisbury dioc.] on 23 Sept.[1] Ind.: official of Chester, or the rector of the Rood.[2] 22 Nov. 1319.

    [[1] MS. *ix kal. Octobris*. This institution is not recorded in the register of Roger
       Martival.
    [2] See **919**.]

1219 Institution of M. Simon Pyte, priest, to Christleton (*Crystelton*) church, vacant by the resignation of M. Walter de Askeby, the last rector,[1] the same day in an exchange[2] of benefices; patrons, abbot and convent of St. Werburgh, Chester. 13 Dec. 1319.

    [[1] Rector by papal provision 28 July 1318, see *CPL*, ii.182.
    [2] Interlined.]

1220 [Fo. 87] Institution of Thomas de Aston, acolyte, to Handley church, which became vacant on 8 Jan. because M. William de Longedon, the last rector, was instituted to Doveridge vicarage;[1] patrons, abbot and convent of St. Werburgh, Chester. Ind.: archd. of Chester. Licence to study for one year from 14 Jan. under the terms of the constitution *Cum ex eo*. Edlaston (*Edulveston*), 12 Jan. 1320.

    [[1] See **1174**.]

1221 Institution of Thomas de Modburlegh, clerk, to Tattenhall church, which became vacant on Tues. 11 Dec. [1319]; patrons, abbot and convent of St. Werburgh, Chester. Ind.: archd. of Chester. 1 Jan. 1320.

1222 Institution of Richard de Pollesworth, chaplain, to the vicarage of Tarvin church; patron, M. Geoffrey de Blaston. Ind.: archd. of Chester. 19 Mar. 1320.

[MCCC] VICESIMO.

1223 Institution of Jordan de Lymme, chaplain, to the moiety of Lymm church vacant by the resignation of Adam de Mascy, the last rector, on Sun. 3 Feb. Ind.: archd. of Chester. 26 Mar. 1320.

1224 Dispensation for Thomas de Modburle, acolyte, to be non-resident for one year under the terms of the constitution *Cum ex eo*. 7 Apr. 1320.
[Margin] Tattenhall.

1225 Institution of Thomas de Colton, chaplain, to Great Budworth (*Budde-worth*) vicarage, vacant by the death of Peter de Middelton, the last rector, on Mon. 14 Apr. last; patrons, prior and convent of Norton. Ind.: archd. of Chester. 26 Apr. 1320.

1226 Institution of Simon de Cestr', chaplain, to the vicarage of Blackburn church, which became vacant on Sun. 8 June last; patrons, abbot and convent of Whalley. Ind.: archd. of Chester. 6 July 1320.

1227 Institution of Adam de Blakeburn, chaplain, to Eccles vicarage, which became vacant on Fri. 11 July because the last vicar obtained a similar cure; patrons, abbot and convent of Whalley. Ind.: archd. of Chester. 25 July 1320.

1228 Institution of Nicholas de Schepeye, priest, to Eccleston church, vacant by the resignation of Richard de Wamberge, [1]the last rector,[1] on 18 June; patrons, prior and monks of Lancaster. Ind.: archd. of Chester. Westhall,[2] 22 July 1320.
[[1-1] Interlined
[2] Interlined.]

1229 Note that the bishop has committed custody of the sequestration placed on the fruits and revenues of Mobberley (*Moburlegh*) church to Thomas de Modburlegh, rector of Tattenhall, during pleasure. He is not obliged to render an account. 26 July 1320.

1230 [Fo. 87v] Dispensation for William Dacre, rector of Prescot (*Prestcot*), to study for one year under the terms of the constitution *Cum ex eo*. 2 Aug. 1320.

1231 Note that on 1 Aug. [1320] at Lichfield, John de Ruston, vicar of Wybunbury, and Henry Savage, rector of Harstshorne, who were present before the bishop, resigned the church and vicarage in an exchange [of benefices]. The resignations were accepted by the bishop. On 7 Aug. at Westhall the bishop collated Henry to Wybunbury vicarage, as patron, and instituted John to Hartshorne church, at the presentation Sir Hugh de Meignel, kt., the patron. Ind. John: archd. of Derby. Ind. Henry: Richard de Haselbech'.[1]
[[1] Rector of Fenny Bentley, see **1164**.]

1232 Institution of Jordan de Marthale, priest, to St. Peter's church in the city of Chester, vacant by the death of Roger de Chew, the last rector, on Tues. 29 July; patrons, abbot and convent of St. Werburgh, Chester. Ind.: archd. of Chester. Westhall,[1] 9 Aug. 1320.
[[1] Interlined.]

1233 Institution of Richard de Par, acolyte, to Prestwich church, vacant by the resignation of John Travers, the last rector, on Mon. 10 Nov.; patron, Sir Richard de Holande, kt. Ind.: archd. of Chester. Brewood, 11 Dec. 1320.

1234 Dispensation for Thomas de Vernon', rector of Davenham, to study until ¹28 May¹ [1321] under the terms of the constitution *Cum ex eo*. 24 Oct. 1320.
    [¹⁻¹ Interlined.]

1235 Grant *in commendam* to Henry de Hanleg', priest, of Mobberley church; patron, William de Modburleg'. Ind.: archd. Eccleshall, 29 Dec. 1320.

1236 Licence to Thomas de Aston, subdeacon, rector of Handley, to study for one year under the terms of the constitution *Cum ex eo*. 11 Jan. 1321.

1237 Note that by letters patent to M. Gilbert de Bruera the bishop has sequestrated whatever money, if any, he owed M. Walter de Thorp, the last rector of Worfield, for the fruits of the same church which he bought from [Walter] when living,¹ into the hands of the said G[ilbert], to be kept under sequestration until another will receive it thereafter. The same day the bishop committed custody of the fruits and revenues belonging to Worfield church and pertaining to the bishop from the time of its vacancy caused by the death of M. W[alter] de Thorp to the same M. Gilbert. He shall be answerable for these. 16 Feb. 1321.
    [¹ Died before 8 Jan. 1321, see *BRUO*, iii.2222.]

1238 Letters patent to his beloved in Christ William de Chavelegh, priest.¹ The hospital of [St. Andrew] Denhall (*Danewell*),² with the church of Burton in Wirral (*Burton in Wirall*), is vacant and belongs to the bishop's provision or collation. He collates and institutes him to the same with all its rights [etc.], provided that he shall have two fellow priests continually dwelling with him in the hospital, according to the ordination of the said hospital, accustomed from of old. Because the hospital exists for the admission of the poor crossing from Ireland, and others, he and his fellow priests shall wear a suitable habit with a regular cross, and he shall perform and exercise the celebration of masses and other [services] with which the hospital is charged. Saving forever the rights [etc.]. Balsall (*Baleshale*), 24 Mar. 1320.
    [¹ Followed by a 13cm. blank space.
    ² *VCH Cheshire*, iii.184–5.]

1239 [Fo. 88] Institution of John de Ellerker, subdeacon, in the person of John de Barneby, chaplain, his proctor, to Eccleston church, vacant by the resignation of Nicholas de Schepeye, the last rector, on 28 Feb. by reason of an exchange with Rolleston church;¹ patrons, prior and monks St. Mary, Lancaster. Ind.: archd. of Chester. Belgrave (*Belegrave*), 28 May 1321.
    [¹ See **1278**.]

1240 Institution of John la Zouche, priest, to Mottram in Longdendale church, vacant by the resignation of William de Legh, the last rector, on 25 Jan.; patron, Sir Robert de Holand, kt. Ind.: archd. of Chester, or the dean of Macclesfield (*Maclesfeld*). Walton on Thames (*Waleton*), 14 June 1321.

1241 Institution of Robert de Chedle, clerk, to Cheadle church, vacant by the death of M. Richard de Trafford, the last rector, on Fri. 26 June last; patron,

Lady Matilda de Sulce, lady of Cheadle. Ind.: archd. of Chester. Bishops Itchington, 21 Sept. 1321.

1242 Institution of Richard de Waverton, priest, to the vicarage of Bolton (*Boulton*) parish church, vacant by the death of Ranulph, the last vicar, on Sun. 16 Aug. last; patrons, prior and convent of Mattersey (*Mathersey*), York dioc. Ind.: archd. of Chester. London, 30 Sept. 1321.

1243 Licence to M. John Waleweyn, junior, subdeacon, rector of Hawarden, to study for one year under the terms of the constitution *Cum ex eo*. 21 Oct. 1321.

1244 Institution of William de Brynynton, acolyte, to Thurstaston church, vacant by the death of M. John Hurel, the last rector, on Tues. 6 Oct. last; patrons, abbot and convent of St. Werburgh, Chester. Ind.: archd. of Chester. London, 31 Oct. 1321.
[The rest of the recto is blank.]

1245 [Fo. 88v] Sixteenth or seventeenth century copy of the ordination of the prebendal vicarage of Alrewas and its chapelries. 11 May 1324.
[The rest of the folio is blank.]

[Fo. 89] ARCHIDIACONATUS STAFFORD'.

1246 Institution of M. Henry de Clif, clerk, to the deanery of Tamworth collegiate church; patron, Joan, widow of Thomas de Lodelowe. Ind.: archd. of Stafford. London, 5 Feb. 1317.

1247 Institution of Br. Gilbert de Bosco, ¹canon of Rocester,¹ to Rocester vicarage; patrons, abbot and convent of Rocester. Ind.: archd. of Stafford. Eccleshall, 29 May 1317.
[¹⁻¹ Interlined.]

1248 Institution of Br. Thomas, canon of Halesowen (*Halesoweyn*), to the vacant vicarage of Walsall; patrons, abbot and convent of Halesowen. Ind.: archd. of Stafford. Aston, 27 Nov. 1317.

1249 Institution of Br. Geoffrey de Whitewell, canon of Kenilworth, to the keepership or rule of the cell of Calwich, without an inquiry as is customary; patrons, prior and convent of Kenilworth. Ind.: archd. of Stafford. 23 Feb. 1318.

1250 Institution of Robert de Overe to the vacant church of Bradley (*Bradelegh*); patron, Sir Thomas de Pipe, kt. The church became vacant from¹ the time of the constraint (*arctacionis*) of Pope John XXII's new constitution

published against pluralism,[2] by [the surrender of] Richard de Camera, the last
rector. 20 Apr. [3]1318.[3]

[[1] MS. *a* over *per* partially erased.
[2] *Execrabilis*, see **1200**, n. 1.
[3-3] Interlined.]

1251 Institution of John de Ellerker to the vacant church of Rolleston; patron,
Thomas, earl of Lancaster and Leicester, steward of England. Ind.: archd. of
Stafford. 23 Apr. 1318.

1252 Letters patent. The most serene prince Lord E[dward], king of England,
has recently granted by his charter the right of advowson which he had in
Worfield church to the bishop and his church of Lichfield.[1] M. Isumbert de
Longa Villa, who was holding the church at the time of the grant, wishes an
exchange with Mapledurham (*Mapeldoreham*) church, Winchester dioc., which
M. Gilbert de Bruera held. With the express agreement of J[ohn Sandale],
bishop of Winchester, diocesan and patron of Mapledurham, Isumbert has
resigned Worfield church. The bishop has accepted and ratified the
resignation. He collates and institutes M. Gilbert de Bruera to Worfield
church, thus vacant, which pertains to his collation, with all its rights, etc.,
saving the right, etc. 28 May 1318.

[[1] *CPR 1317–21*, 145.]

[Fo. 89v] ARCHIDIACONATUS STAFFORD.

1253 Note that the bishop commissioned M. Andrew de Bruge his deputy to
examine Nicholas de Swinnerton, having been presented to Mucklestone
(*Mocleston*) church, and to institute him if suitable. He has instituted him
rector, at the presentation of Adam de Mocleston, the patron. The bishop has
ratified this institution, and confirmed it by his letters. Ind.: archd. of Stafford.
1 June 1318.

1254 Note that Philip Aubyn, clerk, has been admitted to Drayton Bassett
chapel, with cure of souls, vacant by the death of John de Hales on Wed.
21 June; patrons, dean and chapter of Tamworth collegiate church, at the
nomination of Sir Ralph Basset, kt., because it is customary for the dean and
chapter to present a suitable person to the chapel at the nomination of the said
Ralph. Ind.: archd. of Stafford. Sawley, 8 Aug. 1318.

1255 Institution of Nicholas Mauveysin, who has the first tonsure at least, to
Mavesyn Ridware (*Ridwar' Mauveysin*) church, vacant by the death of Nicholas
Mountectus, the last rector, on Fri. 18 Aug. last; patron, Sir Henry de
Mauveysin. Ind.: chancellor of Lichfield, because the right to induct to that
church pertains to him. Fulbrook (*Fulbroc*), 27 Sept. 1318.

1256 Institution of Edmund atte Stone of Newton (*Neuton*), chaplain, to
Buildwas church, vacant by the resignation of Alan de Neuton, the last
rector, on 31 Aug. 1318; presented by King Edward, by reason of his custody

of the lands of Roger, son of John, a minor, the patron. Ind.: archd. of Stafford. 18 Oct. [1318].[1]
[Margin} Shrewsbury [archdeaconry].

[[1] *Anno predicto* interlined.]

1257 Institution of Ralph de Bromcote, priest, to Abbots Bromley (*Bromleye*) vicarage, vacant by the death of Nicholas de Wetote on Fri. 28 July last; patrons, abbot and convent of Burton upon Trent. Ind.: archd. of Stafford. 8 Nov. 1318.

1258 Collation to Roger called Mareschall of the prebend of Darnford in Lichfield church.[1] Ind.: dean and chapter. Pattingham, 7 Jan. 1319.

[[1] *Fasti*, x.32.]

1259 Dispensation for M. Philip Aubyn, rector of Drayton Bassett chapel, [to study] for two years under the terms of the constitution *Cum ex eo*. Coldham, 7 Sept. 1318.

1260 [Fo. 90] Institution of Edmund de Stafford, acolyte, to Draycott (*Draycote*) church, vacant by the death of John Chanei on Fri. 6 Oct. last; patron, Joan, lady of Draycott. Ind.: archd. of Stafford. Coldham, 12 Feb. 1319.

ANNO DOMINI M^o.CCC^{mo}.XIX°.

1261 Institution of Adam de Neuport, acolyte, to Tatenhill (*Tatenhull*) church, vacant because John de Kynardeseye, the last rector, has been instituted to Stoke (*Stok'*) church; patron, Thomas, earl of Lancaster. Ind.: archd. of Stafford. 10 Apr. 1319.

1262 Institution of Robert, son of Adam de Brewode, chaplain, to Brewood vicarage, vacant by resignation of William de Petto, the last vicar, on 30 Apr.; patron, dean of Lichfield. He swore [etc.]. 27 May 1319.

1263 Dispensation for Edmund [de Stafford],[1] rector of Draycott, [to study] for one year from Michaelmas next under the terms of the constitution [2]*Cum ex eo*[2]. 3 June 1319.

[[1] See **1260**.
[2-2] Underlined.]

1264 Note of the exchange between John de Codeshal' and M. Robert de Caumpeden of the vicarages of Dilhorne and Alstonfield (*Astenefeld*) made with the agreement of the patrons: the dean and chapter of Lichfield, the patrons of Dilhorne, and the abbot and convent of Combermere, the patrons of Alstonfield. Institution of John to Alstonfield, and of M. Robert to Dilhorne. Ind. M. Robert: dean of Alton. Ind. John: rector of Cheadle. 12 July 1319.

1265 Licence to M. John Brabazun, priest,[1] to study for one year. 29 Oct. 1319.

[[1] Interlined.]

1266   Institution of Robert de Freford to the prebend of Syerscote (*Cyrescot'*) in Tamworth collegiate church which became vacant on Wed. 30 Jan. last; patron, Sir Alexander de Frevill', kt. Ind.: archd. of Chester.[1] 15 Mar. 1320.

[1 *Sic*]

1267   Institution of John de Smalrys to the vicarage of Caverswall parish church, [Fo. 90v] vacant by the death of Richard de Caverswell, the last vicar, on Wed. 5 Mar. last; patrons, prior and convent of St. Thomas by Stafford. Ind.: archd. of Stafford. 27 Mar. 1320.

1268   Institution of John de Pilardynton, priest, to Drayton in Hales (*Hales*) vicarage, vacant by the death of [Walter de Petling] the last vicar[1] on Tues. 15 Apr.; patron, Br. William, prior of Ware, proctor in England of the abbot and convent of Saint-Evroul [Normandy]. Ind.: archd. of Stafford. 4 June 1320.

[1 See **328**.]

1269   Note that the resignations of M. Walter de Thorp of Astbury church, given at London on 16 June 1320, and that of M. Gilbert de Bruera of Worfield church, given at Lichfield on 21 June 1320, were presented, made on account of an exchange of churches, and no other reason. Having received the presentation made by the abbot and convent of Chester, the patrons, to Astbury church, the bishop, who possesses the advowson of Worfield church, collates M. Walter de Thorp to that church and institutes M. Gilbert de Bruer' to Astbury church. Ind.: the officials or deans of both places. Bishops Itchington, 7 July 1320.

1270   Having produced the grace[1] given previously to Lazarinus, son of George Malocellus concerning the canonry and prebend in Lichfield church which was Theodosius Malocellus's when living, by virtue of the same grace the bishop has admitted Lazarinus to the prebend in the person of his proctor. Ind.: . . .[2] 24 Oct. 1320.
[Margin] Prebend of Freeford.[3]

[1 Papal provision dated 1 May 1320, *CPL*, ii.200.
2 Blank space.
3 *Fasti*, x.38–9.]

1271   Note that on 5 Nov. in the bishop's presence, in a room in his house in London, Br. John de Tannione, monk of Saint-Rémy, Reims, prior of Lapley, in the archdeaconry of Stafford, purely, freely and absolutely resigned the said priorate into the bishop's hands, which resignation the bishop accepted. The same day Br. Gobert de Brabancia was presented to the said priorate by the abbot of Saint-Rémy and, with the presentation and the merits of the presentee having been inquired into summarily by the oaths of certain men, he was instituted prior. Because the presentation of Br. Gobert was incorrectly written, he promised on oath to provide the bishop with another, correct, presentation before 2 Feb. next, on pain of 20 marks (£13 6s. 8d.). [1]An adequate presentation was produced before that time.[1]

[1–1 Added later.]

1272   Licence to the rector of Walton upon Trent to study for one year under the terms of the constitution *Cum ex eo*. 14 Dec. 1320.

1273   Dispensation for M. Philip Aubyn, rector of Drayton Bassett chapel, to study for one year. 21 Dec. 1320.

1274   Collation to M. Walter de Thorp, canon of Lichfield, of the prebend of Dasset Parva in Lichfield church,[1] vacant by the resignation of M. Geoffrey de Eyton, made by reason of an exchange with the prebend of Weeford.[2] Brewood, 17 Dec. 1320.
   [[1] *Fasti*, x.29, 64.
   [2] See **1280**.]

1275   [Fo. 91] Institution of William de Aston, acolyte, to Mavesyn Ridware church, vacant by the death of Nicholas Mauveysyn, the last rector, on Sun. 7 Dec. last; patron, Robert, lord of Mavesyn Ridware. Ind.: archd. of Stafford. Great Haywood, 5 Jan. 1321.

1276   Letters patent to his beloved in Christ William de Ipstanes, acolyte. He has been presented to the bishop for the vacant church of Church Eaton (*Eyton*), near Gnosall, by the abbess and convent of Polesworth, at the nomination of the heir of Adam de Brumpton. He admits and institutes him to the same, saving an annual pension of 20 marks (£13 6s. 8d.) due to the religious women from the church which was canonically established by Roger [Meuland], the bishop's immediate predecessor, which he has pledged on the Holy Gospels to pay. Saving the rights [etc.]. Great Haywood, 6 Jan. 1321.
   The church is vacant by the deprivation (*per privacionem*) of Thomas de Brumpton, the last rector, made in the court of Canterbury on 11 Dec. the same year.

[MCCC] VICESIMO PRIMO.

1277   Licence to Robert de Freford, subdeacon, rector of Elford, to study for one year under the terms of the constitution *Cum ex eo*. Lichfield, 19 Apr. 1321.

1278   Institution of Nicholas de Schepeye, priest, in the person of Ralph de Tuttebur', his proctor, to Rolleston church, vacant by the resignation of John de Ellerker, the last rector, on 4 Feb. by reason of an exchange made with Eccleston church;[1] patron, Thomas, earl of Lancaster. Ind.: archd. of Stafford. Belgrave, 28 May 1321.
   [[1] See **1239**.]

1279   Letters patent to his beloved in Christ M. Ralph de Salop', priest, rector of Walton upon Trent. Worfield parish church is known to pertain to the bishop's collation. It is vacant by the death of M. Walter de Thorp, the former rector. The bishop is unable to ordain finally for the rule of the church, which has a large cure of souls attached to it. Lest the cure of souls and the spiritualities and temporalities suffer, or are neglected in any way, and so that the buildings, chancel and ornaments of the church shall be suitably repaired and duly maintained, the bishop grants him the church *in commendam*, to be held for the lawful time. Saving the right [etc.]. Walton on Thames (*Waleton super Tamis*), 29 June 1321.

1280 Collation to M. Geoffrey de Eyton, canon of Lichfield, of the prebend of Weeford in Lichfield church,[1] vacant by the resignation of M. Walter de Thorp, made by reason of an exchange with the prebend of Dasset Parva.[2] Brewood, 17 Dec. 1320.

[[1] *Fasti*, x.29, 64.
[2] See **1274**.]

1281 [Fo. 91v] Licence to Roger de Crophull, rector of Lullington, to study for one year. 1 July 1321.

1282 Letters patent to his beloved in Christ John de Clipston, clerk. The bishop collates and invests him to the prebend of Dasset Parva in Lichfield church,[1] which belongs to his collation, being vacant by the death of M. Walter de Thorp, with all its rights [etc.], [2]saving the right of any other person to whom the right of it or to it belongs by papal provision.[2] Coldham, 11 Feb. 1321.

[[1] *Fasti*, x.29.
[2-2] Interlined.]

1283 Licence to William de Ippestanes, acolyte, rector of Church Eaton, to study for one year under the terms of the constitution *Cum ex eo*. 1 Oct. 1321.

1284 Letters patent ordaining the vicarage of Seighford parish church. The fruits of holy mother church should support more fully those who devotedly serve God by laudable life. The prior and convent of Ranton live canonically under the rule of St. Augustine. They laudably provide divine services, prayers, vigils, and alms. The bishop wishes to augment their resources. Because of their poverty and their pious devotion to religion, the bishop grants, for himself and his successors, forever, that the religious shall cause Seighford parish church to be served in duties by any canon of Ranton as if by a vicar, provided that the church is not defrauded of duties, and the said canon shall support each and every charge of the vicarage which the vicars of the church have customarily supported.

The said canon shall be presented to the bishop and to his successors for the vicarage of the church, and he shall be canonically instituted to it by him and his successors, and he shall be answerable to the bishop as is fitting, saving the rule of their religion, saving also the rights of the bishop's church [etc.]. Lichfield, 29 Mar. 1311.

[The rest of the folio is blank.]